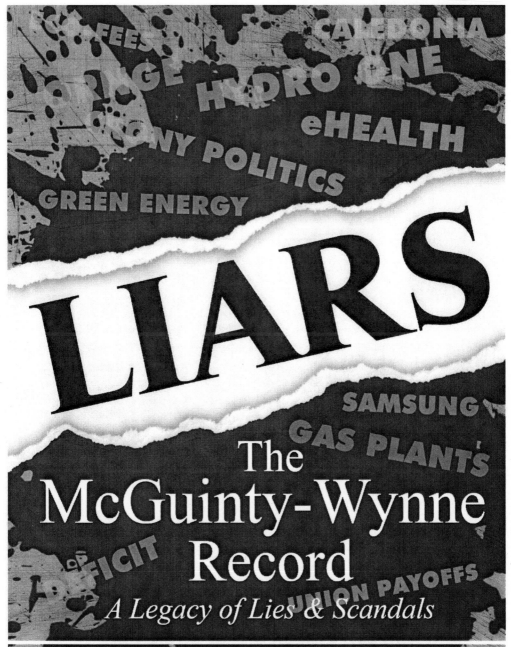

FEES · CALEDONIA · HYDRO ONE · eHEALTH · NY POLITICS · GREEN ENERGY

LIARS

SAMSUNG · GAS PLANTS

The McGuinty-Wynne Record

A Legacy of Lies & Scandals

DEFICIT · UNION PAYOFFS

Daniel Dickin

FRE3DOM PRESS
CANADA INC.

About the Author

Daniel Dickin is a grassroots community leader and self-described political junkie. He obtained his Bachelor's degree in law and political science from Carleton University in 2011. He has worked on federal and provincial election campaigns, including in Dalton McGuinty's former riding of Ottawa South. Daniel is also a legal and political affairs columnist for the *Prince Arthur Herald* and *Huffington Post Canada* publications.

www.danieldickin.ca

Twitter: @DanielDickin

Facebook: facebook.com/DanielDickin

About the Book

Daniel Dickin sees a clear split in Ontario's wealth and prosperity. For the first 136 years following Confederation Ontario was known for its balanced budgets, responsible spending, and prudent political, fiscal, and economic policies. These policies made Ontario the "economic powerhouse" of Canada and the envy of the other provinces.

Unfortunately, all of that changed when Dalton McGuinty's Liberals took the reins of power in Ontario in 2003. The 136 years of substantial progress and good governance were thrown to the side in favour of expensive government experiments, reckless green energy programs, record-setting deficit spending, a ballooning debt, and scandal after scandal after scandal - along with all the lies to cover it up.

While the average Ontario citizen benefitted under the Big Blue Conservative governments of the 20th century, the only people benefiting from the Ontario Liberals are the public sector unions and Liberal Party elites.

Kathleen Wynne took over Dalton McGuinty's legacy in 2013 and had the opportunity to define her new government. She had the opportunity to get Ontario back on track and set herself apart from the scandal-plagued McGuinty past. Unfortunately, Kathleen Wynne only continued McGuinty's legacy of scandals and lies, digging Ontario deeper into the hole of higher debt, more taxes, and fewer jobs.

Dickin's book provides the hard-hitting analysis and inconvenient facts that have been public information for years yet never organized into one strong, cohesive argument. This book presents a compelling argument for the real legacy of Dalton McGuinty and the Ontario Liberal Party - and it isn't pretty – they are liars who have covered up the mismanagement and derailment of a once great and prosperous Ontario.

Freedom Press Canada Inc.

12-111 Fourth Ave., Suite 185 St. Catharines, ON L2S 3P5

Printed in the United States of America

Cover Design: David Strutt

Book Design: David Bolton

ISBN: 978-1-927684-09-2

LIARS

The McGuinty-Wynne Record

A Legacy of Lies and Scandals

By Daniel Dickin

Contents

For: Ontario
May your light once again shine bright

Chapter 1

Introduction

"Dalton McGuinty's legacy is a litany of failure."

- Kelly McParland[1]

"The legacy of Dalton McGuinty is anything but ideal"

- Christina Blizzard[2]

"What can you say about McGuinty? That he introduced all-day kindergarten? That education was his top priority? Who says all-day kindergarten was a good thing? And how did his war with teachers improve the education system? If that's the best you've got – and it is – you've got nada. McGuinty will be remembered as the premier whose incompetence cost us billions of dollars because of Ornge, eHealth and the gas plants scandal. He cost us, and our children, billions of dollars more by doubling spending in just 10 years and running up the debt and deficit."

- *Windsor Star*[3]

Welcome to the Ontario created by Dalton McGuinty's Liberals and sustained by Kathleen Wynne. Thanks to them, Ontario is currently over $288 billion in debt. That's over $21,317 for every man, woman, and child who lives in Ontario. With the $10.3 billion (or $327 *per second*!) Ontario pays just to service that outrageous debt every year, we could cure world hunger in just three short years. The McGuinty-Wynne Ontario has

Liars

grown to favour union interests and Liberal Party elites over the interests of the average Ontario resident. Thanks to Dalton McGuinty, Ontario went from "have" to "have-not" status for the first time in history; Ontario now receives billions of dollars in funding from the federal government because our provincial government has failed to manage its own affairs.

The McGuinty-Wynne Ontario is okay with killing two jobs to create one "green energy" job that costs taxpayers hundreds of thousands of dollars. The McGuinty-Wynne Ontario is okay with giving public servants lavish multi-million dollar bonuses and severance packages. It is okay with standing idly by as armed terrorists take over a community and the police are ordered not to respond. It is okay with teaching grade three children a sexual education curriculum previously reserved for high school students. It is okay with giving their union buddies expensive perks on the backs of taxpayers. It is okay with ballooning health care costs for very few results. It is okay with raising taxes again, and again, and again, and again - whether Dalton McGuinty calls them "eco fees" or Kathleen Wynne calls them "revenue tools."

Ontario is in a state of crisis thanks to the Liberal government policies of Dalton McGuinty and Kathleen Wynne. Our debt is crippling. Our education system is broken. Our healthcare costs are out of control. Our government has racked up deficits so large that great-great-grandchildren will be paying for the reckless McGuinty energy experiments of the twenty-first century. Small, medium, and large businesses alike are fleeing the McGuinty-Wynne Ontario and setting up shop in more affordable provinces and states. Ontarians are rushing to welfare offices to receive government support because they cannot find work in Ontario. Our public servants are better off than ever before, however, taking home handsome paycheques and bonuses and receiving large severance payments.

This is the state of Ontario thanks to the Ontario Liberals. Much of the true Ontario legacy written about in this book is thanks to Dalton McGuinty's action or inaction. For almost a decade, McGuinty led Canada's largest province down a dark road of debt, deficits, reckless experiments, and massive tax hikes. Amidst a criminal investigation, Dalton McGuinty fled his job as Premier in favour of a cushy Harvard fellowship. When Kathleen Wynne came into office in 2013 she did nothing to right the numerous wrongs implemented under McGuinty's time in office. Instead, Kathleen Wynne continued the McGuinty policies without a care in the world for Ontario's families and taxpayers. The McGuinty legacy is the Wynne legacy. Both taken together have created a province in full-blown crisis.

Why hasn't this been written about before? Great question. Since Prime

Minister Stephen Harper was elected in 2006, the Canadian literature marketplace has been saturated with anti-conservative doomsday commentary. These examples have included Lawrence Martin's *Harperland,* Lloyd Mackey's *The Pilgrimage of Stephen Harper,* and Christian Nadeau's *Rogue in Power.* They critique every aspect of the Harper government's policies: his relations with other governments; his foreign policy; his political appointments and staff; his budget and economic management; the way his government handles parliamentary procedure. Even the way he, apparently, didn't send his son off to school 'properly' has made the news. Why, then, aren't the McGuinty Liberals held to the same standard? This book is the answer to that question.

The disastrous McGuinty legacy now being continued by Premier Kathleen Wynne can be viewed in both its immediate and longer-term implications. The McGuinty government policies have crippled Ontario for the past decade, and they will continue to do so for several years longer until we elect a Premier who will make tough, difficult decisions to put Ontario back on track. But the policies of the McGuinty government do not have to be discussed and analyzed as a collective sum. We can also see their effects in the fallout of a single month of provincial politics – a direct result of the policies the Ontario Liberals have implemented (and failed to implement).

In late 2013, Ontario was hit with a string of unfortunate job losses, as companies overburdened and overtaxed decided they had had enough in Ontario. First it was the Heinz plant in Leamington, Ontario, announcing it was closing its processing plant, putting more than 700 full-time employees out of work.[4] Dubbed "the tomato capital of Canada," Heinz was Leamington's largest employer, pulling in hundreds of seasonal and temporary workers during the tomato harvest and paying the city $1 million a year in property taxes. Then came Kellogg's announcement that it would be closing its London plant, putting more than 500 full-time employees out of work from a plant that had been in operation for over 90 years.[5]

It is little conciliation to those employees who found themselves out of work or who will soon be out of work, but these closures were only the latest in a series of closures as businesses – small and large – break under the pressure of an excessive provincial government and move elsewhere. Before Heinz or Kellogg's it was Kraft Canada announcing it was closing its Oakville plant.[6] Plant closures and job losses have lost their sting and become just another announcement, just another reality of the Liberal Ontario.

Think about these businesses' names for a second. These are not small mom-and-pop convenience stores closing their doors because they want

Liars

to spend more time with the grandkids; these are enormous multi-national companies deciding they can no longer do business in Ontario. Kraft had $19 billion in revenues in 2011. Heinz had $11.6 billion in sales in 2012. Kellogg's made almost $14.2 billion in 2012. But it was too expensive, too risky, too unstable for even these multi-nationals to continue to do business here.

These are only three examples of large companies that announced their closures in the span of two years. But before these were several more:

- Navistar, a truck manufacturing company, closed its Chatham plant to go to Indiana[7]
- Xstrata, a mining company in Timmins, closed its doors to move to Quebec[8]
- John Deere, a farm equipment manufacturer, closed its Niagara plant in favour of Wisconsin[9]
- Siemens closed its gas turbine in Hamilton and moved to Charlotte, North Carolina[10]
- Industrial equipment giant Caterpillar closed its London rail locomotive plant and moved to Indiana[11]

If Ontario can't retain some of the world's largest and most successful companies for their enormous job-creating abilities, then Ontario is in serious trouble. If we lose plants from three multi-national companies with almost $50 billion in revenues in a matter of weeks, what can we expect for small and medium businesses? If even the big guys won't put up with doing business in the Liberal Ontario, how can the Liberal government possibly think it can attract the little guys? Job losses and plant closures in Ontario are a symptom of the problem, but Ontario wasn't always this way.

The Ontario Liberals have set countless records in their time in office but, unfortunately, none are to the benefit of you or me. They're benefitting greedy unions reaching ever deeper into the government's coffers while we, the taxpayers, are the ones who pay. They're benefitting Liberal Party cronies hired as government "consultants" – again, with you and I paying for it. When it comes to election time, these unions have no problem activating their membership – often against their will – and forcing them to attend pro-McGuinty rallies. They even force union members to give their union dues – money supposedly given for the benefit of belonging to that union – to McGuinty and his Liberal Party. The union bosses and Liberal cronies stay plump and wealthy, but everyday Ontarians suffer.

But it wasn't always this way. Ontario has a proud tradition with a bright blue history. For the first 136 years of our existence, we were overwhelmingly governed by Progressive Conservative governments. For over 80 years, including a consecutive 42-year dynasty, Conservatives led Ontario to prosperity. When Conservatives were at the helm of Ontario the seas remained calm and the ship steered throughout the waters with ease when they (seldom) got rough. Taxes for citizens and businesses were kept low; the budgets were balanced; the government cautiously approached new ideas while also investing in waves of the future; and transparency was a given.

What happened?

Dalton McGuinty's Liberal Party hijacked Ontario. They took Ontario off its strong, progressive trajectory and placed it instead onto a collision course with enormous debt, default, fewer jobs, and a struggling economy. As it stands right now, Ontario is well on its way to becoming the next Greece, yet the Liberal government has done absolutely nothing to correct its course, make the right investments, encourage businesses to create new jobs, or rein in public spending.

The only way to return to the prestige and responsibility our province once knew is to swiftly throw the McGuinty-Wynne Liberals out of office. This is simply the only possible answer to correcting a Liberal government that is so far off course, so far from implementing the right solutions, and so out of touch with what Ontario residents want and need from their provincial government.

The thesis of this book is straightforward: first, that Ontario was inherently best governed by Conservative governments. Secondly, that Ontario was violently hijacked from our prosperous path to wealth, job creation, and responsible public spending by the McGuinty Liberals.

In chapter two we will examine the first 136 years of Ontario's history and discuss the first attempted hijackings – first with the election of a Liberal government that ended a Conservative dynasty, and next with a shove even farther left with the surprise election of Bob Rae's New Democrats. We will see how Ontario was built upon strong fiscal principles and an overwhelming desire to work, harnessed by a provincial government that was, for a great majority of the time, Progressive Conservative. An impressive 42-year Conservative dynasty once governed Ontario; these successive Conservative governments created the Ontario that was once known as Canada's economic powerhouse, the engine of Canada. Today, under the Ontario Liberals, one can only dream of the former days of Conservative glory.

In the following chapters, I will examine how Ontario was taken radically off-course from wealth and prestige and instead burdened with expensive

Liars

Liberal experiments, massive government debt and deficit spending, and scandal after scandal after scandal. The fall of Mike Harris' Conservative government saw the rise of Dalton McGuinty's Liberals, largely on emotional speculation that Harris had become too mean, too uncaring, and too concerned with reining in public spending. In contrast with that "mean" Harris Premier, McGuinty mercilessly overspent, on throwing our own money at us while simultaneously imposing dozens of new taxes on *everything*. Make no mistake, if Harris' meanness was what caused the pendulum to swing in the Liberals' favour, then McGuinty's meanness takes the cake; his cynical, vote-buying wastefulness is directed towards future generations of children and grandchildren who will inevitably at some point have to rein in public spending and suffer through severe hardship to pay off McGuinty's reckless spending and experiments.

McGuinty has been backed at every step of the way by public sector unions. Not surprisingly, they have also been the largest benefactors of ridiculous salaries and through-the-roof bonuses – all paid for with Ontario taxpayers' money. Numerous backroom deals have also been negotiated between the McGuinty government and unions that have only been exposed by chance or coincidence. While every day Ontario families are struggling to get by, maintain employment, and pay their bills, the McGuinty government *has* been incredibly profitable for two groups of people: unions and Liberal cronies who regularly leave the public sector one day and return the next as a handsomely paid Liberal "advisors" or "consultants." They have been continually exposed and ridiculed, especially by Ontario's Auditor General, yet the scandals continue, even under the Premiership of Kathleen Wynne.

Kathleen Wynne had the opportunity to set the record straight and right all the wrongs created by McGuinty's near-decade in power. She didn't. Instead, she put Ontario further into debt, has continued massive deficits, has continued reckless experiments initiated by McGuinty, and has remained deaf to what Ontario families really need.

Although written from a proudly conservative perspective, this book is meticulously sourced with left-wing, liberal, and right-wing perspectives. Indeed, the Liberal Party has been criticized from the left, the right, and even by its own core centrist supporters. This book analyzes the McGuinty and Wynne governments from angles that will resonate with any voter looking for a change from the disastrous Liberal path Ontario is on.

There is hope. If you're a part of the 99 percent – in other words, not the top one percent of Liberal advisors and unions – then this book is for you. In order to ensure we never repeat the mistakes of the past, we need understand what the past *was*. This book lays out the rise and fall of Ontario. The hope comes in this truth: it is very easy to begin to rebuild Ontario – all we need to do is elect a new government that isn't Liberal.

1   Kelly McParland, "Dalton McGuinty's legacy is a litany of failure," *National Post*, last modified January 25, 2013, http://fullcomment.nationalpost.com/2013/01/25/kelly-mcparland-dalton-mcguintys-legacy-is-a-litany-of-failure/.

2   Christina Blizzard, "Legacy of Dalton McGuinty Anything but Ideal," *Toronto Sun*, last modified June 12, 2013, http://www.torontosun.com/2013/06/12/legacy-of-dalton-mcguinty-anything-but-ideal.

3   "The McGuinty Legacy," *Windsor Star*, last modified July 4, 2013, http://blogs.windsorstar.com/2013/07/04/star-editorial-the-mcguinty-legacy.

4   "Heinz to Close Leamington, Ontario Plant; Hundreds of Jobs Lost," CTV News, last modified November 14, 2013, http://www.ctvnews.ca/canada/heinz-to-close-leamington-ont-plant-hundreds-of-jobs-lost-1.1543663

5   Michael Lewis, "Kellogg's to Close London Plant, 500 Jobs Lost," *Toronto Star*, December 10, 2013, http://www.thestar.com/business/2013/12/10/kelloggs_to_close_london_plant_500_jobs_lost.html

6   "Kraft Canada to close Oakville plant in 2013," *Inside Halton*, last modified November 23, 2012, http://www.insidehalton.com/news-story/2906108-kraft-canada-to-close-oakville-plant-in-2013/.

7   "Navistar to close Chatham, Ont., plant," *CBC News*, last modified August 2, 2011, http://www.cbc.ca/news/canada/windsor/navistar-to-close-chatham-ont-plant-1.1030922.

8   Tanya Talaga, "Xtrata Holds Firm on Decision to cut Chatham Jobs," *CBC News*, last modified April 16, 2010,http://www.thestar.com/business/2010/04/16/xstrata_holds_firm_on_decision_to_cut_timmins_jobs.html

9   Mark Tayti, "John Deere Assembly Line Shuts Down August 6", *Welland Tribune*, last modified July 22, 2009, http://www.wellandtribune.ca/2009/07/22/john-deere-assembly-line-shuts-down-aug-6

10   Richard Blackwell, "Siemens to Close Ontario Plant," *Globe and Mail*, last modified March 11, 2010, http://www.theglobeandmail.com/report-on-business/siemens-to-close-ontario-plant/article4323271/.

11   Rob Ferguson, Robert Benzie and Tanya Talaga, "Caterpillar Closes Electro-Motive Plant in London," *Toronto Star*, last modified February 3, 2012, http://www.thestar.com/news/canada/2012/02/03/caterpillar_closes_electromotive_plant_in_london.html.

Chapter 2

The Lead-Up to Disaster

Mike Harris' "greatest contribution to political life has been to crack the mindset too many Ontarians had of entitlement and limitless public resources. He has taken an axe to the fiscal deficit. He has been prepared to suffer the opposition of many to create a more accountable and cost-efficient public sector for all."

- The Globe and Mail[1]

"Give Harris his due, whether it's luck or whether it's not, it worked out better than I would have thought because it just so happened to coincide that when tax cuts came in place, the U.S. economy started to boom, and in particular all of the Americans decided to buy cars, and a lot of those cars were built in Ontario."

- Don Drummond[2]

In order to understand how Ontario got to where we are today, we need to understand our past. We need to understand our history, our political leaders, and the elections that brought those leaders into office or embarrassingly rejected them. To understand how Ontario came to deserve Premiers like Dalton McGuinty and Kathleen Wynne, we need to understand how and why Ontario rejected Premiers such as Mike Harris. This is not an exhaustive history lesson, but rather a highlight of Ontario's political history as we moved from the Conservative[3] dynasty of the 20th century to the

Liars

Liberals to the New Democrats then back to the Conservatives. This chapter highlights the 20th century provincial politics so that we can understand how Ontario ended up choosing Dalton McGuinty to be its Premier.

The Conservative Dynasty

Ontario was not always the failing province, overburdened with debt and unable to correct its economy. Ontario does know a brighter past: a past which, although smeared by many of today's media and unions was, objectively, a greener, more prosperous, more successful Ontario. In fact, Liberal governments are relatively new to Ontario, which was proudly governed by successive Conservative majority governments for an overwhelming portion of the 20th century.

From Canada's Confederation in 1867 to Dalton McGuinty taking office in 2003, the Ontario PCs held office for over 80 years. Forty-two of those 80 years was an uninterrupted dynasty – a dynasty thrice the length of the longest federal dynasty of Pierre Trudeau (15 years), and twice as long as Ontario's longest serving Premier, Oliver Mowat (23 years). "The Big Blue Machine," as it came to be known, was excellent at governing: their low-tax plans and desire to create jobs while also advocating for fair social programs and personal responsibility meant Ontario's economy was almost constantly growing and expanding.

This well-oiled machine powered its way through the 20th century and raised Ontario's prosperity to levels never before seen. The Conservatives were great at what they did, and Ontario voters rewarded them with large majority governments to ensure the machine carried Ontario forward. Elections throughout most of the 20th century repeatedly re-elected the Conservatives with over 80 percent of the seats.

The Left Turn

Unfortunately, all dynasties must come to an end, and the Ontario PC dynasty would come as the result of several incremental mistakes on the tail end of Conservative Frank Miller's leadership. Only six weeks into his time in office, Miller called an election. The election resulted in a stalemate, and Liberal leader David Peterson and NDP leader Bob Rae began discussions to overthrow the Conservative government and form a coalition government. Under their coalition agreement, *An Agenda for Reform,* the NDP would have some key policy responsibilities in the government (but not cabinet seats), the Liberals would form government under a Premier Peterson, and the NDP would not vote against the Liberals for two years.[4] Their coalition agreement was presented to Lieutenant Governor

John Black Aird, and Rae introduced a motion of no confidence. The Lieutenant Governor accepted the coalition agreement, and Miller, having only served as Premier for 138 days, resigned on June 26, 1985.

Just like that, the second and third-place parties toppled the democratically elected (albeit minority) Conservative government. Their short five-page *Agenda for Reform* brought an end to the 42-year Conservative dynasty, as well as Ontario's position as Canada's leader and solid economic base. The next 10 years would be filled with economic misery, incredibly high unemployment rates, massive government deficits, and new taxes to pay for massive government spending programs.

Peterson's NDP-Liberal Coalition

David Peterson's NDP-Liberal coalition did not rock the boat once in office. One condition of their coalition agreement was that the NDP was given important input into policy considerations, although they were not given cabinet positions. As such, the NDP put forth their best socialist policies for which it is known, including:

- Banning a doctor's right to extra billing
- Creating a rent registry to "protect Ontario tenants"
- Implementing affirmative action and employment equity programs
- Expanding the Ontario Human Rights Commission
- Recognizing state day care and funding as a "basic public service," not welfare

Peterson's first budget introduced a $2.6 billion deficit, followed by subsequent deficits of $2.5 billion, $1.5 billion, and a $90 million surplus heading into the 1990 election.

Peterson was a staunch opponent of free trade with the United States, siding with its NDP allies, creating tensions between the Liberal Premier and Conservative Prime Minister Brian Mulroney. But where Peterson and Mulroney made amends was in their agreement to work together "toward a better Canada" on the Meech Lake Accord. Mulroney noted that they set aside their partisan differences to attempt to enact the Accord, although it failed for multiple reasons.[5] Neither Meech Lake nor the later Charlottetown Accord turned out to be palatable to Canadian voters or provincial representatives once it was brought back to them for ratification. Especially for Canada's largest province, which overwhelmingly speaks English, the Accord was seen as giving too much power to Quebec's Francophones. For Ontario's Premier to be at the forefront, supporting this Accord, was unacceptable to voters.

Liars

The Turn Ever Farther Left

Despite Peterson's Meech Lake baggage, his government was still polling relatively well in the lead-up to the 1990 election. The Liberals called a snap election to capitalize on Peterson's high polling, a move seen as opportunistic. It was also ill-timed from a government perspective: there were several provincial tax hikes planned to come into effect or recently implemented, and angry taxpayers would be more than happy to let the Liberals know how they felt: "There had been hefty rises in Ontario property taxes in the last 2 years. Queen's Park bumped the provincial sales tax to a record 8 percent (then promised to reduce it back to 7 percent during the campaign). These were important irritants to an electorate."[6]

The campaign was also lacklustre and showed the Liberals' enormous complacency. They had spent the last four years in a minority government with the NDP backing them. The Official Opposition Conservatives, having only recently elected new leader Mike Harris, were still divided and not effectively organized to combat the Liberal government's agenda. Voters sent an incredible protest message to Peterson's Liberals: the Liberals lost 59 seats, the NDP gained 55, and the PC's gained four. Peterson lost his own London Centre riding to the NDP. In all, the Liberals lost 14.9 percentage points of their vote, with the NDP gaining 11.9. But it was not the Conservatives to whom the voters returned the keys of Ontario's government. Instead, voters chose Bob Rae to form a majority NDP government.

Rae's NDP Government

Although Rae's government was initially polling as high as 52 percent, the government was destined to be a disaster from the time they introduced their first budget. The NDP's 1991 budget proposed $10.9 billion in deficit spending; in 1992, a $12.4 billion deficit (the largest deficit in Ontario history until Dalton McGuinty's 2010 whopper); and in 1993, a $9 billion deficit and the largest tax hike ever in Ontario history.[7] (The NDP sure seemed to love making history.) Every NDP budget ran incredible deficits, our ratio of debt-to-GDP doubled, and in 1995 Ontario had a deficit-to-GDP ratio of 3.4 percent.[8] Between the Liberal and NDP governments of the 1980s and 1990s, Ontarians saw their taxes raised 65 times.[9]

"Balanced budget" wasn't a phrase in the NDP's vocabulary. As Figure 1 indicates, every NDP budget was passed with significant deficit spending: five budgets were passed totaling $53.6 billion in deficit spending. Rae's NDP also set the record for largest deficit as a percentage of GDP – 4.4 percent – again, until McGuinty broke that record with his 2010 budget.

In 1989 Ontario's debt was $39 billion.[10] With a population then of

10,084,885, this worked out to $3867 per person. By the time the NDP was done in 1995, a population of 10,753,573 was responsible for $98.6 billion in debt – or $9169 per person.[11] In other words, every Ontario resident saw their debt responsibility almost triple in five short years of NDP government. (However, such a number seems miniscule to Ontario's 2010 debt, coming in at a whopping $220 billion, or about $17,000 for every man, woman, and child. More on that later.)

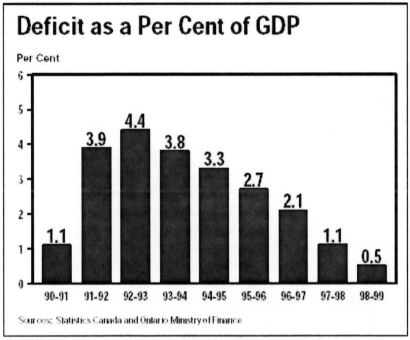

Figure 1: Ontario deficit as a percentage of GDP

But massive debt and deficit spending were not the only portfolios for which Rae wanted to be remembered. Civil servants of the 1990s will also fondly recall "Rae Days." Rae Days were introduced at a time with massive unemployment: in 1992 and 1993, Ontario's unemployment was 10.9 and 10.6 percent respectively.[12] Bob Rae's solution was that civil servants, such as teachers and accountants, take up to 12 unpaid days off per year.[13] Although Rae Days were successful in saving $1.95 billion, Rae did so on the backs of largely unionized workers – his own traditional NDP base. Long-time supporters such as the Canadian Auto Workers (CAW) union and Ontario Public Service Employees Union (OPSEU) openly criticized the NDP for turning its back on their grassroots supporters.

Liars

White Men Not Needed

Halfway through his mandate, in 1993, Rae's NDP racially divided the public service when they began running job advertisements that explicitly stated white men were not eligible to apply. It did not take long for the Ontario public's outrage to cause the Rae government to reverse their decision and allow white men the equal opportunity to apply for public service positions. Equality – what a concept!

Enter Mike Harris

By 1995, Ontarians saw what almost 10 years of Liberal and NDP governments had brought them: higher taxes, expensive government experiments, increasing unemployment, a government willing to give too much power to Quebec, and more. Ten years of Liberal and NDP government meant Ontario voters were fed up with the left-wing parties and were finally ready to return to the right-wing Conservatives. By 1995, Mike Harris had turned his party into a respectable, principled party that could challenge the left-wing ideology. As the third-place party Harris was not the Leader of the Opposition, the Liberals were, which probably gave the PCs the chance they needed to focus on developing a strong platform that would actually deliver real relief to Ontarians. Calls by the Conservatives for lower taxes and reduced government spending were only amplified throughout the nearly-five years of NDP government.

A Common Sense Revolution and Premier Mike Harris

By the 1995 election Ontarians were hungry for change, Harris had the support of his existing party MPPs and core supporters, and he could feel the momentum shifting his way. In the lead-up to the 1995 election unemployment was 8.7 percent, but over 9 percent in manufacturing areas such as Sudbury, St. Catharines, and Niagara.[14]

Liberal leader Lyn McLeod became known as a "flip-flopper" when she withdrew her party's support for a law that would give same sex unions the same benefits as heterosexual couples (Bill 167), introduced by the NDP government. But the campaign's turning point came in the televised leaders' debate when McLeod was seen as being overly aggressive against Bob Rae. Rae defended his government for its actions, but Mike Harris emerged the victor by ignoring Rae and McLeod's questions, looking directly into the camera, and selling his platform, the "Common Sense Revolution."

Today, the slightest mention of Harris' name brings up the famous Common Sense Revolution, but the reaction you will receive is largely negative. Unfortunately, this is the result of a targeted, twisted smear campaign. You're probably much more likely to hear of the platform's supposed negative impacts than its positive ones. It also does not help that campaign platforms in the Harris era were not yet posted on party websites or publicly available in electronic format, leaving today's NDP and Liberals to make up almost any rumour about the platform without it easily being disproven. (To combat this, I was able to locate an elusive electronic copy of the platform and have posted it to my website at http://www.danieldickin.ca/2011/12/common-sense-revolution.html.)

The Revolution was an appropriate balance between fiscal prudence, the ending of "Rae Days," requiring balanced budgets, and cutting taxes. It should come as no surprise that when a government's spending is out of control, costing us money in the name of higher taxes, Ontarians come to favour a populist party that promises lower taxes and less government interference in everyday life. It was simple and straightforward, delivered by a career teacher whose brand became "to do exactly what I say I will do." To summarize, Harris' Revolution planned to:

- Cut income taxes by 30 percent over three years
- Cut total government spending by 20 percent over three years, without affecting health care, law enforcement, or education
- Freeze Ontario Hydro rates for five years
- Introduce 'balanced budget' legislation – the requirement, by law, that the government balance its books and go to the electorate to obtain permission to raise taxes
- Enter into bi-lateral negotiations to end provincial trade barriers
- Eliminate all red tape and reduce the regulatory burden
- Set performance standards for all public employees and reduce the public service by 15%
- Balance the budget in four years (by year five, cut even more taxes and begin paying down the provincial debt)
- Introduce "classroom-based budgeting," to eliminate money spent on "consultants, bureaucracy, and administration" (Harris called them "educrats") and instead focus on in-classroom funding based on the number of students
- Reduce the number of MPPs and replace the MPP pension plan with a retirement savings plan
- Crack down on welfare fraud and creating "workfare" and "learnfare" to get people receiving welfare back on their feet through jobs and/or education
- Eliminate the employer health tax for payrolls making less than $400,000

It should come as no surprise that when such an alternative to Bob Rae's

Liars

NDP government was presented, Ontarians overwhelmingly took the lower taxes and affordable, reasonable government option. Harris gained an impressive 62 seats or 21.3 percentage points, with 44.8 percent of the popular vote. McLeod's Liberals lost six seats and 1.3 percentage points, with 31.1 percent of the popular vote. And Rae's NDP were given a swift kick from office, losing 57 seats and 17 percentage points, with 20.6 percent of the popular vote.

The Harris Golden Years

Brian Crowley, Managing Director of the Macdonald-Laurier Institute, an economic think tank, and former Visiting Economist with Finance Canada, refers to the 1990's as the "redemptive decade" – the decade where provincial and federal governments began to understand their gross overspending was going to ruin their province and the country, and most of them began to amend policies to redeem their previous recklessness.[15] Unfortunately, we know that Ontario's Liberal or NDP governments blatantly failed to take the steps needed, so it was up to Ontario's PCs to begin Ontario's redemption.

Keeping Promises

Harris, to taxpayers' thrill, was a man of his word. He was also very predictable in that he did exactly what he said he would do. The first budget his majority government introduced reduced deficit spending. He reformed welfare exactly as he said he would, creating a temporary program to cover basic costs. Section one of the *Ontario Works Act* established a welfare program that:

> "(a) recognizes individual responsibility and promotes self-reliance through employment;
> (b) provides temporary financial assistance to those most in need while they satisfy obligations to become and stay employed;
> (c) effectively serves people needing assistance; and
> (d) is accountable to the taxpayers of Ontario."

This was a notable break from the previous principle of entitlement – it should be a privilege to be allowed to temporarily live off the taxpayer, not an entitlement which is perpetuated and handed down to future generations like an heirloom.

On the jobs front, within two years the unemployment rate fell by 1.5 percent, and stayed below 7 percent until Harris left office in 2002. In fact, unemployment was two percentage points lower than when the NDP was in government,[16] and every year Harris was in office the unemployment rate was lower than the Canadian unemployment rate.[17] As shown in Figure 2,

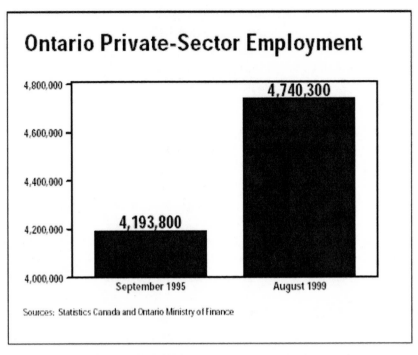

Figure 2:Growth in private sector employment

private sector employment ballooned under Harris' first four years in government, adding over 500,000 jobs.

Harris' pledge to balance the budget within four years without touching health care, law enforcement, or education was a broken promise; in fact, he did it in *three* years with a surplus in his 1999-2000 budget.[18] Their $654 million surplus was over $2.7 billion *better* than the Finance Ministry's original 1999 financial outlook, and was applied to paying down Ontario's debt. It was largely due to Ontario's economy growth of 5.7 percent, lower taxes (meaning Ontarians could spend more), and GDP projections which showed continued growth in Ontario's already booming economy.

A New Liberal Leader

Dalton McGuinty was first elected as the MPP for Ottawa South in 1989, succeeding his father, Dalton Senior. In 1996 McGuinty entered the leadership race to replace Lyn McLeod and won through what even Liberal supporters called "a comically bizarre convention."[19] On the first ballot McGuinty came a distant fourth, behind Gerard Kennedy, Joseph Cordiano, and Dwight Duncan. On the second ballot McGuinty again came fourth behind the same four contestants. But with John Gerretsen and Anna-Marie Castrilli being eliminated and endorsing McGuinty, the third ballot saw

Liars

McGuinty jump over Duncan to third place. With Duncan being eliminated and endorsing Kennedy, the fourth ballot saw McGuinty succeed
Cordiano for second place. Finally, at 4:25am on December 1, McGuinty
beat Kennedy by 140 votes on the fifth ballot. Kennedy had been in first
place in four consecutive votes, and Liberals called McGuinty's win a "a
perverse mistake."[20]

Much like the Conservatives did during their rebuilding period in the 1990s,
the Liberals kept a quiet profile as they focused their efforts on internally
rebuilding their party. When McGuinty did appear in the media, however,
he came off as stiff and inexperienced. By the 1999 election, McGuinty
was still seen as a fresh face even though NDP leader Howard Hampton
had been elected leader of his party six months after McGuinty. McGuinty
was quickly labelled as "not up to the job" by the Tories for his lack of a
clear platform, and Hampton compared McGuinty to fictional serial killer
Norman Bates for his rigidity and awkwardness.

A Winning Re-election Campaign

Harris was in an incredible position by 1999. He promised to do what he
said he would do – and he did it while the both the Liberals and the NDP
were electing new leaders and internally getting ready for the next election. Harris overwhelmingly fulfilled his 1995 election platform, and then
went farther. As a career teacher, he knew the education system needed
serious reforms. He also knew he needed to wrangle the system's control
away from the "educrats" to put the focus back on giving students a quality
education. His government's accomplishments included:

- Creating the Ontario College of Teachers, the licencing, governing,
  and regulating body responsible for Ontario's teachers.
- Reducing the number of school boards from 129 to 72 and the number of trustees from 1900 to 700
- Creating the Education Quality and Assurance Office (EQAO) to
  create and oversee standardized tests for Ontario students, in accor-
  dance with the recommendations made in 1995 by the Royal Commission on Learning.
- Introducing Telehealth Ontario, the free 24-hour 1-800 number to
  call to speak to nurses about medical questions
- Eliminating grade 13
- Funding for research and development through the Ontario R&D
  Challenge Fund, the Ontario Innovation Trust and the Premier's Research Excellence Awards
- Leasing of Highway 407 to a private consortium including the Canada Pension Plan and SNC-Lavalin

Voters love when governments keep their promises, especially during a time when they are increasingly weary of government promises and politicians. Harris setting priorities and then achieving them was a refreshing change from the taxman coming to your door demanding another handout. Indeed, almost 68 percent of people who do not vote in elections do so because they negatively perceive politicians, political parties, the government, and the electoral system.[21] Nineteen percent of the people who do not participate in elections stay away from politics because they swear politicians are "dishonest, selfish, corrupt, immature, and make false promises."[22] Extreme perhaps, but it helps explain the cynicism seen when so many other governments make outlandish promises they fail to follow through.

Harris, as the incumbent responsible for this record, wielded a clear advantage: the memories of massive tax hikes and enormous government deficits under Liberal or NDP rule were still all too fresh in the minds of Ontario voters. Whereas the Conservatives' 1995 election was about "revolution," 1999 was about continuing forward on the same path.

The Conservatives' platform, *Blueprint: Mike Harris' Plan to Keep Ontario on the Right Track,* promised more tax cuts, less government, and better government services. Despite massive cuts to health care funding by Jean Chretien's federal Liberal government, the Harris government promised to increase health care funding by 20 percent. He promised to introduce a Patient's Bill of Rights and guaranteed that education funding could continue to match increasing enrollment. The Ontario PCs would invest $20 billion in upgrading Ontario's hospitals, schools, high-tech links, highways, and universities and colleges. They boasted that by March 1999 372,066 people had been removed from the public welfare roll. On top of the 540,000 jobs already created since they took office, they promised to create an additional 825,000 jobs over five years. Harris' Conservatives cut taxes 69 times in their first three years in office. These were just a few of the promises the Harris Conservatives made in their re-election bid. (Luckily, with increased use of the internet, the 1999 election platform is much more readily available online.)[23]

An Ontario-wide Ekos Research poll showed Harris holding a commanding lead in several aspects of the election, including: the best to deal with health care; the best to deal with crime and violence; the best to deal with employment; the best to deal with public finance and debt; and the best to deal with tax cuts.[24] The second-place Liberals under McGuinty won only as "best to deal with education," while the NDP under Howard Hampton won only as "best to deal with child poverty and homelessness." Decided voters in this poll were 46 percent voting Progressive Conservative, reflecting the final results of the election.

Liars

The 1999 election was the first election in which the provincial electoral districts were redrawn to match the federal districts. This resulted in 27 fewer seats. Because of this, it would be wrong to say the Conservatives "lost" 23 seats, the Liberals "gained" five, or that the NDP "lost" eight. Harris was re-elected with 45.1 percent of the vote, an increase of 0.3 percentage points. McGuinty's Liberals obtained 39.9 percent of the vote, gaining 8.8 percentage points, which were largely taken from Hampton's NDP, who obtained 12.6 percent of the vote and lost eight percentage points. The new legislature had 59 Conservatives, 35 Liberals, and nine New Democrats.

Plain and simple, if voters were really so concerned or disappointed about Harris' government priorities, they would not have given him a second majority mandate to do more of the same. In fact, "Conservatives were re-elected for many reasons, including the power of their election campaign and the reputation of Mike Harris as the most capable leader and one who had proven – in spite of vociferous opposition – that he will actually do what he had promised to do."[25] Some social program funding being reduced to ensure the long-term financial stability and prosperity of Canada's most populous province was clearly worth it to voters. It was an easy victory for a Conservative Premier focused on doing exactly what he said he would do.

No Tolerance for Abuse of Taxpayers Money

As shown through two elections, the Conservative governments of Harris and Eves were proud to stand up for taxpayers. In 2002, Hydro One President and chief executive officer (CEO) Eleanor Clitheroe was fired by the Harris government. Clitheroe was raking in over $2.2 million in annual salary, bonuses, and benefits: $174,000 for a personal car, $172,000 in vacation pay. Her severance package was a ridiculous $6 million if she was to leave for *any* reason, and she would qualify for an annual pension of up to $1 million.[26] She was clearly living the high life, having her personal chauffeur drive her around in her personal limousine to exclusive country clubs – all on the taxpayers' dime.

When she was fired, she took the Ontario government to court. And when she lost that case, she appealed to the Ontario Court of Appeal, claiming – brace yourself – that her $307,000 per-year pension should be raised to $464,000. And when she lost again, she appealed to the Supreme Court of Canada. She lost.[27]

The fall of the Harris Government

This was not to say Mike Harris' government was without controversy or issues. Every dynasty must come to an end, just as the impressive 42-year Ontario PC dynasty came to an end in the 1980s. Harris was a populist, and while the voters may have loved him, the special interest groups and unions did not. This was especially true of the teachers' union, who felt betrayed that Harris, a career teacher, had implemented standardized testing and increased oversight on teachers. It created a poisonous environment, with Harris leading the province and implementing the agenda on which he was elected, and special interest groups, some media, and unions fighting him every step of the way. When juicy political issues came to the fore, it was this triumvirate that effectively did the dirty work of McGuinty's Opposition, selling half-truths and exploiting government oversights to their maximum potential. Here are just three examples:

The Walkerton Tragedy

In 2000, seven people died and hundreds became sick in the town of Walkerton when the water supply became contaminated with E. Coli. In reality, the tragedy was aggravated by a single water facility manager, Stan Koebel, and his brother, who had been falsifying water quality documents.

The Walkerton Commission was formed to find the root cause of this tragedy, headed by Ontario Appeals Court Justice Dennis O'Connor. Those deaths and injuries did not have to happen; they laid entirely at the feet of the Koebels. That is exactly what the Walkerton Commission found, stating:

> The Walkerton Public Utilities Commission operators engaged in a host of improper operating practices, including failing to use adequate doses of chlorine, failing to monitor chlorine residuals daily, making false entries about residuals in daily operating records, and misstating the locations at which microbiological samples were taken. The operators knew that these practices were unacceptable and contrary to Ministry of Environment guidelines and directives.[28]

Norm Sterling, a former Environment Minister, testified at the Commission that any budget cuts resulting in the various government departments were manageable. Premier Harris likewise testified that he was never warned of any public health risks posed by his fiscal measures. Former Liberal Premier David Peterson said such a tragedy could have happened under any government's watch.

However, it did not take much for the Opposition Liberals and NDP to spin the story: here was a government *reducing* spending and then a tragedy like this happens. Could *more* employees have prevented this disaster? Could better equipment and training have saved the lives of those seven people?

Liars

The CBC baldly asked "Did budget cuts and the common sense revolution cause the tainted water tragedy?"[29] We will never know, but those loaded questions penetrated everyone's thoughts.

The Kimberly Rogers Death

Kimberly Rogers was described as "destitute" by the Ontario Supreme Court; she was pregnant, not working, had health issues, and was attending Sudbury's Cambrian College.[30] She was not receiving financial support from her family or the father of her child, and was apparently unable to work full-time due to health issues. When it was revealed that Rogers was drawing both welfare and student loans from the Ontario government without claiming the income, she was ordered to repay $13,486, the amount deemed to be an overpayment from what she should have received if she properly claimed both benefits. When she failed to pay, her welfare payments were garnished and she was criminally charged with welfare fraud.

Rogers pleaded guilty, and Justice Greg Rodgers found that Rogers had engaged in "almost four years of deception and dishonesty." He also pointed out "welfare is there for people who need it, not for people who want it, who want things and who want money." Rogers was suspended from receiving welfare for three months, ordered to repay the overpayment, and sentenced to house arrest, except for traveling for medical, religious, or shopping reasons. Tragically, on August 9, 2001 Rogers committed suicide by drug overdose, taking her own life while nine-months pregnant with her child.

Of course, this was not the story reported in some media sources. Instead, they spun the findings into a case of sexism and discrimination. The *Toronto Star* reported "she was a woman, she was pregnant, she had a disability, those are precisely the issues she was criminalized for."[31] The Feminist Alliance for International Action said it was the courts who caused Rogers' "extreme deprivation, and [ultimately] her death."[32] The FAIA preferred to ignore reality – that Rogers defrauded the system – and instead laid the blame with the courts and the government, proclaiming "Rogers paid the ultimate penalty for the policies of the Ontario government: death."[33] A coroner's inquest was struck and made several reform recommendations, but Community and Social Services Minister Brenda Elliott said the suggestions were unnecessary changes to a system that "was working effectively." None of the inquest's recommendations would be implemented before Eves' government fell to Dalton McGuinty.

Allegations of Misuse of Taxpayers' Money

Thirdly, Cam Jackson, then Conservative minister of tourism and transportation, was accused of lavishly furnishing an expensive lifestyle on the back of taxpayers as he billed the Ontario government over $100,000 for dinners, hotel rooms, and travel expenses.[34] The Integrity Commissioner ruled that Jackson's expenses were "reasonable and appropriate,"[35] but the damage was done the second the story broke. In the public's eyes, this was a minister billing taxpayers excessive amounts of money for food and lodging he used while on official government business. It did not matter that all MPPs were eligible to claim the same expenses.

Unfortunately, the facts did not matter in the Walkerton tragedy, the Rogers suicide, or Cam Jackson's expenses. The *perception* of the Harris' government's culpability in a community suffering because of lax government regulations, a woman dying while under house arrest and on welfare, and a Conservative cabinet minister abusing taxpayers' money was all it took to change the Harris brand and create a negative perception of an impersonal, mean-spirited government.

The *Globe and Mail* gave Harris "much credit for pulling Ontario back from a potentially ruinous fiscal path,"[36] but they surmised Harris' success was largely thanks to a "radical" agenda resulting in a "crumbling" transit system, a "dismantled" government, and a "rudderless" education system.

A New Leader

Harris announced in October 2001 that he would step down as Premier and leader of the Ontario PC Party. Some reporters speculated that after six years as Premier and the implementation of two highly successful election platforms, Harris was losing interest in his job, while others speculated his waning popularity and loss in important by-elections was the reason.[37] Whatever the reason, Harris' resignation sent speculation rifts throughout Ontario and the party Harris had led for almost 12 years.

Candidates for Harris' job were Jim Flaherty, Chris Hodgson, Tony Clement, Janet Ecker, Elizabeth Witmer, and Chris Stockwell. Although not on the original slate of candidates,[38] Ernie Eves joined the campaign after being approached by senior party officials. Each of the candidates had significant experience: all were cabinet ministers, except for Eves, who was Harris' Deputy Premier and Minister of Finance, but had resigned and was replaced in a byelection. All of the candidates from that leadership race continue to have highly successful careers with Flaherty (until his death on April 10, 2014) and Clement currently holding senior federal cabinet portfolios. Witmer remained a trusted Ontario PC MPP and Critic, and was even voted Ontario's Greatest [Potential] Female Premier by Equal Voice.[39] Witmer left provincial politics in 2013, resigning as an MPP to become

Liars

head of the Workplace Safety and Insurance Board (WSIB); more on that in chapter nine.

Eves emerged as a frontrunner, with almost unanimous support amongst sitting MPPs. He ran on a centralist platform, stating that he was neither left – nor right-wing while simultaneously distancing himself from Harris' Common Sense Revolution platform. It was this distancing from the Revolution platform that would eventually doom the Conservatives a few years later. Such a position drew criticism from eventual runner-up and former federal Finance Minister Jim Flaherty, who was running a hard-right platform which he hoped would appeal to the party's grassroots.

Flaherty attempted to keep the party's sights in the future, asking "Do we want the kind of conservatism that continues to build on the gains of the Common Sense Revolution, or do we want to go back to that outdated conservatism of the past, when Tories governed blandly from the comfort of the country club?"[40] Flaherty answered his own question: "Members of our party tell me overwhelmingly they want more Common Sense Revolution, not a country-club restoration." Flaherty drew criticism from the same interview when he called Eves a "serial waffler" and nothing more than a "pale, pink imitation of Dalton McGuinty."[41]

By the time Flaherty made that statement, according to an SES Research survey he was already a distant fourth place, behind every candidate except Chris Stockwell, with just 6.9 percent support.[42] Eves won the contest on the second ballot, with leadership candidates Tony Clement and Elizabeth Witmer withdrawing after the first ballot and endorsing Eves. Eves won with 54.6 percent support, behind Flaherty's 37.8 percent, and was sworn in as Premier on April 15, 2002.

The Downwards Slide

Eves came to office during a chaotic time when the PC government was already under increased scrutiny. Indeed, in much of Eves' 18 months as premier, he was seemingly constantly embattled with questions and scandals surrounding his government. And although most of these "scandals" were not scandals at all – like the Walkerton tragedy or Cam Jackson's expenses or the Kimberly Rogers death – it was the public's ongoing perception of them as scandals which ultimately toppled Eves' government. Left-leaning media sources bent the truth, instead choosing to report on the very worst case scenarios which painted Eves' government as one of disrepute. It did not hurt that the Liberals also lied about cabinet ministers. By the time the truth came to surface, the public had already made up its mind; they did not appreciate Eves' Conservative government and were swinging to the left one more time.

24

Eves also reversed a Harris-era decision to privatize the Ontario power grid. Almost ten years of consultations, evaluations, and government reviews went into the original decision to put Ontario hydro generation, at the time monopolized by Hydro One, on the competitive market. Two electricity unions challenged the move in court, which ended in the courts blocking the privatization move.[43] A hot summer combined with cost-overruns at Ontario's plants meant hydro prices rose significantly. Eves announced the government's reversal on the decision, stating that they would be holding public consultations on how to best fund Ontario's hydro system, without privatization as an option.[44] It was the death of a strong Conservative plank in Harris' Revolution platform, one that Harris could not implement during his time in office.

Indeed, Eves' government seemed to be always in reaction mode for most of his 18 months as Premier. Yet there were several strong points during his premiership, such as his exceptional leadership during the 2003 North American blackout – a power failure which left 10 million people in Ontario and 45 million people across North America without electricity for up to five days. The failure, which originated in the United States, spread to Ontario after power plants simultaneously took themselves off the grid to protect them from a surge. Eves handled the event swiftly and competently, providing daily media briefs and updates regarding the status of the Ontario power grid, and calling on businesses and households to conserve their electricity usage until the power grid was stable.

Although some residents were understandably agitated, the blackout actually increased Eves' popularity: true to his leadership campaign, Eves demonstrated he could be calm under pressure, organize and control the government's response, and deliver relief for most people within a few days of the blackout. Fifty four percent of Ontarians agreed with the job Eves was doing according to an Ipsos-Reid poll, a five percent boost in his approval rating. Ipsos-Reid Vice President John Wright said Eves "owns the airways. He's eclipsing Liberal Leader Dalton McGuinty and NDP Leader Howard Hampton."[45]

The time was right for Eves' government to call a snap election to capitalize on his recently popularity boost. This, however, would prove to be the final nail in the Ontario PC coffin, echoing back to the same fateful decision Peterson's Liberal government made in the 1990 election.

In summary, the overwhelming majority of the 20th century saw Ontario led by successive Conservative governments. They paved the way for Ontario to become the economic powerhouse, the largest and most reliable province in the Canadian union. When Ontario did decide to take a turn to

Liars

the left, first through Liberal government, then to New Democrats, it was an unmitigated disaster. Between NDP and Liberal governments, Ontarians saw their taxes raised 69 times over 10 years. New Democrats introduced job-killing regulations, and Liberals were bent on raising taxes to pay for government experiments. Bob Rae, as Ontario's first and only socialist Premier plunged Ontario into years of deficit spending, doubling Ontario's debt between the two governments. When Ontario needed to be rescued, Mike Harris' Progressive Conservative government was there, cutting income taxes by a third, creating over half a million jobs in four years, and reforming some of Ontario's social services to be more responsive, transparent, and affordable. But by 2003, under the new Conservative leadership of Ernie Eves, Ontario once again became hungry for change, and it would turn back to the same political ideology that brought Ontario to the brink of disaster in the 1980s and 1990s.

1   *Globe and Mail*, Mike Harris's Legacy, *Globe and Mail*, October 17, 2001, http://www. theglobeandmail.com/globe-debate/mike-harriss-legacy/article763723/

2   Don Drummond, Mike Harris: His Political Legacy, CBC Learning, May 2002, http:// newsinreview.cbclearning.ca/wp-content/uploads/2002/05/harris.pdf

3   I use "Conservative" to describe the Progressive Conservative Party of Ontario, or the "Ontario PC Party." Conservatives are inherently progressive, in that they seek progress, making the title Progressive Conservative somewhat redundant.

4   Muriel Draaisma, How it Might Work in Canada, *CBC News*, November 28, 2008, http://www.cbc.ca/news/canada/story/2008/11/28/f-faq-coalition.html

5   Brian Mulroney, *Memoirs: 1939-1993* (Toronto: McClelland & Stewart Ltd., 2007).

6   Jim Henderson, *The 1990 Ontario Election: Lessons for Canadians*, Canadian Parliamentary Review, 1991, http://www.revparl.ca/english/issue.asp?art=889&param=136

7   Patrick Grady, Ontario NDP Tax Increases, Canadian Business Economics, 1993, http:// global-economics.ca/ONTTAX93.pdf

8   Ernie Eves, Restructuring the Government of Ontario, Fraser Institute, http://oldfraser. lexi.net/publications/books/fiscal_surplus/chapter8.html

9   Ibid.

10   Livio di Matteo, Ontario: After the Orgy, Winnipeg Free Press, November 4, 2009, http://www.winnipegfreepress.com/opinion/westview/ontario-after-the-orgy.html

11   Ontario Ministry of Finance, Public Accounts: 1995-1996 Annual Report, http://www. fin.gov.on.ca/en/budget/paccts/1996/96_ar.html

12   Dave Gower, Canada's Unemployment Mosaic in the 1990s, Statistics Canada, 1996, http://www.statcan.gc.ca/studies-etudes/75-001/archive/1996/5018477-eng.pdf

13   Richard Brennan, No Regrets about Days that Bear his name, Rae Says, *Toronto Star*, November 6, 2009, http://www.thestar.com/news/canada/article/721995---no-regrets-about-days-that-bear-his-name-rae-says

14   Dave Gower, supra note 12.

15   Brian Crowley, Jason Clemens, and Niels Veldhuis, The Canadian Century (Toronto: Key Porter Books, 2010).

16   Ontario Ministry of Finance, Public Accounts: 1998-1999 Annual Report, http://www.fin.gov.on.ca/en/budget/paccts/1999/99_ar.html

17   Ontario Ministry of Finance, 2009 Ontario Economic Outlook and Fiscal Review, http://www.fin.gov.on.ca/en/budget/fallstatement/2009/ecotables.html

18   Ontario Financing Authority, 2000 Ontario Budget Highlights, May 2000, http://www.ofina.on.ca/pdf/budget00.pdf

19   *Toronto Star*, How Dalton McGuinty Changed Ontario – and why he Resigned, Toronto Star, January 10, 2013, http://www.thestar.com/news/insight/2013/01/10/star_dispatches_how_dalton_mcguinty_changed_ontario_and_why_he_resigned.html

20   Ibid.

21   Jon Pammett and Lawrence LeDuc, *Explaining the Turnout Decline in Canadian Federal Elections: A New Survey of Non-Voters, Elections Canada*, March 2003, http://www.elections.ca/res/rec/part/tud/TurnoutDecline.pdf

22   Ibid.

23   *Ontario PC Party, Blueprint: Mike Harris' Plan to Keep Ontario on the Right Track*, 1999, http://www.poltext.org/sites/poltext.org/files/plateformes/on1999pc_plt._26122008_84857.pdf

24   EKOS Research, Ontario Election Campaign Survey, May 1999, http://www.ekos.com/admin/articles/5-25-99.pdf

25   Canada Watch, The Harris Second Term: Is the Revolution Over? Canada Watch, York University, December 1999, http://www.yorku.ca/robarts/projects/canada-watch/pdf/vol_7_6/armstrong.pdf

26   CBC News, Hydro One CEO Eleanor Clitheroe Fired, CBC News, July 22, 2002, http://www.cbc.ca/news/business/hydro-one-ceo-eleanor-clitheroe-fired-1.339806

27   *Globe and Mail*, Supreme Court Rejects former Hydro One CEO Clitheroe's Bid for $464,000 Pension, *Globe and Mail*, December 23, 2010, http://www.theglobeandmail.com/news/national/supreme-court-rejects-former-hydro-one-ceo-clitheroes-bid-for-464000-pension/article1320991/

28   Dennis O'Connor, Report of the Walkerton Inquiry: The Events of May 2000 and Related Issues, Walkerton Commission, http://www.attorneygeneral.jus.gov.on.ca/english/about/pubs/walkerton/part1/WI_Summary.pdf

29   *CBC News*, Walkerton was a Wakeup Call for all of Us, CBC News, http://www.cbc.ca/archives/categories/environment/pollution/death-on-tap-extra-clips/walkerton-was-a-wake-up-call-for-all-of-us.html

30   Rogers v. Sudbury (Administrator of Ontario Works), 2001 CanLII 28086 (ON SC).

31   Kate Harries, Groups Fight Inquest Ruling in Sudbury, Toronto Star, November 18, 2002, http://www.fact.on.ca/news/news0211/ts021118.htm

32   Canadian Feminist Alliance for International Action, Canada's Failure to Act: Women's Inequality Deepens, January 2003, http://www.iwrp.org/pdf/fafia_report.pdf

33   Ibid.

34   Barry Brimbecom, Ontario Votes 2003, CBC News, http://www.cbc.ca/ontariovotes2003/features/cabinet_090803.html

Liars

35   Office of the Integrity Commissioner of Ontario, Guidelines for Expense Claims for Cabinet Ministers, Opposition Leaders, and their Staff, November 2010, http://oico.on.ca/web-att.nsf/vw/EXP/$FILE/Guidelines-Nov2010.pdf

36   *Globe and Mail*, supra note 1.

37   CBC News, Ontario Premier to Resign, CBC News, October 16, 2001, http://www.cbc.ca/news/canada/story/2001/10/16/harris011016.html

38   Ibid.

39   Equal Voice, Ontario's Greatest Female Premier, http://www.equalvoice.ca/mmp/

40   Robert Benzie, Flaherty Gets Personal With Attack on Eves, National Post, January 31, 2002, http://www.sesresearch.com/news/in_the_news/NationalPostJ31.pdf

41   Ibid.

42   Ibid.

43   Roy Hrab, Privatization: Experience and Prospects, University of Toronto Law School, February 2004, http://www.law-lib.utoronto.ca/investing/reports/rp22.pdf

44   Toronto Star, Tories scrap Hydro sell-off, Toronto Star, January 21, 2003, p. A1.

45   Richard Mackie, Blackout Gives Eves Boost: Poll, Globe and Mail, August 21, 2003, http://www.theglobeandmail.com/news/national/blackout-gives-eves-boost-poll/article1165062/

Chapter 3

Bye-Bye Balanced Budgets!

"I promise not to raise taxes"

"I'm telling Ontario families that their taxes will not go up tomorrow or any day under a Liberal government."

"We will not raise taxes one cent on Ontario families"

"We will not be raising taxes. Families are carrying enough of burden as it is."

"We're not going to raise taxes. That's just not on the table."

"I, Dalton McGuinty, leader of the Liberal party of Ontario, promise, if my party is elected as the next government, I will not raise taxes or implement any new taxes without the explicit consent of Ontario voters and not run deficits. I promise to abide by the Taxpayer Protection and Balanced Budget Act."

- Dalton McGuinty in 2003

The shift from reasonable conservatism to radical liberalism

For the past eight years before Dalton McGuinty came to power, Ontario had done remarkably well. It was recovering from almost 10 years of Liberal and New Democrat rule. Under those governments, unemployment sky-rocketed, individuals and businesses were constantly being saddled

Liars

with an endless list of new taxes and regulations, and the economy was suffering. Ontario needed a hero to rescue the province from disaster, and it found one in the leadership of Mike Harris, a career teacher and straight-shooter whose pledge to do exactly what the voters elected him to do was simple and refreshing.

But with Harris' early departure in 2001, Ontario came to loathe the more centrist and less popular Ernie Eves. For most of Eves' 18 months in office, he was criticized and his government went from scandal to scandal, forcing Eves to defend the Harris government's policies while also attempting to craft his own legacy. When Eves received a popularity boost in the polls due to his calm and professional handling of the 2003 North American blackout, he called a snap election. It would be a fateful decision for Ontario's Conservatives and a decision which all of Ontario would regret.

The Issues

The central theme of the 2003 election was how well the Progressive Conservatives could rebrand their party as moving on from Harris' majority governments. Indeed, polling by Nik Nanos at SES Research found that all the talk about the Common Sense Revolution had become tired and voters were looking for a less-confrontational government.[1] However, while they were searching for a "kinder, gentler Mike Harris," they were still seeking someone with Harris' wisdom and principles: Harris scored 21 percent higher as the preferred choice for Premier over Dalton McGuinty. Even when Eves took office as Premier, he remained the favourite. According to an Ipsos-Reid poll, 39 percent of Ontarians said Eves made the best Premier, over McGuinty's 28 percent.[2] Ontarians still wanted a conservative government, even if the previous Harris government was too pushy with its reform policies. Questions about Eves' government were largely baseless. In Eves' relatively short time in office, he had really only dealt with the blackout, which helped his popularity, and a SARS outbreak, which was relatively well-contained to the Greater Toronto Area.

It was up to the each political party to define their leaders and the best road forward for Ontario:

Conservatives

With eight years in government, the Ontario PC platform was about maintaining the successful government Harris has built with his two majorities government. *The road ahead: Premier Ernie Eves' plan for Ontario's Future* was about highlighting this success and ensuring Ontario stayed on the right track. The central slogan, "Experience You Can Trust," was intended to send a simple yet powerful message: you could trust the incumbent Premier, but you could not trust anyone else. This was in contrast to McGuinty who had still shown himself as an awkward amateur in front of the camera and in Queen's Park. In fact, McGuinty would become known as "the accidental Premier... a man seemingly without natural attributes for politics."[3] And the NDP have never been serious contenders in almost a generation, since too many people still remember the Rae Days.

Eves' plan for Ontario's future focused on five platform planks: tax deductions for mortgage payments; a tax rebate to seniors for the education portion they paid on their property taxes; tax credits to parents who send their children to private schools; getting rid of teachers' strikes in favour of sending any negotiations to binding arbitration; and creating a "Made in Ontario" immigration system.

Each of the five planks was targeted at the overwhelmingly majority of Ontarians. Being able to reduce the amount of taxes paid on mortgage interest would allow home owners to keep more money in their pockets (some stated it was up to $500 per year). Seniors did not feel their taxes should go towards an education system their children (if they had any) had left long ago. Ditto for parents sending their children to private schools. The parents who did send their children to public schools overwhelmingly felt their kids should actually be in school and be given an education rather than seeing the teachers disrupt this process through strikes. Finally, with the economy doing better under the Harris government than first projected, Ontario was going to be able to reduce even more of the net provincial debt.

Eves also touched upon the health care and the post-secondary education systems. His government would hire 650 doctors and 8,000 nurses over five years. They would guarantee wait times for surgeries, cancer treatment, and MRI scans. They would inject $2.3 billion in creating 135,000 student spaces at colleges and universities across the province. Spending would be further reduced by $7 billion, which would free up more money to further reduce personal income taxes.[4]

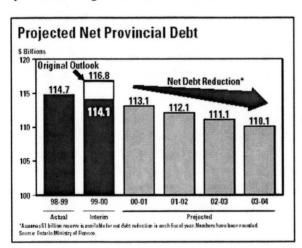

Figure 3: Ontario's debt reduction[5]

Liars

It was a platform aimed at maintaining the status quo – which was excellent – while continuing to offer new ideas to support Ontario's families.

New Democrats

The Ontario NDP have rarely ever had a realistic opportunity of forming a government. When they did come to power in 1990 it was a huge upset, a shocking result very few people saw coming. The reasons for that election's outcome were discussed in chapter two, and many people, even in 2003, did not forget the incredible mess Bob Rae's NDP created in the years they were in government.

By 2003, Howard Hampton's New Democrats were tired and uninspired. In the 1999 election which gave Mike Harris his second majority government, Hampton led his New Democrats to their worst showing to-date – even worse than when Rae's NDP were resoundingly kicked from office in 1995.[6] The CBC, which is known for being sympathetic to left-wing and liberal parties, summarized bluntly: "Barring a miracle – or campaign disasters of truly mythic proportions for the Liberals and Conservatives – there's no chance that Hampton will lead the next government of Ontario. In fact, it's extremely unlikely that Hampton will ever occupy the premier's office." In fact, the NDP would have lost their status as an official party if it were not for a Conservative motion that lowered the threshold of official party status to accommodate the NDP's smaller numbers following the 1999 election.

Where the NDP have usually done well is in opposing whichever government is in power. In the days of Conservative governments, it was easy for the NDP to claim the Conservatives were unkind, wealthy, white men who failed to represent women, visible minorities, and the "little guy" down on his or her luck. Indeed, the CBC said it was "easy" for the NDP because they were the automatic antithesis to conservatism. Hampton's NDP, if it were ever to reform government or give a fair showing in an election, could capitalize on this through a populist platform that would show the NDP as principled individuals with good judgment.

The NDP promised to increase taxes on anyone making over $100,000 per year. They would balance the budget. They would get rid of the private school tax credit. They would make junior and senior kindergarten full-day programs. They would replace Harris' standardized testing "bureaucracy" with "student testing" that would better identify the students' strengths and needs. They would raise corporate taxes by $3 billion a year over the following four years. They would implement a state-regulated child care program that would cost parents only $10 per day.[7]

The NDP were the obvious antithesis to Eves' Conservatives. They were the ones who directly opposed *everything* the Conservatives were doing, while the McGuinty Liberals were more selective in picking and choosing which Ontario PC policies they would repeal, without going into too many specifics. As a protest vote, the NDP had real promise in making an impact.

Liberals

Dalton McGuinty, now a leader with a campaign under his belt, took the cake for the most over-the-top and outrageous campaign platform of the three. He went to the voters with a cumbersome, apocalyptic message that Ontario needed to change. McGuinty manufactured a crisis from which only he and his party could rescue Ontario. Their platform, *Government that Works for You: The Ontario Liberal Plan for a More Democratic Ontario*,[8] suggested that Ontario was inherently undemocratic. What was Mc-Guinty's justification for such a statement? The early 1970s saw voter turnout of 73 percent, yet (they claimed) barely 50 percent voted in the 1999 provincial election which saw Mike Harris earn his second majority (it was actually 58 percent[9]). To McGuinty, this spoke of Mike Harris' and Ernie Eves' "dramatic acceleration of the erosion of our democratic institutions." Of course, it was laughably false, as McGuinty entirely ignored the fact that the Conservative government was elected to not one but *two* majority governments, both times with over 40 percent of the vote. If they were not liked after the first election, they would not have been re-elected a second time.

In reality, voter turnout is a complex issue that elections agencies have struggled with for some time. While turnout has, in general, declined across federal, provincial, and municipal elections since the 1970s, no one has ever before suggested the turnout made the governments elected inherently undemocratic or illegitimate. (Municipal elections, for example, rarely see a voter turnout above 30 percent, few people would argue the elected council and mayor were illegitimate.) Indeed, voter turnout only declined throughout McGuinty's near-decade in power, including the 2011 election, which saw the worst ever turnout in Ontario's history. Unless the 2003 version of McGuinty was declaring that his future 2007 and 2011 governments were inherently illegitimate, his complaints simply failed to hold water.

Other promises from McGuinty's platform included:

- "We will live within our means by balancing the budget and not adding to the debt"
- "We will protect jobs in the North"
- "We will freeze taxes for individuals and small businesses"

Liars

- "We will not raise the debt"
- "We will build North America's best workforce"
- "We will bring stability to Ontario's electricity market"
- "We will stop the waste of taxpayer dollars"
- "We will protect health care and education and tailor these essential services to the specific needs of rural Ontario"
- "We will freeze tuition and help our neediest students with tuition waivers"
- "We will hold elections on fixed dates, introduce Internet voting and work to increase voter turnout by at least 10%"

These promises are direct quotes from McGuinty's platform. Looking back on McGuinty's 2003 promises in retrospect, they are a sad list of pathetic failures. On every pledge, McGuinty has failed abysmally.

According to the Ontario public service's own costing analysis, the McGuinty platform would cost a whopping $18 billion.[10] Somehow, that price tag did not make it to the public's ears in time to vote. Premier Eves warned "Dalton McGuinty's Liberals will promise you anything and everything to get elected." Few people heeded Eves' warning, which – more than 10 years later – would come back to haunt us.

Broken Promises Start Early

On Taxes

Indeed, promise Ontario anything to get elected, then do something completely different was exactly the McGuinty way. And McGuinty would continue his promise-break promise-apologize cycle hundreds of time throughout his tenure as Premier. One of Harris' greatest legacies was the *Taxpayer Protection and Balance Budget Act*: it made it *the law* that balanced budgets would be passed, and that government would go to the people with a referendum question if they wished to raise or impose new taxes. It was precisely the answer needed after a decade of massive Liberal and NDP deficits, where they spent money like it grew on trees. It was also just common sense that the government, like every day families, should have to live within its means and balance its books every year, going into deficit or debt territory only when absolutely necessary.

McGuinty realized the Liberals and NDP were known for their tax-and-spend liberalism and incessant tax hikes during the Peterson and Rae Years. He knew the Conservatives were the only party seen as holding in high regard respect for taxpayers' money, which is why McGuinty promised to continue to uphold this important legislation: "We will comply with the *Taxpayer Protection Act* and balanced budget legislation," said Dalton

McGuinty's platform. In fact, McGuinty knew the level of distrust against his Liberal Party was so high that he spent most of 2003 confirming that his party would not raise taxes. He continually repeated "I promise not to raise taxes," "I'm telling Ontario families that their taxes will not go up tomorrow or any day under a Liberal government," "We will not raise taxes one cent on Ontario families," "We will not be raising taxes. Families are carrying enough of burden as it is," and "We're not going to raise taxes. That's just not on the table." After repeating it for the better part of a year, Ontarians actually began to believe a Liberal government could be trusted to do as they said they would and not raise taxes.

Selling out Commuters?

Another amusing claim was that Harris and Eves "sold out commuters" by allowing the privately-owned Highway 407 to charge user tolls. Its purpose, after all, was to be a more convenient option than the highway 401, an option that might not have been possible to build were it not for the private-public partnership. Perhaps you're asking "well, who owns the highway? I bet it's some greedy corporation, personally headed by a close friend of Mike Harris who's stuffing his pockets by charging a toll to ride on an express highway! Ugh, those Conservatives!" In reality, however, Highway 407 is privately leased to a consortium of companies including the Canada Pension Plan and SNC-Lavalin. It being a private highway, responsible for its own upkeep, of course the highway owners are free to charge a user toll. With the Canada Pension Plan being an investor, you and I both profit from those who travel on the 407.

The Press Release that Sealed their Fate

The Progressive Conservative campaign was carrying on, not necessarily performing to its best, but still focusing on defending its record of two successful majority governments. An Ekos Research poll showed the electorate split, with roughly one third saying the Eves government was doing well, another third saying the Eves government was doing okay, and the final third saying the government was doing poorly.

However, the scales tipped the moment they put out a bizarre press release. Almost half way through the campaign, the Progressive Conservatives called Dalton McGuinty an "evil reptilian kitten-eater from another planet." It instantly raised questions that doomed Eves' campaign: was this supposed to be funny? Was it a joke? Was it a rogue campaign staffer acting against Eves' campaign team? Would Eves stand by this ridiculous statement? What was its purpose? No one could answer why such a bizarre blast of negativity was released by a political party previously mature

Liars

enough to hold government for the overwhelming majority of the 20th century. The comments highlighted an issue within the PCs themselves that called into question their competence: that Eves couldn't find someone to hold responsible for the press release. McGuinty capitalized on his opportunity to show the Conservatives' hyper-negativity was not accountable in the public light.

The Conservatives never recovered. McGuinty performed significantly better in the 2003 leaders' debate than he did in 1999, surpassing Eves by four percent to become the favoured candidate for Premier (37 percent).[11] According to an Ekos Research poll, while Eves offered the best leadership and the best ideas for Ontario, McGuinty was more believable and more likeable.

A New Government

Eight years of Conservative government was not without its missteps and miscalculations. The issues noted above, whether legitimate or merely ridiculous political spin, took a substantial toll in the minds of voters. When combined with other negative perceptions, such as the provincial government's handling of the 1995 Ipperwash crisis,[12] voters came to see the Harris and Eves Conservatives as entitled and mean-spirited.

This attitude was affirmed on October 2, 2003, when Eves' Conservatives lost 35 seats and 10.5 percentage points, and McGuinty formed a Liberal majority government, gaining 37 seats and 6.6 percentage points. The NDP lost two seats, but increased their vote percentage by 2.1 percentage points. The tide had turned, with 60 percent of Ontarians polled saying the election of Dalton McGuinty was good for Ontario, and 75 percent saying he would do a good job as Premier.[13] Of course, Ontario had just been promised the world – the paradox of lower taxes and more government – from an untested McGuinty who promised to keep his promises. When Mike Harris promised to keep his promises, he did; to McGuinty, promises were just a part of politicking in order to win the election.

Ontario had a new Premier, Liberal Dalton McGuinty and would never again be the same. Its eight years of glory and stability under the Harris' and Eves' Conservative governments was negated in a single night, culminating in the election of the accidental Premier. In the following years to come, the election of Dalton McGuinty would doom Ontario to massive job losses, increasing unemployment rates, endless tax increases on Ontario families, and reckless and expensive energy experiments that pathetically never lived up to their expectations. In a single night, Ontario's voters gave McGuinty's Liberals a majority government. Just that quickly, Ontario was hijacked.

1   Nik Nanos, *From Harris to McGuinty: The Ontario Election Roller Coaster,* SES Research, October 2003, http://www.sesresearch.com/news/press_releases/Nikita%20 Nanos%20October%2030%202003.pdf

2   Jay Makarenko, 2003 Ontario General Election, Mapleleafweb, September 2003, http:// mapleleafweb.com/features/2003-ontario-general-election

3   Toronto Star, *How Dalton McGuinty Changed Ontario – and why he Resigned,* Toronto Star, January 10, 2013, http://www.thestar.com/news/insight/2013/01/10/star_dispatches_ how_dalton_mcguinty_changed_ontario_and_why_he_resigned.html

4   CBC News, *Ontario Votes: the Election of 2003,* CBC News in Review, October 2003, http://newsinreview.cbclearning.ca/wp-content/uploads/2003/10/election.pdf

5   Ontario Ministry of Finance, *Ontario Budget 2000: Budget Paper D – Ontario's Financing Plan: Cutting Ontario's Debt,* http://www.fin.gov.on.ca/en/budget/ ontariobudgets/2000/00d.html

6   CBC News, *Ontario Votes 2003: Parties and Leaders,* CBC News, October 2003, http:// www.cbc.ca/ontariovotes2003/parties/hampton_052103.html

7   CBC News, supra note 4.

8   Ontario Liberal Party, Government that Works for You, April 2003, http://www.leonard-domino.com/news/platform-ontarioliberal2003.pdf

9   National Post, *Graphic: Ontario's Downward Trend in Voter Turnout Continues,* National Post, October 7, 2011, http://news.nationalpost.com/2011/10/07/graphic-ontarios-downward-trend-in-voter-turnout-continues/

10   Christina Blizzard, *10-Year Anniversary of Ontario Liberals' Broken Promises,* Toronto Sun, October 1, 2013, http://www.sunnewsnetwork.ca/sunnews/straighttalk/archives/2013/10/20131001-183330.html

11   EKOS Research, Ontario Election Campaign Survey, EKOS Research, September 5, 2003, http://ekos.com/media/default.asp

12   Harris is alleged to have said "I want the fucking Indians out of the park!" during a cabinet meeting. While witnesses disputed the allegation, many in the media took it to be true. See, for example, Transcript of the Ipperwash Public Inquiry before the Honourable Justice Sidney Linden, November 28, 2005, http://mail.tscript.com/trans/ipperwash/nov_28_05/text. htm

13   Ipsos, *Six in Ten Ontarians Say Election of Liberals is Good News for Province as Even More Feel McGuinty will do a Good Job as Premier,* Ipsos, http://www.ipsos-na.com/news-polls/pressrelease.aspx?id=1966

Chapter 4

The Chance for Change I
McGuinty's First Four Years in Office
and the 2007 Election

"His manner is plodding, his oratory is cloying and self-righteous, his governments were beset by no small number of scandals — and in the dying days of his premiership he invited us all to conclude that his Most Benevolent Premier act was just another political put-on."

-Chris Selley, National Post¹

"At the time of the last election I told Ontarians that I wouldn't raise their taxes, and I broke that promise and I did raise their taxes... I still think it was the right call to make."

"We won't have to increase taxes on a go-forward basis"

- Dalton McGuinty in 2007

The First 100 Days

Dalton McGuinty's first four years in office were an unmitigated failure, but it turned out to only be the tip of the iceberg, as the largest and most expensive controversies would come in his second term.

Ontario had recovered so well and accomplished so much under the Conservative governments of Mike Harris and Ernie Eves, rebuilding after a decade of darkness under Liberal and New Democrat governments. One confusing and short-sighted Progressive Conservative press release was

Liars

all it took for the McGuinty Liberals to successfully seal the narrative of Conservative governments being mean, partisan, and uncaring. Suddenly, with one stupid mistake, the PCs were thrown from government and the McGuinty Liberals took their seats as leaders of Canada's economic powerhouse, Canada's largest province, the heart of Canada that had driven and led our country through previous disasters and challenges. In one night, Ontario was hijacked, and we were going to regret it.

What *exactly* Dalton McGuinty and his fresh cabinet were doing in its first days was anyone's guess. The accidental Premier was rarely heard from or seen in his first few months in office. Whatever he was doing, it wasn't working. As soon as McGuinty was elected Premier, his favour in the eyes of the electorate plummeted: after just one month in office, McGuinty's approval rating was a dismal nine percent – *nine percent!* – an approval rating never seen before by pollster Nik Nanos.

McGuinty did recall the legislature for a short period at the end of 2003, ironically, to implement the auto insurance reforms Ernie Eves promised if re-elected.[2] McGuinty also began musing about a possible "hidden deficit" left by the Conservatives that would require substantial tax increases. Bizarrely, 58 percent of Ontarians polled actually agreed McGuinty would be justified in breaking his campaign promises in order to get rid of this "hidden deficit."[3] However, less than half (49 percent) said the McGuinty government was doing a good job three months into its majority mandate.

McGuinty's First Budget

The first McGuinty budget was the first chance Ontarians really got to see the Liberal leader in action. Premier McGuinty had promised Ontarians a premier who would balance the books and not raise taxes – he was the friendlier, more likeable version of Ernie Eves. What Ontario was promised and what it ended up getting were completely different.

Finance Minister Greg Sorbara tabled the budget in late spring 2004, already into the new fiscal year. On the surface, Ontarians could actually be mistaken for thinking they got a good deal. Kindergarten-to-grade three classes would be no larger than 20 students. Hospital wait times would be reduced for cancer patients, and 3,760 long-term care beds would be added. Immunizations for children against chicken pox, meningitis, and pneumonia would be free. One thousand more teachers would be trained and 4,000 more teachers would be trained as specialists in literacy and numeracy. One billion dollars would be spent on repairing and expanding highways. The property tax credit and the basic needs and maximum shelter allowances would be increased for low-income seniors and individuals collecting welfare.[4] This was a budget that did exactly what the McGuinty Liberals promised – or so it seemed. They promised the world in exchange for no new taxes. Mike Harris could be trusted to do what he said he would do – but with the McGuinty Liberals, you always had to read the fine print.

The Health Care Premium & Raising the Corporate Tax Rate

There was indeed just a *minor* detail in the fine print: "we are proposing to introduce the Ontario Health Premium."[5] Health premium? That nine-word sentence in the first McGuinty budget was the easy way of saying "we know we promised not to raise taxes, but we lied, and we're going to raise them anyway." It was only the first in what would be hundreds of broken promises and tax hikes under McGuinty government rule. In fact, Conservative leadership candidates had warned that McGuinty would implement a health tax as far back as 2002, which he had denied.

The "Health Care Premium" – let's be honest, the health tax – costs the average Ontarian up to $900 per year and applies to everyone making more than $20,000 per year. That's a new $2.4 billion tax being collected by the McGuinty Liberals. The question of where exactly the roughly $3 billion goes every year remains unanswered. Precisely *which* "additional investments in health care" (the supposed purpose of the health tax) are now being funded by each Ontarian's $900? Which of these investments were not being made before the McGuinty Health Tax? Why are they needed now? Why weren't taxpayers consulted about this new tax like McGuinty promised he would?

But just raising taxes to cover new health care expenses that were never articulated wasn't enough. On the same day that McGuinty brought in the largest-ever tax increase on Ontarians, he also delisted optometry, chiropractic, and physiotherapy services from being covered by the Ontario Health Insurance Plan (OHIP). Let me say that again: on the same day McGuinty was raising taxes to supposedly pay for *more* health care and medical services, he *removed* his government's coverage of several important medical services. McGuinty wasn't just raising taxes – he was raising taxes while reducing the services that could be covered by those taxes. Finance Minister Greg Sorbara said these were "less critical" services that Ontarians could do without.[6] The President of the Ontario Chiropractic Association called the budget "incredibly short-sighted" and said it would affect over 1.2 million people. An EKOS Research poll confirmed the obvious: the majority (54 percent) described the budget as "bad" or "terrible," and 14 percent suggested it was just "good." Not one person thought the budget was "excellent."

Liars

There was another small detail: the McGuinty Liberals were increasing the corporate income tax rate by 1.5 percent, from 12.5 to 14 percent. It would remain at 14 percent for most of McGuinty's time as Premier. By the time he acknowledged the shrinking investments corporations were making compared to GDP (since more of their revenue was going towards taxes), McGuinty pledged to reduce the corporate income tax rate to 10 percent, but later changed that to 11.5 percent.[7]

Massive Deficit Spending

McGuinty's maiden budget did not just add new taxes and reduce government services, it also ramped up spending enormously, plunging Ontario into a $2.2 billion deficit.[8] Sorbara complained the Conservative government left "hidden" deficits – "the health deficit, the education deficit, the infrastructure deficit, and the fiscal deficit" as he liked to call them – which was complete nonsense. It was proof from the very outset that McGuinty had no intention to actually live by his promise; his Liberals were already elected, and they would break the law and raise taxes anyway. Even if we do believe the Liberals were secretly left a "hidden" deficit, their own numbers did not add up: they claimed the hidden deficit was $5.5 billion, yet they engaged in deficit spending that far exceeded the $5.5 billion supposedly caused by the Progressive Conservatives. Indeed, the Liberals have never been held to account for their blatant lie about raising taxes. Remember, also, that the *Taxpayer Protection Act* was still Ontario law, meaning McGuinty required a referendum vote of Ontarians before being allowed to impose new taxes and plunge Ontario into deficit spending.

Ontarians were rightly furious that their new Liberal government had so casually lied in order to be elected. "The honeymoon is over," declared an Ipsos poll just seven months after McGuinty was elected. By April, 60 percent of Ontarians believed the McGuinty government had "no clear plan and is managing day-to-day."[9] The Liberal approval rating slipped to 45 percent, an 11 percent drop since November 2003. And McGuinty was faring worse than his own party, with 46 percent of Ontarians saying they disapproved of his performance. However, that same poll found that 62 percent of Ontarians were okay with the Liberals running a deficit as long as the books were balanced by 2007. Almost half (49 percent) thought the *Taxpayers Protection Act* could be thrown to the wayside in favour of McGuinty's deficit.

By June, Ontarians were nostalgic for the old days. Not once did a Conservative government raise their taxes, and not once did they lie to Ontarians. Conservatives took on challenges and were honest with taxpayers; the Liberals proudly promised the world then hiked taxes. An SES Research poll showed 41 percent of decided voters wanted the Conservatives back, compared to the "free-falling" Liberals at 34 percent.[10] Even considering Eves' imminent departure as Conservative leader, Ontarians were desperate for a Premier who kept his word and respected their wallets. Likewise, a December 2004 Environics poll showed the Conservatives with a narrow, two percent lead over the Liberals (39 to 37 percent) – a lead that widened by the spring to six percent (41 to 35 percent). But what could Ontarians do? They had been baldly lied to by a Liberal government that had already been elected with a majority government.

The McGuinty Liberals – in your wallet, your house, your school, and at your dinner table

Dalton McGuinty had your wallet with a new $900 tax he unilaterally imposed contrary to Ontario law. Now he was going to meddle in your personal affairs and your children's schools. He required restaurants to allow patrons to bring in their own wine. He banned smoking in public (and would later go on to legislate smoking in almost every other area too). He made it the law that students stay in school until age 18. And he mercilessly banned pit bull dogs, sending living dogs to be heartlessly sterilized or euthanized. Pit bulls were banned because of the potential harm they *could* do, but cigarettes were not banned for what they *actually* do – they were simply regulated and controlled.

All of these new laws were enacted without a single consultation with the public. Nowhere in the 2003 McGuinty platform was anything about his desire to ban children from eating potato chips or requiring that you stand inside a thin yellow box while smoking. These were the early makings of "Premier Dad" who knew was best for you, your family, and your children, and his government would make sure you followed his rules. This was a government bent on clamping down on every aspect of Ontarians lives; they would tell you what to do, and you would comply. Was limiting smoking in public places a good idea? Absolutely. Should it have been high on the priority list for a government that had just introduced a $900 annual tax? Probably not. McGuinty came to power promising transparency and accountability, yet he provided neither when it came to imposing regulations and laws that were never asked for and never publicly discussed.

Fixed Election Dates

To McGuinty's credit, one of few good policies his government enacted was to set fixed election dates. The *Election Statute Law Amendment Act*, passed in 2005, set the date of the 2007 election at Thursday, October 4. Elections thereafter would be held "on the first Thursday in October in the fourth calendar year following polling day in the most recent general election." Nothing in McGuinty's law, however, affected "the powers of the Lieutenant Governor, including the power to dissolve the legislature... when the Lieutenant Governor sees fit." In a parliamentary system, the Lieutenant Governor dissolves the legislature on the advice of the legislature's Prime Minister, meaning Premier McGuinty could still request that the Lieutenant Governor dissolve the legislature and trigger an election at any time. Such an exemption clause is necessary to allow a parliamentary government to operate.[11]

A Union of Love

Dalton McGuinty's Liberals did not care much what you thought about his euthanizing of undesirable dogs or his telling your son or daughter what they could eat at lunch. Who he really cared about keeping happy were his public sector union buddies – the public servants, the teachers, the doctors – who would happily prop up his Liberal Party come election time in exchange for lavish union contracts paid for with taxpayers' money.

Health Minister George Smitherman gave Ontario's 20,000 doctors a sweetheart $6.9 billion deal to work longer hours, take on more patients, and establish "family health teams" that could treat more patients.[12] Next came Education Minister Gerard Kennedy's "negotiating framework" that gave the teachers a 10.5 percent salary increase over four years.[13] Finally, Management Board Chair Gerry Phillips' deal with the Ontario Public Sector Employees Union (OPSEU). Union members were given a 9.75 percent wage increase over four years, with correctional officers gaining an additional three percent. Drug benefits were added. Over 1400 "casual" employees were given permanent jobs with full benefits, and fewer casual employees would be used in favour of termed employees.[14] It was the price of "labour peace" (as it would later be called) and Liberal votes; there was no other justification for such high wage increases in any of the three cases.

Those promises were just suggestions

If Ontarians were okay with being lied to by the McGuinty Liberals when it came to jacking up taxes after they promised they wouldn't, why not lie about coal plants too? A central promise of the Liberals in their 2003 platform was to close all coal-powered electricity plants by 2004.[15] Then it became 2006. And in 2006 it became 2014. As of March 2014, Ontario is still powering about 35,000 homes with coal.[16] McGuinty complained his "experts" gave him poor advice that was "too ambitious" on a portfolio as "sophisticated" as electricity policy.[17]

What about his "promise" to cap class sizes? By late 2005 it turned out not all class sizes were following the 20-student cap, meaning students were still (in the Liberals' own words) in overcrowded classrooms. Was that just poor advice too?

The McGuinty government's second budget further entrenched the fact that McGuinty's "promises" were nothing more than cheap political suggestions to get elected. His second budget projected a deficit of "only" $3 billion, and the Liberals *promised* to have the budget balanced by 2008-2009.[18] But what about that "promise" to balance the budget without raising taxes? Or what about the fact that McGuinty's maiden budget promised to balance the books by 2007-2008, and that promise was now being pushed to 2008-2009? You didn't read the fine print in the Liberal election platform; merely half-way into McGuinty's mandate, it turned out most of his promises were just suggestions – maybe his government would fulfill their promises, or maybe not. They were wildly unpopular, and McGuinty was okay with that – after all, he had a majority government for another two years.

OLG is out of Control – Part 1

The first of three (to-date) Ontario lottery scandals began in 2006, when it was revealed that a disproportionate number of lottery retailers, such as store clerks and convenience store owners, were winning lottery jackpots. Cancer survivor Bob Edmonds, for example, was scammed out of a $250,000 winning ticket by a store clerk who told him the ticket was a loser, then claimed the ticket for himself. OLG ignored Edmonds' complaints. It was not until four years later, in 2005, that the store clerk and his wife were arrested and charged with fraud. But OLG refused to give Edmonds the winnings, saying there was no evidence he had been tricked by the store clerk. Luckily, an Ontario judge disagreed, ordering the OLG to pay Edmonds his winnings – but OLG insisted it would only comply if Edmonds signed a confidentiality agreement to hide the specific details of his settlement.

OLG wasn't much of a lottery. Between 1999 and 2006, over 200 lottery retailers had won major prizes totaling approximately $100 million. The chances of that happening were one in a quindecillion (1 followed by 48 zeroes). Then came the largest Canadian recall of lottery tickets in March 2007, when a customer claimed there was a marking on the ticket that showed whether it was a winner without actually scratching the ticket. Over one million Super Bingo tickets were recalled. That same month, OLG President and CEO Duncan Brown was fired.[19]

Liars

Scandal Touches the Premier's Inner Circle

It was only the first in a number of scandals that would plague OLG and, indeed, nearly the entire McGuinty cabinet. In June 2005, Economic Development and Trade Minister Joseph Cordiano was caught being reimbursed to the tune of $17,000 for fancy dinners in Paris and Milan. According to Cordiano, they were an appropriate expense for which he could bill his Liberal riding association. McGuinty agreed. That same month came revelations that Transportation Minister Harinder Takhar had made a personal visit to a company in which he held a blind trust, a huge no-no according to the Integrity Commissioner, who ruled Takhar breached the *Integrity Act* by failing to maintain an arms-length distance.[20] But neither Cordiano nor Takhar were fired from cabinet for their ethical breaches and significant lapses in judgement – in fact, McGuinty reaffirmed his support for both by leaving them in their cabinet posts following a cabinet shuffle at the end of the month. Their actions were perfectly acceptable in McGuinty's Liberal Party.

Only months later, the police raided Finance Minister Greg Sorbara's company owned by him and his brothers as part of a fraud investigation.[21] At last, a McGuinty cabinet minister was forced to resign. Three cases of alleged or proven impropriety barely two years into McGuinty's mandate was setting a troubling precedent: not only was the McGuinty cabinet open for "business," but they had the direct support and approval of the Premier. This disturbing attitude – a complete lack of respect for taxpayers' money and independent Officers of Parliament – would only become more obvious as the McGuinty years went on.

Crisis in Caledonia – McGuinty Does Nothing

Many people talk about their "rights," but fail to understand that without the rule of law – the legal and social contract that makes all of us, from poorest to richest, powerful to weak, equally subject to the law and the requirement to use the state's judicial system to settle our differences instead of violence – there can be no exercise of rights possible.

In fact, the rule of law is such a pre-eminent condition for liberty that the Preamble to the Canadian Constitution's Charter of Rights reads as follows: "Whereas Canada is founded upon principles that recognize the supremacy of God **and the rule of law**." (emphasis by author)

Our rights can only be exercised freely when citizens obey the law in return for a promise from government to enforce it so that the community can live in peace. When either of these conditions are absent there is anarchy or even civil war, which is not only bad for human and civil rights, but exceptionally bad for business. After all, who wants to invest money in a community where employees are not safe, where the company's equipment can be stolen and vandalized, and its land and buildings stolen, all because the government refuses to protect the innocent from thuggery?

Welcome to the Caledonia crisis, the greatest rule of law failure in modern Ontario history. It began in 2006 when two women from Six Nations walked onto a subdivision under construction and claimed (falsely) that it was stolen land. Once other radicals realized the Ontario Provincial Police (OPP) were not going to stop them, intimidation, violence, and vandalism against innocent residents, business owners, and even police escalated exponentially and spread to other communities in the area.

What did the McGuinty government do? Nothing. Worse than nothing, actually; it not only allowed the OPP to act as taxpayer-funded security guards for those terrorizing the community, it provided lawyers to go into court to oppose those who wanted the rule of law upheld; and it watched knowingly as its police force conducted racial policing, targeting non-Natives who spoke out against the injustices.

At an estimated $4.1 billion in lost economic activity (and another nearly $3 billion due to native lawlessness elsewhere in Ontario), combined with the terrorization of an innocent community enabled by the people who were supposed to protect it, the Caledonia crisis would become – as you will see in the next chapter – the Liberal's most expensive boondoggle of all in both economic and human costs.

The Third & Fourth Budgets

The 2006-2007 budget projected a minor $310 million surplus, yet laughably stated "this budget has no new taxes or tax increases." In reality, the statement meant very little coming from a government that successively raised taxes having just promised to not raise them. Nor was it actually true: deficit spending is still a tax, it's simply a pledge to collect taxes at a *future* date from future taxpayers rather than those in the present day, presumably benefitting from government programs at that time. McGuinty's fourth budget included a $1.7 billion surplus, miraculously, just in time for the election.

With the 2007 election approaching, McGuinty needed another pet project: enter his new obsession with "green energy." Maybe the Liberals could not keep their promise as to when they would close all the coal plants, but they could release an elaborate plan to spend a whopping $46 billion to build more nuclear reactors – a plan that contained the familiar McGuinty fine print that included the fact that his energy plan would not be subject to an environmental assessment. Groups like the left-wing Pembina Institute and Greenpeace Canada pounced on McGuinty for his choice of "dirty, dangerous and expensive nuclear power" when he should have been looking into "meaningful investment in green energy options."[22] Unfortunately, McGuinty's initial policy was right: nuclear energy is one of the cleanest and safest energy technologies available. But he had angered a very sensitive part of his base, and he would never make that mistake again. In the coming years, McGuinty's aversion to the clean, safe, and reliable nuclear energy that angered his supporters would drive him into reckless experiments with the most unpredictable of all energy sources: wind and solar power.

The McGuinty Slush Fund

Although McGuinty was angering his base of environmental fanatics with his choice to invest in nuclear energy, his government was making some other Liberal cronies very, very happy by bestowing taxpayers' money on them disguised as government grants. Citizenship and Immigration Minister Mike Colle was a fan of distributing taxpayers' money to his Liberal friends and colleagues without a care in the world for the people footing the bill. In a personal effort to distribute government "grants" before the end of the year, the Minister fast-tracked a cool $250,000 to the Bengali Cultural Society.[23] The Society's President also happened to be the Vice President of the Beaches-East York Liberal association, represented at Queen's Park by Liberal MPP Maria Minna. Colle admitted Minna approached him directly and asked for the money, and after Colle verified there was some money "available" from his department, he asked for a formal proposal.

Like so many McGuinty government scandals, what seemed like a minor one-off issue with the Bengali Society quickly grew out of control. When the Ontario Cricket Association asked for a grant of $150,000, the Liberals gave them $1 million instead![24] (Why the Citizenship and Immigration department was doling out taxpayers' money to cricket associations has never been answered.) The Chinese Professional Association of Canada received $250,000 within months of conveniently meeting with Colle at a Liberal fundraiser in Toronto. Two directors of the association also had direct Liberal ties: one was a Liberal association Treasurer and another worked in Colle's office.

In all, $32 million of Ontario taxpayers' money went into the pockets of the Liberals and Liberal friends. At least in the federal Liberal Adscam scandal, Canadians ostensibly got *some* work for the $40 million they paid Chretien's Liberal cronies, but the McGuinty government was shoveling taxpayers' money out the door and into their friends' pockets without a care in the world!

The Auditor General's Report

The Auditor General intervened to determine what was really going on in this mess. It was clear from the early days of the McGuinty government – as it continues today under Kathleen Wynne – that the Auditor General, not the Premier or the Liberal cabinet, would be the guardian of the public interest and the public's money.

In his July report, the Auditor General did not hold back:

> [The government grant scheme] was one of the worst I have ever seen, with virtually no controls. Many organizations received grants simply because the minister of citizenship and immigration or his staff had some knowledge of their needs or because a member of the organization had had a discussion with, or had made verbal requests to, the minister or his staff.[25]

The year-end grants that were given out were "not open, transparent, or accountable."[26] The "decisions were based on conversations, not applications." Documentation supporting *most* of the requests for funding was insufficient, and, "in fact, for many of these grants there was no documentation at all. In most cases, it was also not possible to determine how the amount of funding that an organization would receive was decided."

While the Immigration Minister may have tried to lay the blame on public servants, the Auditor General saw it another way. The Deputy Minister raised her concerns as far back as 2006 about "not having proper names of the organizations, the very sketchy information her staff had about most of the proposals put forth by the Minister's office, and the fact that many of the proposals had nothing to do with her Ministry's mandate or responsibilities." The response to the Deputy Minister was that these names came directly from the minister's office – in other words, she was to shut up and comply.

Colle became the second McGuinty minister to resign in disgrace,[27] and McGuinty prorogued the legislature in order to avoid Colle having to testify at committee.[28] After all, there was an election barely three months away and McGuinty wasn't going to allow the scandal to get in the way of a Liberal victory.

Liars

The Lost Four Years – McGuinty's First Mandate of Broken Promises and the Chance for Change

The 2007 election was Ontario's first chance for change. Ontarians had four years of a Liberal government that proudly, and with a straight face, promised" we will not raise taxes" – several times – yet came into office and introduced a $900 annual health tax and increased the corporate income tax rate by 1.5 percent. The cruel reality of Dalton McGuinty's government was, in stark contrast to Mike Harris's Conservatives, that it could not be trusted to do what it said it would do. This was reflected in McGuinty's continually low polling numbers throughout his first mandate. He was unpopular – but he didn't care.

The 2007 election was also the first testing ground for new Progressive Conservative leader John Tory. Fresh off a bid to become mayor of Toronto, and with the resignation of Ernie Eves as leader of the Ontario PCs, Tory was elected leader in 2004.

As was within the limits of McGuinty's fixed election date law, the October 4 election date set under McGuinty's law was pushed back six days, to October 10, to avoid conflicting with a Jewish holiday. The Liberal strategy, touted by campaign chair Greg Sorbara, was to campaign on the Liberals' first four years as representing good governance and positive achievements for Ontario residents. It was hard to understand whether Sorbara was seeing what the rest of Ontario was seeing.

By 2007 Ontarians were fed up. Many of the promises made by McGuinty in 2003 were shamelessly broken: "We will live within our means by balancing the budget and not adding to the debt." This was a sore joke by 2007. Three of McGuinty's budgets introduced a total of $7.6 billion in deficits. "We will freeze taxes for individuals and small businesses." Barely seven months into his first mandate, he introduced a $900 health care tax – a tax that costs us over $2.4 billion per year[29] – and raised the corporate income tax rate by 1.5 percent. "We will not raise the debt." By 2007, the McGuinty government had added $17.8 billion to the debt. McGuinty knew he was unpopular for his bald-faced lies, so he addressed the issue head on by telling CTV News: "At the time of the

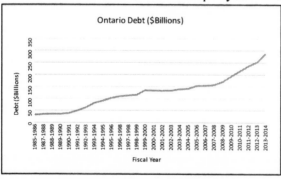

Figure 4: Ontario Net Debt

50

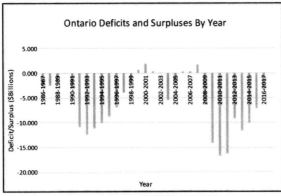

Figure 5: Deficit Spending

last election I told Ontarians that I wouldn't raise their taxes, and I broke that promise and I did raise their taxes." Yet he arrogantly concluded "I still think it was the right call to make."

So, what about those promises to increase voter turnout by 10 percent and introduce electronic voting?

Increasing Voter Turnout

McGuinty promised to increase voter turnout by at least 10 percent. Remember, his apocalyptic message was that the Eves government was illegitimate because the voter turnout was only 58 percent. Yet voter turnout in the election that brought McGuinty to power was only 56.8 percent, rendering, by McGuinty's own standard, his government illegitimate. In fact, voter turnout has only decreased under the McGuinty government, reaching an all-time record low in 2011.

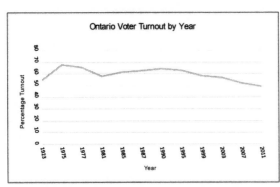

Figure 6: Voter Turnout in Ontario

By pledging to raise Ontario's voter turnout by 10 percent, McGuinty would have put Ontario back into the high-60 percent range that elected Mike Harris in 1995. But that election was to elect a Premier who actually did what he promised – a key difference McGuinty never seemed to grasp.

Electronic Voting

Another McGuinty promise seemingly forgotten was electronic voting: the ability to vote via the internet from home or work, or, to start with, at least saving paper by voting electronically at the local polling station. It wasn't for lack of cooperation on the part of the bureaucracy: within months of being elected Premier, Dalton McGuinty was presented with a plan from Elections Ontario's Chief Electoral Officer to phase in internet voting.[30] That report advocates for further study into "non-paper" methods of voting, and compares the successes and challenges other governments have had around the world with studying or implementing internet voting. Yet the McGuinty Liberals did nothing to fulfill their campaign promise.

The Withering Health Care Record

The "health care Premier," as he liked to call himself, was also seeing his record on that very file fade. In a scathing *Toronto Star* article, Thomas Walkom laid McGuinty's true record on the table:[31] McGuinty complained about doctor and nurse shortages in 2003; by 2007, the number of doctors-per-capita was still "static." In fact, despite being Canada's most populace province, Ontario was the fourth-worst for doctors-per-capita. More nurses were being trained, but "barely" enough to keep up with Ontario's population growth. Nine out of 10 Ontarians diagnosed with cancer had to wait at least two months from the time they were scheduled until they actually received surgery. Cataract surgery was even worse – with an average 153-day wait – but the McGuinty government had the nerve to say this was an "improvement" because the target it set for itself was 311 days. Ninety percent of patients requiring MRI scans had to wait at least 110 days.

This was the true record of a Premier who aimed to be "the health care Premier." Worst of all, these severe deficiencies in health care wait times persisted even with McGuinty's $900 health tax. After his true record was exposed, as it was in 2007, he amusingly tried to change his tune and become "the education Premier."

The Unions are Back

McGuinty's Liberals were not alone when it came to defining their "achievements." In exchange for lavish public sector union contracts, the Liberals had all the support they needed come election time. In 2003, that came in the form of the innocently-named Working Families Coalition, a non-profit group supposedly created to make "voters aware of policies that were threatening the well-being of working families across Ontario."[32] The WFC, however, was never were about helping voters make honest, informed choices; it existed to spread half-truths and lies about the Conservatives.

In fact, in 2007 a resounding 88 percent of the WFC's "members" were trade unions.[33] Teachers, autoworkers, millwrights, steelworkers – they all supposedly decided to get together and make sure their interests were known. This wasn't a coalition of working families at all: this was a pro-union lobby group set up to be the kingmaker of whichever political party would be most sympathetic to their demands. Not surprisingly, due to the direct involvement of former McGuinty aides, staffers, and consultants, the WFC just so happened to side with the Liberals as they ruthlessly attacked the Conservatives. Canadian Autoworkers President Buzz Hargrove was less obscure about what this lobby group was really all about: "Our goal is to make sure the Tories don't get elected here."[34]

Unfortunately, it was not until 2011 that Ontarians would really understand who the WFC was and what their motivations were, thanks in part to an investigation by Elections Ontario which will be discussed in chapter seven.

The Platforms

The McGuinty Liberals put forth a platform that would allow them to continue to implement their agenda; they thought their first four years had actually gone well. Thus, they "re-announced" that the provincial government would take on the full cost of the Ontario Disability Support Program and the Ontario Drug Benefit over four years. In other words, it was a promise McGuinty already made, but he was repeating it because it was election time. Laughably, they once again promised balanced budgets and annual surpluses: a re-elected Liberal government would bring in $107 billion and spend $96.6 billion in 2007-2008 – a sizeable $10.4 billion surplus.[35] McGuinty also said he would demand the federal government ban handguns; ban "cosmetic" pesticides; reduce greenhouse gases by six percent below 1990 levels by 2014; spend $650 million so companies could develop clean cars; plant 50 million trees; and yes – he swore this time it was true – completely close all coal power plants by 2014.

Meanwhile, the NDP advocated for an immediate $10 per-hour minimum wage (the Liberals would only pledge $10.25 per hour by 2010), a rebate on the McGuinty heath tax, and a balanced budget with a surplus. The NDP projected $109.5 billion in revenue and $108.4 billion in spending: a $1.1 billion surplus was much less impressive than McGuinty's surplus but, clearly, the NDP had come a long way from their reckless spending days of Bob Rae. However, they did not forget where they came from: to increase revenue and thus government spending, the NDP would have raised taxes on tobacco; increased personal income taxes by two percent; created a new tax bracket for high income earners; increased the corporate tax rate; and continued to tax corporate capital.

The Progressive Conservatives, too, had a plan to balance the budget. They were the only party with any credibility for actually balancing the budget.

Liars

Their plan projected $105.4 billion in revenue and $104.2 billion in government spending – a $1.2 billion surplus after scrapping the McGuinty health tax. They also pledged to get the homeless out of shelters and into permanent housing more quickly; appoint more justices of the peace; eliminate the corporate capital tax; raise the standard of care for 35,000 long-term care beds; increase education funding by $2.4 billion by 2011-2012; and fund additional faith-based schools with $400 million.

The Bombshell that Would end the Campaign

If you glanced over that last sentence, you shouldn't have. PC leader John Tory's $400 million for faith-based schools was about to become the bombshell that would end the PC's campaign.

The 2007 election should have been about the incredible failures throughout McGuinty's first four years in office, and voters should have judged each of the party's platforms for the best replacement. Instead, all it took was that one pledge of funding, and the Conservative campaign was derailed. In a theme that would be repeated in the 2011 election, the Tories' steady ride towards victory was brought to a drastic halt. The focus suddenly shifted from McGuinty's first term in office to what McGuinty's Conservative successor would do if elected.

Tory pledged $400 million to schools based on teaching Islam, Hinduism, Judaism, and other religions beyond the Catholic/Public divide Ontario continues to see.[36] Tory's reasoning was that children were being excluded from receiving a faith-based education by being forced to attend a public school program, when instead they could be educated in a school based on their faith. Tory would appoint former Premier Bill Davis as the head of a commission that would examine how to best implement faith-based schooling in Ontario – an ironic choice considering Davis' government was kicked out of office for touching that same proverbial third rail (funding Catholic schools).

As Education Minister at the time, Kathleen Wynne's response was that the Conservatives were sending children into the stone age by dividing children based on their religious beliefs. (She would have no trouble, however – only years later – implementing a radical sexual education curriculum that was entirely inappropriate for the targeted age groups.) Wynne also found some sensationalist figures to make the Conservative proposal even worse: she suggested that by implementing faith-based schools, Tory would have to fire 6300 teachers, 3800 specialist teachers, and 8500 support staff; and would cut $102,000 from every school and $7 million from every school board. It was nonsense, considering Tory's proposal was to establish a commission to study the idea's implementation, not necessarily approve certain levels of funding.

It didn't matter. A May 2007 SES Research poll had the Conservatives and Liberals tied at 35 percent support. When Tory made the religious schools announcement in July, the Liberals shot up to 41 percent support and the Conservatives went as low as 33 percent. The Conservatives recovered somewhat by September, coming within two percent of the Liberals, but voters could not shake the thought that a Conservative government under John Tory would cut millions of dollars from the education system to be given to religious schools.

Referendum on Electoral Reform

The 2007 election also included a provincial referendum on electoral reform. The question was whether Ontario's election system would change from a first-past-the-post system to a mixed-member proportional system. The former, which had been used since Confederation, means the person with the largest plurality of votes would be elected. This system works well in two-party states, where the winner is the one who receives more than 50 percent of the vote, but its weakness is in multiple-party systems, where a person with as little as 30 percent of the vote can receive the largest plurality compared to his multiple competitors. The latter, which is used in countries such as Germany and New Zealand, takes into account both an individual's vote count in proportion to his or her competitors, but also the portion of votes received by that person's party as a whole. The Ontario Citizens' Assembly on Electoral Reform was struck by McGuinty in 2006 and consisted of one person from each riding. It recommended the government adopt the MMP system.[37]

Party leaders were also clear on whether they supported the change to MMP: Howard Hampton's New Democrats and the Green Party said yes, Ontario PC leader John Tory said no, and McGuinty's Liberals never released an official for-or-against position.

The proposal to switch to a MMP system failed, with only 37 percent of voters voting in favour. Similar proposals in Prince Edward Island and British Columbia have been flatly rejected by voters.[38] It does not appear that the political parties' positions on the electoral system had an effect on the 2007 election result.

Conclusion

The 2007 election was a wash. McGuinty's Liberals lost one seat, Tory's Conservatives gained two seats, and Hampton's Democrats gained three

Liars

seats. At 42 percent of the vote, McGuinty's Liberals were able to pull off another majority, followed by the Conservatives at 31.62 percent and the NDP at 16.76 percent. In terms of percentage points, it was actually the Green Party that did the best, gaining 5.2. However, despite having eight percent of the popular vote, it was not enough to elect a Green Party MP. It was interesting that, despite Tory's religious schools announcement, the Liberals were the only party to actually lose any seats.

It was a shame that Ontario's first chance for change – our first chance to end the McGuinty hijacking and return to balanced budgets and prosperity – was so easily derailed by a Liberal counter-attack that amounted to "look at those guys, at least we're not *that* bad!" John Tory lost his own seat – to Kathleen Wynne – but said he would stay on as leader unless the Progressive Conservative Party decided otherwise.

If the first four years were bad, McGuinty was about to shatter even the worst expectations. If you thought 2003 to 2007 was enough to define McGuinty as a lying, promise-breaking, tax-raising, law-avoiding, scandal-fueled Premier, you hadn't seen anything yet! In his affinity for setting records, the McGuinty government saw a record low 52.8 percent of voters turn out to vote. (McGuinty would break this record in 2011, with less than 50 percent of voters turning out to vote for the first time in Ontario history.) If McGuinty thought the Eves government was illegitimate because only 58 percent of voters gave them their mandate, he certainly could not govern with an even smaller voter turnout. McGuinty's second majority government would be defined by even more reckless experiments, massive deficits, a ballooning debt, and government corruption and scandals to an extent never before seen in any Canadian government.

1   Chris Selley, *How does a Premier Like This Stay in Office?*, National Post, January 24, 2013, http://fullcomment.nationalpost.com/2013/01/24/chris-selley-on-the-mcguinty-years-how-does-a-premier-like-this-stay-in-office/

2   Canadian Underwriter, *Eves' Government Announces Additional Auto Insurance Reforms*, Canadian Underwriter, September 2, 2003, http://www.canadianunderwriter.ca/news/eves-government-announces-additional-auto-insurance-reforms/1000010188

3   Ipsos, *58 Percent Say New Ontario McGuinty Government Justified In Breaking Promises: Bring Down Deficit First*, Ipsos, http://www.ipsos-na.com/news-polls/pressrelease.aspx?id=1997

4   Ontario Ministry of Finance, *Ontario Budget 2004 Highlights The Plan For Change*, http://www.fin.gov.on.ca/en/budget/ontariobudgets/2004/budhi1.html

5   Ibid.

6   Michael Devitt, Ontario Removes Chiropractic from Provincial Health Plan, Dynamic Chiropractic Canada, http://www.chiroweb.com/mpacms/dc_ca/article.php?id=46289

7   Charles Lammam and Milagros Palacios, *Dalton McGuinty's Legacy of Poor Fiscal Management*, Fraser Institute, January 2013, http://www.fraserinstitute.org/uploadedFiles/fraser-ca/Content/research-news/research/articles/dalton-mcguintys-legacy-of-poor-fiscal-management.pdf

8   Ontario Ministry of Finance, *2004 Ontario Budget*, http://www.fin.gov.on.ca/en/budget/ontariobudgets/2004/pdf/papers_all.pdf

9   Ipsos, *Honeymoon Over for Provincial Liberals*, Ipsos, April 19, 2004, http://www.ipsos-na.com/news-polls/pressrelease.aspx?id=2129

10   Ian Urquhart, *In Politics, Misery Loves Company*, Toronto Star, June 13, 2004, http://www.sesresearch.com/news/in_the_news/Toronto%20Star%20June%2012%202004.pdf

11   John Pepall, *We Don't Have Fixed Election Dates, and Can't*, Globe and Mail, March 29, 2011, http://www.theglobeandmail.com/globe-debate/we-dont-have-fixed-election-dates-and-cant/article574553/

12   Ontario Ministry of Health and Long-Term Care, *500,000 More Ontarians with Access to a Family Doctor as a Result of Investments in Family Doctors*, Newswire, June 21, 2007, http://www.newswire.ca/fr/story/104783/500-000-more-ontarians-with-access-to-a-family-doctor-as-a-result-of-investments-in-family-doctors

13   Michael Posner, *Kennedy is the One to Watch*, Globe and Mail, September 21, 2006, http://v1.theglobeandmail.com/servlet/story/RTGAM.20060921.wkennedy0922/front/Front/Front/

14   Fort Frances Times, *OPSEU, Province Reach Tentative Agreement*, Fort Frances Times, June 15, 2005, http://www.fftimes.com/node/71651

15   CBC News, *McGuinty Takes Blame For Broken Promises on Coal Plant Closures*, CBC News, November 16, 2006, http://www.cbc.ca/news/canada/toronto/mcguinty-takes-blame-for-broken-promise-on-coal-plant-closures-1.612604

16   Canadian Nuclear Society, *Where is my Electricity Coming From at this Hour?*, http://media.cns-snc.ca/ontarioelectricity/ontarioelectricity.html

17   CBC News, supra note 15.

18   Ontario Ministry of Finance, *2005 Ontario Budget*, http://www.fin.gov.on.ca/en/budget/ontariobudgets/2005/pdf/papers_all.pdf

19   Robert Benzie, *Fired Lotto Chief "In Shock,"* Toronto Star, March 24, 2007, http://www.thestar.com/news/2007/03/24/fired_lotto_chief_in_shock.html

20   Office of the Integrity Commissioner of Ontario, *Report of The Honourable Coulter A. Osborne, Integrity Commissioner, Re: The Honourable Harinder Takhar, Minister Of Transportation & Member For Mississauga Centre*, January 4, 2006, http://oico.on.ca/oic/oicweb2.nsf/(CommReports)/27/$FILE/report.pdf

21   An Ontario court would later rule there was no reason for Sorbara to have been named on the initial search warrant, and McGuinty re-named Sorbara to the Finance Minister post.

22   Greenpeace Canada, *The Campaign Starts Now – No to Nuclear*, Greenpeace Canada,

Liars

June 24, 2006, http://www.greenpeace.org/canada/en/archive/press-centre/press-releases/no-to-nuclear/

23 Rob Ferguson, *Opposition Alleges Liberal Slush Fund*, Toronto Star, April 19, 2007, http://www.thestar.com/news/2007/04/19/opposition_alleges_liberal_slush_fund.html

24 CBC News, *Ontario Citizenship Minister Quits in Wake of Auditor's Report*, CBC News, July 26, 2007, http://www.cbc.ca/news/canada/ottawa/ont-citizenship-minister-quits-in-wake-of-auditor-s-report-1.632556

25 Windsor Star, *Liberal Grants*, Windsor Star, July 28, 2007, http://www.canada.com/story_print.html?id=b1ad992a-3762-4df5-9815-c021f5fa4890

26 Office of the Auditor General of Ontario, *Special Review for the Premier of Ontario: Year-end Grants Provided by the Ministry of Citizenship and Immigration*, July 26, 2007, http://www.auditor.on.ca/en/reports_en/MCI_special_en.pdf

27 CBC News, supra note 26.

28 Windsor Star, supra note 27.

29 CBC News, *Ontario Health Premium Kicks In*, CBC News, July 1, 2004, http://www.cbc.ca/news/canada/story/2004/07/01/ontario_healthtax040701.html

30 Elections Ontario, *Access, Integrity and Participation: Towards Responsive Electoral Processes for Ontario*, September 2004, http://www.elections.on.ca/NR/rdonlyres/063715FC-A692-4473-A756-CC43663D27F0/0/election_report_2003_en.pdf

31 Thomas Walkom, *Liberal Health-Care Record Withers Under the Microscope*, Toronto Star, September 15, 2007, http://www.thestar.com/opinion/columnists/2007/09/15/liberal_healthcare_record_withers_under_microscope.html

32 Working Families Coalition, *Who is Working Families?*, http://www.workingfamilies.ca/about/

33 Vince Versace, *Working Families Coalition Not a Front for Liberal Party: Dillon*, Daily Commercial News, January 1, 2007, http://dcnonl.com/article/id24446

34 Ian Urquhart, *Tory Faces Union Ad Campaign*, Toronto Star, June 15, 2007, http://www.thestar.com/opinion/2007/06/15/tory_faces_union_ad_campaign.html

35 City of Toronto, *2007 Ontario General Election: Party Platform Positions of Interest to Toronto*, http://www.toronto.ca/legdocs/mmis/2007/ex/bgrd/backgroundfile-7811.pdf

36 Kerry Gillespie, *John Tory Puts Faith in School Religion*, Toronto Star, July 24, 2007, http://www.thestar.com/news/ontario/2007/07/24/john_tory_puts_faith_in_school_religion.html

37 Citizens' Assembly on Electoral Reform, http://www.citizensassembly.gov.on.ca

38 Andre Barnes and James Robertson, *Electoral Reform Initiatives in Canadian Provinces*, Parliament of Canada, August 18, 2009, http://www.parl.gc.ca/Content/LOP/research-publications/prb0417-e.htm

Chapter 5

Caledonia - Dual Classes of Citizens in the McGuinty-Wynne Ontario

"The protesters' lawlessness has been allowed to go on too long. More importantly, their behaviour is getting worse, not better. Rewarding it with further deference – with promises that their grievances will be heard before their violence and illegality have ended – will only provoke more such criminal behaviour in Caledonia and elsewhere."

Lorne Gunter[1]

"The line has to be drawn at enforcing the law. There cannot be different classes of law for different classes of people. That undermines the very equality we strive for and cherish in Canada."

Toronto Star[2]

"'It's rural terrorism,' said one police officer at the scene. 'Technically he's right. It's doubtful the government would tolerate this kind of action from any other group.' As of last night, no one seemed to have been charged with anything."

Joe Warmington[3]

The Biggest Liberal Boondoggle of Them All? $7B and the Greatest Rule of Law Failure in Modern Ontario History

There are no shortage of Liberal scandals and billion dollar boondoggles, but the one that, arguably, trumps them all (and the one least likely to be cited by commentators) is the despicable willingness of the McGuinty government to stand by and do nothing while the Ontario Provincial Police (OPP) allowed innocent Canadian citizens in Caledonia and other communities to be terrorized after the 2006 occupation began.

In a February 22, 2010 email to constituents on the 4th anniversary of the occupation Haldimand-Norfolk MPP Toby Barrett outlined the terrible human impact and the staggering economic costs of the government's refusal to uphold the rule of law:

How much are these land disputes costing us?

February 28th marks four years to the day that Haldimand and area began bearing the brunt of the illegal occupation of a Caledonia subdivision.

Four years of chaos, and a compromised policing and justice system have taken their toll. As costs accumulate for the ongoing dispute, the real toll personally and in lost economic opportunity, is much less obvious.

Recently we saw an out-of-court settlement between Dave Brown/ Dana Chatwell and the Ontario Government/Ontario Provincial Police over claims the OPP abandoned the family to chaos and lawlessness. But as those suffering through these past four years are well aware, the Brown/Chatwell harassment is the tip of the iceberg.

I think of other residents on Argyle, as well as Braemar, Thistlemoor, Kinross, Oneida and Sixth Line, all adjacent to Douglas Creek Estates. I think of the lost economic opportunity across Haldimand, Brantford and Brant as investments are scared away by the threat of land disputes.

Aside from the social and psychological stress Caledonia and much of Haldimand and Brant has been under over four years, real investment has been lost and development has ground to a halt.

Just two years into the ongoing standoffs, I presented a locally-derived accounting of lost economic activity from Brantford to Dunnville before the Standing Committee on Estimates – it came in at $4.1 billion, rising to $7 billion if one includes other occupations and protests across the province. These are figures of two years ago.

Testimony before Ontario's Finance Committee – three years ago – pegged the drop in property values of homes adjacent to DCE at anywhere from 15 to 40 percent. There was also an unconfirmed figure of $150 million in additional expenses at Imperial Oil, Ontario Power Generation and the former Stelco because the railway was barricaded for a month.

For four years I have been apprising the Ontario Legislature of the Niagara to Middleport electricity corridor being sabotaged and halted. This was a $116 million project. And whoever torched the Caledonia Transfer Station caused $1 million in direct damage plus four years of security costs up and down the system.

Dunnville did not get a Walmart, a TSC store and a major food chain because of threats. Throughout Haldimand you rarely hear a skilsaw or hammer as builders have had to confront masked trespassers. Hundreds of homes have not been built bringing negative repercussions for the sustainability of Haldimand's socio-economic growth and tax revenue.

I have also received recent data that the Ontario Government has been under-reporting the costs of policing since the occupation in 2006. The report states: "It is entirely possible that the total number of man-hours spent in Caledonia could be as high as two million, with an average cost as high as $100 per man hour, or even more. Based on these figures, the cost of policing could be $200 million, which is over four times more than the province has reported." It concludes, "Dalton McGuinty is hiding the true costs of Caledonia from Ontario taxpayers."

So just how much are these disputes costing us?[4]

Keep in mind that the economic figures cited by Barrett are based on 2008 statistics; the Wynne government continues to allow the derelict eyesore that is the Douglas Creek Estates subdivision to be occupied by native militants to this day.

One Standard for Them, Another for the Rest of Us

The abject failures of Dalton McGuinty and Kathleen Wynne's Liberal governments cannot only be expressed in economic terms. Indeed, while there is plenty of economic evidence highlighting Ontario's fall under the Liberal Party, there are plenty of other ways we can evaluate the true McGuinty-Wynne legacy. Under Dalton McGuinty, Ontario became a more divided society, with two classes of citizens living under two sets of rules and being treated in two different ways. There is no rule of law and equality for all – instead, there's one standard for them, and another standard for the rest of us. This trend only continued under Kathleen Wynne, who has either been purposely complacent or paralyzed from doing anything to end the dual classes of Ontario citizens. Of course, I'm speaking of the plight of aboriginals living in Ontario.

Starting under McGuinty and continuing under Wynne, the supposed special status aboriginals hold within our province has been exacerbated by a provincial government that has no interest in rectifying this embarrassing and shameful divide. A basic principle of most democracies is that each person is equal under the law – there are no special standards for black or white, for men or women, or for right or left. However, this principle has become just another suggestion – an afterthought – of the McGuinty-Wynne Liberals.

Caledonia: Residential Terrorism while the Government does Nothing

One of the most fundamental responsibilities of a government is to protect its citizens, but, apparently, the McGuinty government could not be bothered when it came to the residents of Caledonia, a small community of about 10,000 people about 30 minutes south of Hamilton. The dispute erupted in 2006, when aboriginal protesters occupied a subdivision under construction in Haldimand County being built on a patch of land they claimed was theirs. What occurred thereafter would become Ontario's disgrace: for years, residents who rightfully owned property in Haldimand could not exercise their ownership of that property in peace.

For years, property owners sought and obtained numerous court injunctions and warrants for arrest from judges which were delivered to the occupiers who quickly destroyed and ignored them. For years, the people of Caledonia were arbitrarily deprived of their fundamental human rights: the streets were blocked on a whim by "protesting" aboriginals who constantly showed force by carrying baseball bats, tire irons, guns, large pieces of wood, and by wearing masks over their faces. And they would routinely exercise that force: houses were broken into, ransacked, and trashed. Business properties were trashed and set on fire. Residents were beaten up. Emergency vehicles were blocked from doing their job.

Infrastructure was also being attacked: a hydro station destroyed, roads blocked (the main road through Caledonia was dug up to stop traffic for weeks), and even a bridge was burnt to the ground. Intimidation, assault, forcible confinement, attempted murder, motor vehicle thefts, and vandalism were rampant.

It was clear early in the Caledonia occupation that court orders to the militants would not be sufficient – the people of Caledonia needed real *police* intervention to stop the violence and restore order. In what must be one of the greatest disgraces to the police uniform, the OPP did nothing to stop it. Personal and legal appeals to the McGuinty government went nowhere.

The residents of Caledonia lived in a state of terror for years because the police were completely enabled by a McGuinty government that refused to get involved. Its refusal to order the OPP to uphold the Charter and their duties under the Police Services Act to prevent crime meant that police were replaced by a self-appointed group of aboriginal thugs who terrorized residents – and police – with impunity.

Just one of the thousands of criminal occurrences that exemplified the aboriginals' attitude during the illegal occupation was when a group of aboriginals hijacked a U.S. Border Patrol vehicle: the three Border Patrol officers were assaulted and car-jacked while two OPP officers stood by, doing nothing. The Border Patrol vehicle was then driven directly at an OPP officer in an attempt to run him over. Eventually, the carjackers exited the Border Patrol vehicle, and one of them taunted the police and onlookers by holding his wrists out and screaming, "Arrest me, come on arrest me!" When the police did not arrest him, the carjacker turned to the terrified residents and screamed, "You see, your fucking cops can't touch us, you're all next." The carjackers finally abandoned the vehicle where it could be recovered – covered in feces and urine.[5] Eventually, police arrested eight aboriginals who were charged with various offences, but most of the charges were withdrawn by the Crown, including one of attempted murder.[6] The OPP failed to protect their American colleagues during the incident and Ontario's justice system failed them afterwards. The McGuinty double standard was on full display that day.

The *National Post* did not mince words about the government's pathetic response (and lack thereof):

> Dalton McGuinty's pathetic response to Caledonia is an embarrassment. The Premier is so petrified of being accused of launching into another Ipperwash-type confrontation – where, God forbid, an aboriginal, and not just a white real-estate developer building a home for his daughter, might get hurt – that he is willing to risk turning large parts of his country into a lawless enclave.[7]

On May 23, 2006, the Haldimand Law Association sent the McGuinty government a powerful message - which McGuinty promptly ignored:

> The refusal of the Ontario Provincial Police to comply with and enforce valid and outstanding court orders issued by the Ontario Superior Court of Justice in respect of the land occupation by Natives of the Douglas Creek Estates Development is of great concern to

our membership. We believe that the failures of the Ontario Provincial Police to enforce direct court orders has serious implications in respect of the administration of justice, both real and perceived, and the rights of landowners not only in Caledonia and Haldimand County, but throughout the Province...

A fundamental characteristic of any democratic civilization is the governance of the Rule of Law. When the Rule of Law comes under attack so do the rights and freedoms of every individual in that society. The Rule of Law is under attack in Haldimand County and the powers that be, that have been entrusted to ensure the operation of the Rule of Law and to protect the rights and freedoms of the residents of Canada, are either refusing or neglecting to act...

The Haldimand Law Association, in the interests of the administration of justice in Haldimand County and all parts of the Province, calls upon the Ontario Provincial Police and those other individuals and authorities with the power and duty to enforce and protect the operation of the Rule of Law in this Country to take action to do so. For as long as they refuse, they fail us all and all of our rights and freedoms remain under attack.[8]

Karl Walsh, then-President of the Ontario Provincial Police Association, verified the grave situation in Caledonia and the disconnect between the police commanders and the officers on the ground. In fact, Walsh was one of the many individuals to cite the "two tier justice" hypocrisy:

I got numerous calls from members [OPP Officers] who will tell you that they were petrified of the repercussions of acting... they've got all these examples of people on the ground [Officers] who have already been persecuted, disciplined, had repercussions career-wise. I still don't understand why we took different approaches to law enforcement in Caledonia...

I can't forgive them for a lot of the approaches they took to this and I think numerous officers got unnecessarily injured, I think people from the general public got unnecessarily injured, I think everybody that was involved in this suffered injuries that could have been avoided had they just stuck to their training, stuck to their policies and stuck to the law. You know, the law doesn't discern colour of skin or ethnic background, and it's not supposed to. Justice is supposed to be blind.[9]

The courts repeatedly ruled against how the McGuinty government wanted the OPP to handle the lawlessness in Caledonia. In fact, then-OPP Commissioner Julian Fantino was criminally charged with interfering in municipal affairs and then-Deputy Commissioner Chris Lewis was charged with obstruction of justice.[10] Yet, even after these charges were laid, McGuinty continued to support their style of policing. It was McGuinty who appointed Fantino as Commissioner, and it was McGuinty who appointed Lewis as the new Commissioner when Fantino resigned.

Activist Gary McHale, a former Richmond Hill resident now living near Caledonia, first got involved in 2006 in order to give Caledonia victims a voice. His book, *Victory in the No Go Zone*[11] documents the illegal behaviour of OPP officers and Crown lawyers to ensure McGuinty's policy of appeasement was not interfered with by law-abiding citizens who expected to live in peace and under the rule of law. McHale details how the OPP not only covered up for the criminal behaviour of aboriginal protesters, but how senior OPP officers authorized and supported criminal behaviour on the part of OPP officers themselves.

In his book, McHale, who convinced various courts to issue the criminal charges against Fantino and Lewis, publishes Fantino's and Lewis' own emails that led to those charges and provides a mountain of evidence that demonstrates how the McGuinty government willfully covered up for criminal behaviour. McHale's evidence was never presented at trial – the Crown dropped the charges against Fantino and Lewis, saying there was no likely prospect of a conviction.

Peter Worthington of the *Toronto Sun* described the OPP's handling of Caledonia:

> It is a horror story for ordinary people who were the victims of thuggery. But it's a greater horror story for the OPP which behaved with negligence, dereliction of duty and, yes, cowardice. Officers on the job turned a blind eye to people being beaten, homes threatened, curfews imposed, road blocks established. On occasion, the OPP even refused to come to the aid of a fellow officer being beaten. And now Julian Fantino wants to be a federal MP and cabinet minister. Shame on him for Caledonia, and for his failure to lead.[12]

Caledonia is more than just about the failure of the McGuinty government to protect its citizens from violent thugs. Caledonia is a demonstration of the willingness of the McGuinty government to force upon the Ontario public race-based policing: a double standard with two classes of residents that any reasonable person would see as directly undermining our democracy. In the end, the government would settle the dispute not by arresting, charging, and prosecuting those criminal thugs but, instead, by throwing money at the victims. Attorney General Chris Bentley announced it was paying $20 million to settle a class-action lawsuit brought on behalf of the 440 residents and 400 businesses of Caledonia whose lives were forever changed by what the Liberal government insisted to the end was just a "protest."[13]

What happened at Caledonia was a disgrace, a monumental scandal that cannot be fully done justice here. For a full and thorough account of the nightmare the residents of Caledonia lived through, I strongly suggest Christie Blatchford's book, *Helpless*.[14] I also recommend McHale's *Victory in the No Go Zone*.[15]

Illegal Burger Shack puts Public at Risk

When the E. Coli tragedy hit Walkerton (see chapter two), it created a provincial hysteria about the safety of Ontario's water and food systems. Even with the water facility managers, Stan and Frank Koebel, being found guilty for their neglect of duties and attempts to cover up not actually doing work, the liberal media and the Liberal Party repeatedly blamed Mike Harris for the E. Coli outbreak.

However, when it came to aboriginals operating an illegal burger stand on Ontario government property, the Wynne government changed its tune. In the summer of 2013, a burger shack operating in Caledonia came to the attention of regional health officials. It was built in 2010 during McGuinty's government next to a smokeshack built illegally on government land. As with OPP policy in Caledonia, whereby aboriginals are free to commit criminal acts, the Wynne government wasn't about to take steps to ensure public health if it meant telling aboriginals they had to obey health and safety laws.

Doctor Malcolm Lock, the region's Medical Officer of Health, ordered that the burger shack be shut down because: it could not provide "reliable refrigeration," they were not sure whether the water being used was "pathogen-free," the washrooms for the food stand were just port-a-johns, and the food stand did not have access to hot water or a proper hand-washing station.[16] In other words, basic requirements and expectations for any business that deals with food or the public.

Nevertheless, the food stand refused to close: it was on provincial land and not under the jurisdiction of Caledonia's laws, or so they argued. So Doctor Lock went to court and obtained a cease and desist order – not only against the food stand operators, but also against the Ontario Minister of Infrastructure. The Wynne government refused to enforce it. Both Premier Wynne and Infrastructure Minister Glen Murray were invited for a burger and fries at the illegal shack. After all, if the burger shack was serving safe food, what was there to worry about?[17] Strangely, neither ever made it to their lunch date with the concerned residents and health officials. MPP Toby Barrett baldly asked the Wynne government: "Why do you feel your government is above the law in disobeying this court injunction?"[18]

On September 5, 2013, faced with a provincial government that refused to recognize the court order, Doctor Lock and the Haldimand-Norfolk Health Unit did the only thing they could do; issue a press release that advised the public not to eat there.[19] Once again, the blatant hypocrisy and persistence of two sets of rules for two sets of citizens was readily apparent. If a Tim Horton's or a Burger King were set up with such shoddy food safety policies, they would be immediately shut down. And if they refused to follow the orders of the local health unit, they would quickly be shut down by their own head offices, if not for the ensuing mass citizen outrage. But because this burger shack was run by aboriginals near an aboriginal community, the Ontario Liberals granted them a special status and refused to enforce basic health safety rules that any other restaurant would be required to follow.

Also in September, the Health Unit again filed an injunction in court, both against the illegal burger shack and an illegal cigarette shack; neither had building permits and they violated fire safety laws. Kathleen Wynne actually sent in government lawyers to argue that the Superior Court had no jurisdiction to hear cases regarding buildings on provincial property! On October 2, judge Harrison Arrell responded by adding the Wynne government to the injunction case, saying they were involved since they allowed the shacks to be illegally built in the first place and failed to intervene for over seven years.[20] As of October 2013, faced with a potential finding of contempt of court, the illegal shack's owners agreed to work with health officials and keep their doors closed until standards were drastically increased.

Remember the context in which this debate is situated: Ontario residents tragically died in Walkerton because of water contaminated with E. Coli. The Ontario Liberals and the media refused to lay the blame on the corrupt water managers, and instead chose to blame Mike Harris and his Conservative government for their supposed lack of enforcement of public health rules. Yet, when the Wynne government refused to act to close down a dangerous burger shack, which could reasonably contain an E. Coli risk, there was nary a peep from most of the media. Kathleen Wynne has only continued the McGuinty legacy of two classes of Ontario citizens. In the McGuinty-Wynne Ontario, two sets of rules for two classes of citizens is the norm, even when it threatens our public health.

Liars

Illegal Smoke Shacks built on Government Land

For years, the McGuinty government allowed government property to be used to build illegal smoke shacks and sell illegal cigarettes. But if this was a government that refused to crack down on some dangerous burgers and fries coming from an illegal burger shack, how could they even begin to police dangerous products like tobacco? True to her reputation, Kathleen Wynne only continued this McGuinty hands-off legacy.

It is not hard to imagine how quick law enforcement officers would move to shut down any business illegally built on government land, if it was you or me breaking the law. However, the McGuinty-Wynne government has sent a powerful message over the years that aboriginals will not be arrested or prosecuted for violating laws that apply to every other Ontarian. Across Ontario, the government has consistently allowed aboriginal-run illegal smoke shacks to function without the OPP taking any steps to prevent them. Several of these illegal shacks are built on Ontario government property. However, the McGuinty-Wynne governments have simultaneously abdicated their duty to uphold the law.

The dangers of tobacco are incredibly well-known in terms of health consequences, let alone the dangers of illegal tobacco products that are not controlled, regulated, or overseen in any way. Beyond the health concerns, there are issues with who is producing the tobacco and who is benefiting from its sale: organized crime and terrorists. From an RCMP flyer:

The sale of illegal tobacco products often benefits criminal organizations. The profits are used to: finance drug trafficking in Canada; purchase illegal weapons; and fund other illicit activities. These activities affect the safety and security of our communities and our children.[21]

In 2008, the United States' Department of Homeland Security issued a report that echoed the RCMP's concerns:

> Cigarette smuggling is generating millions of dollars every year that can be reaching terrorist groups, including Hezbollah, Hamas and Al Qaeda, according to law enforcement sources. In a single case, $100,000 was sent to Hezbollah.

> 'This is a very serious homeland security issue, one that has gone unnoticed for far too long,' said Rep. Peter King, (R-N.Y.), the ranking member of the House Homeland Security Committee, who called for the investigation. 'Cigarette smugglers are able to generate millions of dollars in illegal profits with a great deal of this wealth being sent to terrorist groups overseas – groups that would like nothing more than to inflict devastating harm on our country and its citizens.'[22]

While both the Department of Homeland Security and the RCMP understand the seriousness to public safety because of the sale of illegal cigarettes, the McGuinty government would rather spend taxpayers' money to encourage aboriginal youth *to use* aboriginal tobacco. Yes, you read that correctly.

Not only have the McGuinty-Wynne governments refused to shut down illegal smoke shops, they have actively targeted some of those most susceptible to its abuse: young aboriginal children. According to statistics from the *First Nations Regional Longitudinal Health Survey 2002/03* indicate the smoking rate for First Nation's people is about triple the rate for Canadians in general. Sixty-one percent of aboriginal girls between the ages of 15-17 smoke versus only 15 percent of girls in the general public of the same age. The rate for aboriginal boys of the same age is 47 percent, whereas in the general public it is only 13 percent.[23]

The Ontario Aboriginal Cancer Strategy was a program of Cancer Care Ontario, which spent millions of dollars on radio and newspaper advertisements using children as young as eight years-old. In 2006-2007, Cancer Care Ontario published a poster that appallingly pictured a young boy with half of his normal face as if he were healthy and the other half a skeleton. On the skeleton half, the poster states "Commercial Tobacco is a KILLER!" while on the healthy side the poster states "Traditional Tobacco is a HEALER!" (emphasis in original).[24]

In 2005, the McGuinty government supported the Aboriginal Tobacco Strategy Working Group (ATSWG) to fight against that supposedly evil commercial tobacco while promoting traditional tobacco. While it is illegal to promote tobacco at sports events (for those evil "commercial tobacco" producers), the McGuinty government created a strategy to target aboriginal sports events to encourage the use of traditional tobacco.[25] Ontario taxpayers actually paid for the production of magazines which encourage the use of traditional tobacco and government grants to sporting events.[26]

For example, "Grants of $500 to $3,000 are available if you want to set up, promote, and enforce tobacco-wise policies [commercial tobacco is bad but traditional tobacco is a healer], band council resolution, or by-laws in your community. Funding for grants comes from the Aboriginal Tobacco Program of Cancer Care Ontario." The stated goal of Promoting Tobacco-Wise Sports is "Prevent youth from using commercial tobacco products; Prevent youth from being exposed to second-hand smoke; Improve athletic performance of players; [and] Provide further understanding of the role and uses of traditional tobacco."[27]

Liars

While preventing aboriginals from using "commercial" tobacco is noble, it is difficult to understand how "traditional" tobacco doesn't cause any second-hand smoke-related harm to people. It is especially difficult to understand how these recommendations – and even government money! - were coming from an *anti-cancer* organization to help support the "appropriate" use of tobacco. Which specific scientific tests have been done to prove traditional tobacco doesn't create any harm? Why were aboriginals being directed to use "traditional" tobacco, but "commercial" tobacco use was apparently fine for the rest of Ontarians? The proliferation of illegal tobacco smoke shacks is just another example of the McGuinty-Wynne governments having one law for the aboriginals, and one law for everyone else.

McGuinty's Ipperwash Report

Dalton McGuinty first staked his career on being the kinder, gentler Mike Harris. McGuinty said he would balance the books, would not raise taxes, and would be more respectful of Ontario residents. He attempted to live up to his reputation by criticizing and blaming the Harris government at every chance possible, whether it was 2004 or 2012. One of the most blatant abuses of McGuinty's powers as Premier was the vilification of the Harris government through the Ipperwash Inquiry.[28]

The Ipperwash report was issued in 2007, and not surprisingly it supported McGuinty's approach to violence committed by aboriginals: blame the police for lawlessness during aboriginal protests, yet order that they do nothing. The violence in Ipperwash actually started in 1992, when Bob Rae was premier; Mike Harris was not elected until the spring of 1995. Somehow, the inquiry bizarrely twisted the events, conveniently applying different standards to different governments: when Rae was Premier, Ipperwash was a calm negotiation. But when Harris took over, he became that mean government bully. Very little of the inquiry's conclusions laid blame on the aboriginal protesters for their actions. By the time the McGuinty government was in office and the report was set to be released, it conveniently excused Bob Rae, blamed Mike Harris, and fit right into McGuinty's view of Ontario as a province of two classes of citizens.

Gary's McHale's book, *Victory in the No Go Zone*,[29] has a whole chapter explaining how the Ipperwash Inquiry covered up for aboriginal violence. Not one non-aboriginal resident of Ipperwash was permitted to testify at the inquiry and the inquiry made no attempt to deal with the violence committed against residents in Ipperwash. The inquiry was all about ensuring McGuinty's views of non-enforcement of laws against aboriginals were endorsed by the report. As Andrew Coyne perfectly summarized: "So the police badly mishandled the occupation, yes. But had this particular group of natives not taken it into their heads to break the law, defy their band council, and seize the provincial park, they would never have come into conflict with the police. Yet throughout his report, Judge Linden takes the existence of this and other such native occupations as a given."[30]

Or, as another report summarized: "the report by commissioner Sidney Linden essentially tells natives across Canada that they are not responsible for their own actions. Nothing they do will be punished. Indeed, if they protest long enough and loud enough, they will be rewarded with land and money, even if their illegal acts end in violence."[31] The aboriginal protesters were more than happy to indulge in their new-found impunity. Terry Nelson, a Manitoba aboriginal chief, boasted that they would be targeting "the white man" by going after oil, gas, and railway lines. It was their only option, Nelson said, since "there are only two ways of dealing with the white man. One, either you pick up a gun, or you stand between the white man and his money."[32] The McGuinty government failed to respond to such an obviously racist and racially-motivated threat.

The Dual Class Legacy

Although Caledonia was tragic, it was only the explosive tip of the iceberg that exposed how the McGuinty-Wynne Liberals view the dual classes of Ontario's residents. What happened at Caledonia should rightly be called Ontario's disgrace, for it demonstrated the fundamental abrogation of the rights of Ontario's residents and the orders via failure of the McGuinty government to ensure police force upheld the rule of law.

But it has not stopped at the illegal occupation of Caledonia: the attitude of the Ontario Liberals under Dalton McGuinty and Kathleen Wynne has been to create two classes of citizens - the aboriginals, and the rest of us. The aboriginals have been free to operate with impunity, whether illegally occupying land, operating illegal burger shacks, or selling illegal tobacco products. McGuinty and Wynne, uninterested in the terrible damage their policies have done and can do in the future, have turned a blind eye to the provincial government's most fundamental responsibility: to protect Ontario residents, whether black or white, man or woman, aboriginal or non-aboriginal.

This impunity and contempt for the rule of law has continued in other forms, too. The media is constantly filled with stories of aboriginals blocking Highway 401 and other roads[33] or blocking the Via Rail tracks between Toronto and Montreal.[34] They know they can operate with impunity, with the police standing back with orders (tacit certainly; direct, we do not know) from the McGuinty or Wynne governments to not intervene. As the

Liars

Toronto Star stated, there should be absolutely no tolerance for a democracy to legitimately uphold two classes of citizens who operate under two very different standards of laws and rules.

McGuinty's legacy in Ontario has radically changed the rule of law in Ontario and the view that all people are equal under the law. After years of Liberal rule, police forces and government lawyers are well-trained to ensure that aboriginals are not subject to the same laws as the rest of us, regardless of the danger to the public. This is the McGuinty-Wynne Ontario.

1   Lorne Gunter, *Doing Nothing While Natives Run Riot*, National Post, June 12, 2006, http://www.nationalpost.com/story.html?id=f43b6434-789d-4007-a1c0-e2922211c4d4&k=19953

2   Toronto Star, *Time for a Reality Check on Caledonia*, Toronto Star, December 21, 2006, http://www.caledoniawakeupcall.com/apr17press/vandermaas/4.%20Toronto%20Star%20Dec%2021-06.PDF

3   Joe Warmington, *"It's Rural Terrorism," Said one Officer at the Scene*, Toronto Sun, April 22, 2007, http://www.caledoniawakeupcall.com/updates/070422sun.html

4   MPP Toby Barrett (Haldimand-Norfolk, Ontario), *How much are these land disputes costing us?* 'Caledonia Update' email to constituents, February 22, 2010, http://caledoniavictimsproject.files.wordpress.com/2010/05/100222-mpp-barrett-costs-4-1b.pdf

5   Ian Austen, *Mob in Ontario Hijacks Vehicle from U.S. Patrol*, New York Times, June 11, 2006, http://www.nytimes.com/2006/06/11/world/americas/11ontario.html

6   Christie Blatchford, Helpless (Toronto: Anchor Canada, 2010).

7   National Post, How did it come to this? National Post, January 17, 2008, http://www.caledoniawakeupcall.com/updates/080117post3.html

8   Michael J. McLachlin, President, Haldimand Law Association, http://www.caledoniawakeupcall.com/opp/lawassoc.html

9   Gary McHale, Misplaced Moral Outrage, The Regional, August 24, 2011, http://www.caledoniawakeupcall.com/updates/110824regional.html

10   Stephanie Dearing, *Ontario's Top Cop Julian Fantino Facing Criminal Charge*, Digital Journal, January 2, 2010, http://digitaljournal.com/article/284886

11   Gary McHale, *Victory In The No Go Zone*, (Toronto: Freedom Press Canada, 2013).

12   Peter Worthington, *Helpless in Caledonia*, Toronto Sun, October 27, 2010, http://www.torontosun.com/comment/columnists/peter_worthington/2010/10/27/15855826.html

13   Government of Ontario, *Class Action Settlement for Caledonia Community*, July 8, 2011, http://news.ontario.ca/mag/en/2011/07/class-action-settlement-for-caledonia-community.html

14   Christie Blatchford, *Helpless* (Toronto: Anchor Canada, 2010).

15   Gary McHale, *Victory In The No Go Zone*, (Toronto: Freedom Press Canada, 2013).

16   Monte Sonnenberg, Brantford Expositor, September 19, 2013, http://www.brantfordexpositor.ca/213/09/19/health-unit-seeks-contempt-ruling-against-burger-shack

17   Antonella Artuso, *Activist to premier: Come eat at illegal burger shack*, Toronto Sun, September 13, 2013, http://www.torontosun.com/2013/09/16/activist-to-premier-come-eat-at-

illegal-burger-shack

18   Toby Barrett, MPP, Barrett calls for Minister to "Step Aside" over Burger Shack, The Algoma News, October 4, 2013, http://www.thealgomanews.ca/news/regional/barrett-calls-for-minister-to-step-aside-over-burger-shack/

19   Haldimand-Norfolk Health Unit, *Diners Advised to Avoid Burger Stand until Health Concerns Addressed,* Norfolk County, September 5, 2013, http://www.norfolkcounty.ca/media-releases/diners-advised-avoid-burger-stand-health-concerns-addressed/

20   Jennifer Vo, *Caledonia Hamburger Stand will work with Health Officials,* Sachem and Glanbrook Gazette, October 4, 2013, http://www.sachem.ca/news/caledonia-hamburger-stand-will-work-with-health-officials/

21   Royal Canadian Mounted Police, *Illegal Tobacco – the Consequences,* http://www.caledoniawakeupcall.com/documents/RCMPtobacco-tabac-broch-eng.pdf

22   Catherine Herridge, *Cigarette Smugglers Funnel Money to Terror Group, Report finds,* Fox News, Apr 29, 2008, http://www.foxnews.com/story/2008/04/29/cigarette-smugglers-funnel-money-to-terror-groups-report-finds/

23   Health Canada, *First Nations Regional Longitudinal Health Survey,* 2002-2003, http://fnigc.ca/sites/default/files/ENpdf/RHS_2002/rhs2002-03-technical_report.pdf

24   Cancer Care Ontario, *Are you Tobacco Wise?,* http://www.caledoniawakeupcall.com/tobacco/tobaccoad_l.jpg

25   Cancer Care Ontario, *Aboriginal Tobacco Strategy,* 2006, http://www.caledoniawake-upcall.com/tobacco/ATS-RFP-2006-2007-August-18-06.pdf

26   Aboriginal Tobacco Program, *Breathing Life into our Communities: March 2011,* Government of Ontario, http://www.tobaccowise.com/common/pages/UserFile.aspx?fileId=88331

27   Aboriginal Tobacco Program, *Tobacco-Wise Sports and Recreation,* Government of Ontario, http://www.tobaccowise.com/tobacco_wise_sports/

28   Sidney Linden, The Ipperwash Inquiry, June 6, 2007, http://www.attorneygeneral.jus.gov.on.ca/inquiries/ipperwash/index.html

29   Gary McHale, *Victory in the No Go Zone,* (Toronto: Freedom Press Canada, 2013).

30   Andrew Coyne, *Native violence becomes blameless - Ipperwash report effectively legitimizes illegal protests,* National Post, June 2, 2007, http://www.caledoniawakeupcall.com/updates/070602post.html

31   National Post, *For natives, a legal free-for-all,* National Post, June 2, 2007, http://www.canada.com/nationalpost/story.html?id=dbd74d75-5450-4f66-9cfd-203c53fd3213&p=2

32   Kevin Steel, *Protection Racket,* Western Standard – July 2007, http://www.westernstandard.ca/website/article.php?id=2620

33   Toronto Star, *Protests Block 401, Rail Lines,* Toronto Star, June 29, 2007, http://www.thestar.com/news/canada/2007/06/29/protests_block_401_rail_lines.html

34   CBC News, *Via Rail Blockade by First Nations that Halted Montreal-Toronto Train Ends,* CBC News, March 19, 2014, http://www.cbc.ca/news/canada/montreal/via-rail-blockade-by-first-nations-that-halted-montreal-toronto-trains-ends-1.2578221

Chapter 6

Deficits, Scandals, and Expensive Experiments – the Second McGuinty Majority (2007-2011)

"For each job created through renewable energy programs, about two to four jobs are often lost in other sectors of the economy because of higher electricity prices."

-Auditor General on the McGuinty government's
green energy investments

"It is unconscionable to teach eight-year-old children same-sex marriage, sexual orientation and gender identity. It is even more absurd to subject sixth graders to instruction on the pleasures of masturbation, vaginal lubrication, and 12-year-olds to lessons on oral sex and anal intercourse."

-Charles McVety on the McGuinty government's
radical sex education reforms

A Disappointing Result

Despite the winds shifting back towards the Progressive Conservatives, they were unable to capture the win and save Ontario. When John Tory's Conservatives promised government funding for religious schools, the Liberals were able to successfully capitalize on a contentious issue. The 2007 election was basically a wash, but it highlighted several important issues. Among them, Ontarians were concerned about government spending, the increasing debt, and expensive government experiments. This was

Liars

why the Liberals actually lost one seat while the Progressive Conservatives and NDP gained two and three seats respectively. If only they knew what was coming. Ontario remained on its hijacked course to failure, unable to be rescued from a Conservative Party that stepped on the divisive third rail and an NDP that struggled to gain any relevance.

McGuinty's second majority mandate spoke volumes about the state of politics in Ontario. Voters were unwilling to trust the brands of Progressive Conservative John Tory and New Democrat Howard Hampton. McGuinty's second mandate went forward in the same fashion as his first. Ontario was plagued by growing job losses and smaller investments from the private sector. It was becoming more burdensome and expensive to do business in Ontario, and employers were beginning to look to Quebec, Manitoba, or the Maritimes as cheaper alternatives than Ontario; or they simply abandoned Canada and took their jobs to the United States. The second McGuinty government would also be marred in scandal after scandal after scandal, as public sector executives were revealed to be living the high-class lifestyle of private limousines and lavish expense accounts on the taxpayers' money. But for McGuinty, government from 2007 to 2011 was just business as usual.

The New Cabinet

Twenty days after being re-elected, McGuinty announced his new cabinet – a total of 28 cabinet assignments, among them nine women. Several ministers appointed to Ontario's 39th Parliament would become key players in notorious portfolios in the years to come:

- Gerry Phillips was promoted to Minister of Energy
- Dwight Duncan became the Minister of Finance
- Michael Bryant moved from Attorney General to Minister of Aboriginal Affairs
- Chris Bentley became Attorney General
- Donna Cansfield became Minister of Natural Resources
- John Gerretsen became the Minister of the Environment
- Laurel Broten became Parliamentary Assistant to the Minister of Health and Long-term Care
- Margaret Best, who had just been elected in the 2007 election, became the Minister of Health Promotion
- David Ramsay was removed from cabinet

In his cabinet announcement, McGuinty promised his second mandate would see his government become an "activist."[1] Among those "activist" policies would be:

- Addressing chronic diseases and hiring more physicians and nurses
- Expanding public transit
- Creating the "Next Generation Jobs Fund" as a way of supporting innovative jobs
- Expanding home care for seniors and assisting them in paying their property taxes

Broken Promises Start Quickly

After winning the 2007 election, McGuinty promised he would review the massive $2.6 billion health care levy he imposed on Ontarians following the 2003 election – despite his pledge to not raise taxes in that same election. Yet he pre-emptively kyboshed any sort of "review" by saying the $2.6 billion tax would stay regardless of what the review found or recommended.[2] It was a telling sign of a Premier who had already made up his mind, and was simply going through the motions of "reviewing" a tax he decided to impose on Ontarians before unilaterally deciding the tax needed to stay anyway. What was the purpose of the review if the Premier had already declared he knew what was best? What was the purpose of government at all if Dalton McGuinty had all the answers?

The New Leaders

Ontario's Opposition parties were also regrouping, electing two new leaders who could better take on McGuinty's Liberals. The NDP needed to replace the ineffective Howard Hampton and the Progressive Conservatives needed to replace the divisive John Tory. In 2009, Andrea Horwath, the union's favourite candidate and a self-described "CAW [Canadian Auto Workers] brat,"[3] beat out the other candidates, including those financed by then-federal NDP leader Jack Layton. On that same weekend, the Progressive Conservatives elected Tim Hudak as their leader. Hudak had been a Niagara Falls MPP since 1995 and a former cabinet minister in Mike Harris' government. Hudak had an impressive endorsement list from several prominent former and current provincial and federal cabinet ministers. Both Hudak and Horwath faced opponents in the leadership race, and both won on the third ballots.

The Green Energy Nightmare

In 2009, McGuinty's government introduced the *Green Energy and Green Economy Act*, an act which was intended to stimulate the economy while investing in green energy – "the wave of the future," McGuinty proclaimed. This wave of the future would cost a minimal one percent electricity cost increase – a minimal price to pay if Ontario was shifting to clean energy,

Liars

McGuinty reasoned. Wrong! Like everything else the McGuinty government touched, McGuinty's green energy dream became a green energy nightmare. McGuinty's reckless green energy experiments became the sad hallmark that highlighted everything wrong with the McGuinty government. It didn't work the way the Liberals said it would; projects were constantly under-delivered and over budget, and it killed jobs! The only "green" associated with these experiments was the millions of dollars sucked clean from taxpayers' pockets.

Auditor General Steps In

Once again, the Auditor General stepped in. It was clear from the outset that the McGuinty government would pursue its ideological quest for green energy regardless of the costs. The Auditor General, instead of the Liberal government, had to be the voice of reason and the defender of taxpayers' money. His report would abruptly shatter the myths surrounding McGuinty's green energy nightmare.

The Approval Process

McGuinty's green energy agenda was a pet project from the beginning, so why should it have to be put through the inconvenient vetting process? He was Premier – couldn't he just override the rules and avoid his independent bureaucracy as he pleased? In fact, the Auditor General noted much of the Liberal government's green energy agenda was done by ministerial prerogative, avoiding those pesky independent regulators such as the Ontario Energy Board (OEB),[4] the approving authority for Ontario's long-term energy plans. The Liberal government delegated the creation of Ontario's long-term energy plan to the Ontario Power Authority. The OPA spent $10.7 million developing this plan, which was submitted to the OEB. Yet the McGuinty government suspended the OEB review, and instead released its own energy plan. Such politicking, the Auditor General said, made it unclear to the public who was responsible for implementing the green energy agenda: the independent government regulator, or the Premier's Office?

Power Generation

The Liberals projected that their investments in wind turbines would generate 1500 megawatts (MW) per day in 2010, and 10,700 MW by 2018. At the time of writing, wind power accounts for a dismal 198 MW of the total 17,025 MW being used, barely 1.2 percent of all electricity generation.[5]

Ontario has also had a power surplus for some time now, meaning suppliers who were paid a flat-rate to produce electricity are being paid to have that electricity sent to other provinces and states. Between 2005 and 2011, Ontario taxpayers paid $1.8 billion to produce electricity then send it to

New York, Quebec, and Manitoba. In fact, in 2013 it was revealed the provincial government was paying wind farmers to *not* produce wind energy![6]

Electricity Prices

McGuinty promised the increase to electricity bills would be a paltry one percent increase – peanuts if that was the price of a cleaner environment and cheaper electricity in the long run. In fact, the Auditor General said that "electricity prices for the average Ontario consumer are projected to rise 46 per cent in the next five years."[7] The overwhelming source of Ontario's electricity is nuclear power, followed by hydro, gas, and then wind power. Even the McGuinty government estimated a household's electricity costs would almost double, from $1400 per year in 2010 to over $2600 by 2022. But an analysis conducted by the C.D. Howe Institute concluded that an *additional* $310 per year was being added to each household's bill as a direct result of the government's green energy investments.[8]

Jobs

But maybe – just maybe – these costs were worth it if they were creating jobs for our province. The Liberal government boasted that its green energy plan would create 50,000 jobs at a time when the economy desperately needed them, 40,000 of which were directly related to renewable energy. However, the Auditor General concluded 30,000 of those jobs were construction jobs that would last one-to-three years. In fact, as of May 2013, the Liberal government admitted the *Green Energy Act* had only created 62 percent – or 31,000 jobs – of the 50,000 it promised.[9]

The worst was yet to come. "Studies in other jurisdictions have shown that for each job created through renewable energy programs, about two to four jobs are often lost in other sectors of the economy because of higher electricity prices," concluded the Auditor General. In other words, even if the McGuinty government could create 50,000 jobs, they were killing 100,000-400,000 jobs because of the rising electricity costs. Furthermore, the Auditor General said the cost of creating just one green energy job was enormous: between $100,000 and $300,000.[10]

The enormous investment in green energy simply did not add up in the ways the Liberals said it would: the process was not followed; wind power remained a minute source in lieu of more reliable energy, like nuclear power; electricity prices were set to skyrocket; and most of the jobs the green shift would create were temporary construction jobs. All in the name of McGuinty's strange infatuation with wind turbines.

In light of the massive cost of $5.4 billion, or $1100 per year per household, some have noted that the real outrage against the McGuinty government

Liars

should not come from the gas plants cancellation (see chapter ten), but from McGuinty's expensive green energy nightmare.[11]

Learn From Experience

As much as McGuinty wanted to portray Ontario as being the government on the cutting edge, it really wasn't. States and provinces around the world were already dabbling in the renewable wind energy business – and they were failing miserably. In the United Kingdom, investments in wind power simply weren't adding up. One turbine installed in Hampshire, at a cost of £30,000, generated a dismal 520 kilowatt hours of electricity (kWh) *in one year*.[12] At the average of 30 pence per kWh, that *one* turbine would take a ridiculous 190 years to pay for itself! Other turbines were installed throughout the UK at a cost up to £89,000 a piece, yet they were constantly down due to "faults." Even when the wind was blowing, these expensive eye sores were not generating electricity because they didn't work.

Or what about Spain's green energy experiment? With a similar population and GDP to Canada, Spain is another example from which the McGuinty government could have learned instead of wasting billions of dollars. In March 2009, a study by Spain's King Juan Carlos University questioned whether that country's massive investments in green energy were really worth it.[13] Much like Ontario would find, green energy wasn't all it was trumpeted up to be. "The Spanish/EU-style 'green jobs' agenda" being admired and implemented around the world "in fact destroys jobs," concluded the study. Every "green job" that was created in Spain cost 2.2 other Spanish jobs – like Ontario, usually due to the higher electricity costs. Every green MW of power produced killed five Spanish jobs.

Furthermore, like Ontario, most of the jobs that green energy investments created in Spain were not created out of private sector entrepreneurialism, but out of direct government subsidies. The result was a whopping €571,138 per job, or about $850,000 in 2009 exchange rates – on top of the €1 million it took just to create that job! In total, the Spanish government was spending the equivalent of 4.35 percent of all value-added taxes collected, 3.45 percent of household income taxes, or 5.6 percent of corporate income taxes.

And finally, once again just like Ontario, the enormous cost of creating such expensive and unsustainable green jobs simply was not worth the output. Despite the €29 billion ($43 billion) in Spanish subsidies to encourage the use of renewable energies, only 23 percent of its electricity came from solar and wind power in 2010.[14]

The cases of reckless green energy experiments in the United Kingdom and

Spain should have underscored the case against wind power: it's expensive, unpredictable, and unreliable. The Spanish threw billions away – why did Ontario need to experience the same disastrous investment for ourselves?

The Multi-Billion Dollar Samsung Deal

McGuinty's pet project was in trouble and it needed help. The Auditor General had added a dose of reality to the discussion about just how much the Liberals were willing to spend on reckless and untested renewable energy technologies. But instead of heeding the Auditor's advice and taking some time to further study the issue, McGuinty doubled down. In January 2010 he announced a massive "landmark" $7 billion deal with Samsung that would supposedly create 16,000 jobs and 2500 megawatts of electricity with wind turbines. That was no small investment, at almost $500,000 per job or $2.8 million per megawatt.

There was that pesky Auditor General again, inconveniencing the Liberals with a bit of reality: "No formal economic analysis was done to determine whether the [Samsung] deal was prudent, and neither the OPA nor the Ontario Energy Board was consulted about the deal."[15] Analyses about whether Samsung offered what Ontario apparently needed? Nah! Questions about why Samsung was offered a sole-source deal without a competitive bidding process? Who cares! Ask the Power Authority or the Energy Board about whether they thought it was a good deal? Hogwash! McGuinty was set on wind turbines, and he was going to get them regardless of the cost.

Smart Meters

Not only would each household be paying $1100 a year so McGuinty could live out his wind turbine fantasy, they would also be paying more to do their laundry in the afternoon or take showers in the morning. In 2010, the Liberal government forced its way into Ontarians' homes to learn about our dishes and underwear – and they wanted to learn how to charge us more to clean both.

So-called "smart meters" were forcibly installed in Ontario households; they send time-of-use data back to the power companies. Suddenly it was more expensive to shower after 7:00 am on weekdays or do laundry before 7:00 pm. The McGuinty government had successfully conquered any shred of decency Ontarians once had by taxing them into behaving as his government pleased.

The way Dalton McGuinty and his Liberal government handled the green energy fiasco was indicative of the way his government would treat Ontario taxpayers: here was a Premier who would do anything and say anything to get elected – then do something else. He completely disregarded his government's independent regulatory agencies and failed to look at examples in other countries. This was a Premier who wanted what he wanted and was going to get it when he wanted it – regardless of the cost to taxpayers.

Increasing Hydro Rates

The Liberals' obsession with wind turbines and controlling when we do our laundry or bathe did not come cheap. Hydro rates have exploded out of control since the Liberals took office. Ontario used to have some of the cheapest electricity in Canada: in 2002, Ontario's electricity was 4.2 cents per kilowatt hour (kWh). Today, Ontario's hydro bills are the third highest in Canada, behind only Nova Scotia and Prince Edward Island. The average Canadian pays $113.72 for 1000 kWh per month. Not so for Ontarians, who pay $141.69. That's an extra $27.97 a month and $335.64 per year.

As of November 1, 2013, the per kWh electricity rates were set at 12.9 cents for "on peak" use, 10.9 cents for "mid-peak" use, and 7.2 cents for "off peak" use.[16] The on peak price is more than *triple* the 2002 flat rate; even off-peak use is almost *double* the flat rate for electricity that existed before McGuinty came to office.[17]

But that still wasn't enough. In late December 2013, just as Canada was being plunged into record-setting low temperatures the Ontario Liberals announced they were going to set their own record for deepest dive into taxpayers' pockets: they were increasing hydro rates by a suffocating 42 percent. (Those record-setting low temperatures would last into January 2014 and caused the worst power outage since the 2003 blackout – more on that in chapter ten.) The plan, led by Energy Minister Bob Chiarelli, would mean the average household electricity bill would climb from $125 per month in 2013 to $167 by 2016.[18] By 2018 that would equal a 42 percent increase, and a 68 percent increase by 2032.[19] Of course, the average homeowner would have been straddled with $100 a year *less* than they would have been if it weren't for the McGuinty government's $1.1 Billion decision to cancel the Oakville and Mississauga power plants (see chapter ten).

Chiarelli's energy plan also meant a decrease in Ontario's use of nuclear and coal energy plants in favour of the untested and unreliable solar and wind power. By 2025, Chiarelli said, nuclear would account for 17 percent *less* of Ontario's power supply, while reliance on wind power would triple by 2032.[20]

The picture painted by Chiarelli makes it appear as if Ontario is in an energy crisis, desperate for any and all electricity we can generate. Not so: at the time the Liberal minister was raising electricity rates by 42 percent, Ontario was actually giving away over $1 billion in electricity. The scheme

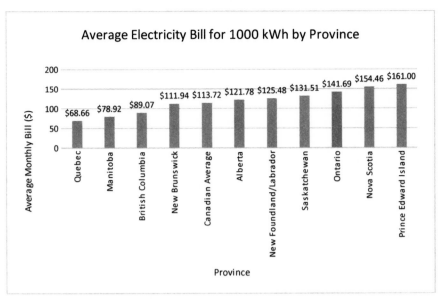

Figure 7: Average electricity bill by province

the Liberals have set up is this: we purchase electricity from provinces and states like Manitoba, Quebec, Michigan, Minnesota, or New York for 8.5 cents per kWh. Yet, the over-purchased electricity is sold back to those same states for less than 3 cents per kWh.[21] That's over $1 billion in electricity being given away, or another $220 per year being added to your average hydro bill and mindlessly thrown away by the McGuinty Liberals due to poor planning and the over-purchasing of foreign electricity. If only we had those new power plants in Oakville and Mississauga, perhaps we could be saving the $1 billion being thrown to our neighbours. But again, the Ontario Liberals give little attention or care to what's good for Ontario. This attitude would come to define the McGuinty government's second majority government, and indeed, his entire legacy.

More Tax Grabs by the McGuinty Liberals

Harmonized Sales Tax (HST)

In 2009, the McGuinty government added yet another tax onto the backs of Ontario's families by reaching an agreement with the federal government to merge the separate Provincial Sales Tax (PST) with the federal Goods and Services Tax (GST) into one tax: the Harmonized Sales Tax (HST).[22]

To be clear, I support the fact that Ontario uses a harmonized sales tax rather than keeping separate the provincial and federal sales tax. A single value-added tax offers significant savings for businesses that no longer have to track and remit two separate sales taxes. For one, businesses ab-

Liars

sorbed an estimated $5 billion in provincial sales taxes just in getting the product onto their shelves (because the end product was taxed at each step along its production or refining). Secondly, streamlined taxes offered businesses an estimated $500 million in administrative costs.[23] These savings are then passed onto consumers.

Where the McGuinty government went wrong was firstly in unilaterally implementing the HST with little notice or consultation with Ontarians and secondly, in failing to provide tax relief for items previously only taxed provincially now being taxed federally as well. By harmonizing the sales taxes and charging a flat 13 percent, the federal GST portion (five percent) was added to many items that were previously only taxed provincially. This meant the province was raising taxes on gasoline, home heating, electricity, tobacco, newspapers and magazines, any fast food over $4, taxi fares, dry cleaning, lawn care and landscaping, accountants, gym memberships, internet bills, haircuts, hotels, home renovations, real estate fees – and more![24] The McGuinty government could have provided tax relief or updated its exceptions list to balance out the new items that would be taxed at 13 percent that were previously only taxed at eight percent. Both of these reasons speak about the *process* of implementing the HST rather than the HST itself – something the Liberal government was perfectly capable of controlling.

The HST was not without its critics, which is why the implementation process should have required more public information and outreach. Seventy four percent of Ontarians opposed the introduction of the HST, to a large degree because the government failed to articulate the significant benefits for customers and businesses of implementing a single sales tax.[25] McGuinty claimed the HST would create jobs rather than kill them,[26] a common response to a common concern many people expressed.

The HST was implemented, so what were its effects? The Canadian Centre for Policy Studies attempted to quantify this answer one month after the HST was implemented in British Columbia and Ontario.[27] They found a net tax *increase* of approximately $290 per household. One year after the HST was implemented, the Liberal government was confident consumers and businesses were seeing lower prices. Finance Minister Dwight Duncan said:

> There's a debate as to how long it takes for [savings to be passed onto consumers], but there's unanimity that it does. Small business people especially who originally opposed the HST are now starting to see their input tax credits coming back and they realize just what an enormous change this was. My sense is they are passing some of those savings on to consumers.[28]

84

Yet, all the McGuinty Liberals succeeded in doing was offering a rare moment for both the Ontario Conservatives and NDP to agree: both Tim Hudak and Andrea Horwath agreed business savings from implementing HST had been passed along in the form of lower prices for consumers.[29]

The Sneaky Eco-Tax

If implementing the HST without notice or consultation wasn't sneaky enough, the McGuinty "eco tax" sure was. Ontarians had their taxes hiked a second day on July 1, 2010, the same day the HST was implemented. Suddenly over 10,000 common consumer items were hit with a new "eco-tax." Apparently, adding another tax onto your grocery bill would make you want to "recycle or dispose of" those items.[30] Sunblock, mouse traps, cleaning supplies, hairspray, calculators, toothbrushes, batteries... all were suddenly taxed thanks to the McGuinty government. The *Toronto Star* called it a "scam" and rightly noted the McGuinty Liberals got it backwards: "instead of first making it easy to recycle, say, flashlight batteries and then charging a fee to pay for that service, it did the reverse. It first charged the fee, but without making recycling any easier."[31] Some lawyers stepped forward to say McGuinty's sneaky eco-fees were illegal, since they amounted to a form of indirect taxation.[32]

In a matter of days, public outrage forced the McGuinty government to repeal the eco tax for 90 days while they could figure out what they were doing. It was shocking that such a sudden and unadvertised tax grab was not thought through in advance. But that didn't stop McGuinty from implementing a tire tax – $6.60 per tire (including tax) for the Liberal government to "store, transport, recycle, and process used tires" and to "fund research and development and be used to educate consumers."[33] Oh, but it wasn't a tax like the eco-tax – in fact an agency under the Minister of the Environment said "describing the fee (levied on stewards) as a tax may be considered a false, misleading, or deceptive representations under the *Consumer Protection Act.*"[34] It's a tax – but the McGuinty government may sue you if you call it a tax. (At a University of Toronto speech in June 2005 McGuinty promised "There will be no tire tax. Did everybody get that? There will be no tire tax." He must have forgotten.)

In November 2013, the Wynne government introduced Bill 91: *The Waste Reduction Act,* which abolishes the McGuinty eco-tax charged on consumers' bills in favour of an eco-tax charged on industry's bills.[35] And when businesses and industries are charged fees, who foots the bill? Consumers! So it's still a tax on Ontarians – it's just no longer written on our grocery receipts. Call it the new Wynne eco-tax. (At the time of writing, the bill is in its second reading.)

Liars

The Health Tax

Let's ignore that McGuinty broke his repeated promises to not raise taxes, and instead ask whether the health tax actually reduces wait times. According to the Auditor General, "only 10% to 15% of the patients with emergent and urgent conditions were seen by physicians within the recommended timelines, and sometimes waited for more than six hours after triage before being seen by nurses or physicians."[36] In fact, the Auditor's office found that it was not uncommon for patients to wait between 10 and 26 hours for a bed. Despite the Canadian Acuity and Triage Scale recommending that all patients be triaged within 10 minutes of their arrival in the emergency room, it was also not uncommon for patients to wait for more than an hour. Patients are still struggling in desperate conditions and are unable to receive the help and surgery they need.[37] These results are simply unacceptable for a $2.4 billion tax with the explicit promise of reducing wait times and improving services in our hospitals.

OLG Gets Caught A Second Time

On August 31, 2009, Finance Minister Dwight Duncan announced he was "taking action to ensure protection of taxpayers money" by firing Ontario Lottery and Gaming Corporation (OLG) President and Chief Executive Officer Kelly McDougald and accepting the resignations of OLG's entire board of directors.[38] Duncan said he had reviewed two years' worth of expense claims by the OLG executives, and he did not like what he saw: Vice President of Security and Surveillance Michael Sharland billed the Ontario government for cancelling a deposit on a Florida condo. Another executive billed $500 for a nanny. Another charged $7 for a pen refill, $1.12 for a grocery bag, and $30 for a car wash without a receipt.

Apparently, just two years after the previous OLG CEO was fired, the McGuinty government had still failed to enforce the rules on how one of its agencies handled public money. The Auditor General actually had to reiterate that the Crown corporation "should be spending public tax-payer dollars with the same care they would take in spending their own money."[39]

Duncan's house cleaning was an attempt to get a leg up on another impending scandal. For some reason, while the McGuinty government sent eHealth CEO Kramer off with a lavish severance package (see below), they had no issues firing the OLG chief executive for cause. So McDougald responded with a $9 million lawsuit.[40] That lawsuit was quietly settled on Christmas Eve for $750,000 – a move the McGuinty government tried to spin as "a good deal" since it was less than 10 percent of what

McDougald was asking for.[41] McDougald said the settlement cleared her name and reputation, yet the specifics of the settlement are secret.

The Auditor General's Report

When Auditor General Jim McCarter reported on the corporation's expense claims 10 months later, he confirmed much of what had been suspected. The policies on certain types of expenses were not covered in OLG's policy, such as the maximum limits for employee meals at official meetings and for hotels when travelling on official business. More than 20 percent of the claims examined by the Auditor General had no itemized receipts and 10 percent had no list of attendees, even though both *were* required by existing OLG policy. OLG spent approximately $1 million on hospitality expenses in the 2008/2009 year, but it could not breakdown "in-house meetings," which were regularly held at restaurants, and meals for which employees were reimbursed while travelling on official business.

The executive staff bought themselves season tickets and corporate boxes at several sporting events, at a cost of over $100,000 per year, not including the food and drink consumed at those events. They regularly held "team-building" meetings at spas and resorts, onboard private boats, and at a privately-rented arcade. They rented out a resort casino for four days for an astonishing $551,000 – and you and I paid for it!

They leased an executive fleet of vehicles between $41,000 and $58,000 a piece for 26 senior executives, and gave another 16 executives vehicle allowances between $17,000 and $24,000 per year. The Auditor General was especially perplexed by this, since only deputy ministers are given a private vehicle and it has to cost less than $30,000.

As with the eHealth scandal discussed below, the generous perks of working at OLG could not be simply dismissed as a rogue agency. OLG was responsible to the government of Ontario – and thus the people of Ontario – through Dalton McGuinty's cabinet. Yet it was not until May 2007 that an official memorandum was signed that OLG would report to the Minister of Public Infrastructure Renewal. But even with this signed memo, OLG failed to follow the government-approved policies on expenses and employee reimbursement and, seven months later, applied to be exempted from those policies. When the McGuinty government did not respond, OLG thought its exemption was approved. Another nine months went by before the McGuinty government directed OLG to follow the government standard. This was not a rogue agency. This was a systemic problem that fully belonged to the McGuinty government leadership, from the premier down to the cabinet ministers. No one could be bothered to enforce the rules that protect taxpayers' money.

Liars

The eHealth Scandal

Two months after the OLG scandal, the McGuinty government was hit with yet another scandal involving questionable business practices and the abuse of public funds. The eHealth scandal is one of the largest blights on Dalton McGuinty's government, and will forever define his legacy. eHealth Ontario was created in September 2008 with the mandate of having electronic health records for all Ontario patients by 2015.

The SSHA Legacy

eHealth was the new agency resulting from a merger between the Ontario Health Ministry's Electronic Health Program and the Smart Systems for Health Agency (SSHA), established in 2003 based on a 2000 provincial-federal agreement to create electronic health records. Three years into its mandate, in 2006, auditing firm Deloitte & Touche LLP released a scathing indictment of SSHA: there was "little or no meaningful progress," the agency was "not well regarded in the health-care community and lack[ed] strategic direction," and policies regarding privacy were "incomplete and not widely understood."[42]

In 2007 SSHA was hit again by the information and privacy Commissioner, who challenged SSHA's privacy and security violations.[43] Furthermore, while SSHA was supposed to eliminate the need for private contractors, they spent an average of 17 percent of their annual budget on them. Thus, eHealth Ontario was born. Chief executive officer (CEO) Sarah Kramer was personally appointed by the Health Minister and had her employment terms directly ratified by the Premier's Office. The Chairman of the Board, Doctor Alan Hudson, was also personally appointed by McGuinty into the volunteer role. Both Hudson and Kramer had worked together at Cancer Care Ontario.

Sole-Source Contracts and Blatant Nepotism

To ensure taxpayers receive the best services or products for the best value, the Ontario procurement system requires a competitive bidding process for any contract over $100,000. The only exceptions to this are: if it involves legal services; to respond to an "urgent circumstance;" or if the government requires a patented product unique to a single supplier. Roughly nine months after eHealth Ontario was created, CBC News revealed that in its first four months of operation, Kramer had awarded $4.8 million in contracts that completely avoided the procurement system. These were contractors charging up to $300 per hour for their services.[44] Kramer said following the bidding process would have slowed down the agency's start-up and discouraged the recruitment of "specialized services." The contracts included $915,000 to the Courtyard Group, a health care consulting firm, $300,000 to Anzen Consulting, and two separate $1 million contracts to Accenture, a management and technology consulting firm.

But how did Kramer choose these particular contractors? One of the managing partners of Courtyard Group, Michael Guerriere, was a former eHealth Senior Vice President – another consultant hired in the early eHealth days who bills more than $3000 per day. And Guerriere's wife, Miyo Yamashita, is the head of Anzen Consulting. But Yamashita came at a discount compared to her husband – she only charged $300 per hour for "communications services" that included reading the *New York Times,* reviewing the holiday greeting left on Kramer's voicemail, and giving a debriefing during a chat on the subway.[45]

It was blatant nepotism as Kramer showered former eHealth consultants with new contracts without ever stopping to implement a competitive bidding process to ensure Ontario would receive the best value for our dollars. It was corruption and the patent abuse of taxpayers' money, not seen in such an obvious and deliberate fashion since the federal Liberals' AdScam.

The Luxurious Lifestyle

But it didn't end there. Kramer also spent $51,500 refurnishing her office, begging the question of how its original furnishings became inadequate in less than one year. Also, within her first year at eHealth, Kramer spent at least $800 on limousine rides, including a $408 ride which picked her up at her home and another while she was visiting Boston.[46] Working at eHealth was apparently worthy of a luxurious lifestyle, as demonstrated by Kramer's $380,000 salary, more than Ontario's Premier or Canada's Prime Minister. And she was doing something right according to the McGuinty government – they gave her a $114,000 bonus after just five months in the job. In fact, the bonus, at 30 percent of her annual salary, was more than double what the eHealth policy was for bonuses (a maximum of 15 percent), but the Minister of Health personally approved it anyway.

Kramer did not keep all the wealth to herself: two Senior Vice Presidents, whose primary residences were in Alberta, were being flown to Ontario – on the taxpayers' dime. Each of those Vice Presidents billed, on average, $2700 per day for their services. Their bills even got so ridiculous as to include a $3.26 reimbursement for a can of pop and muffin! In total, the two Vice Presidents cost Ontario taxpayers $1.5 million per year.

The Golden Severance Ticket

When Kramer was fired in June 2009, she took with her a plentiful $317,000 severance package on top of 10 months' worth of benefits.[47] All told, Kram-

Liars

er personally fleeced over half a million dollars from Ontarians' pockets for leading an organization that did... what exactly?

McGuinty's Inner Circle

McGuinty's Liberals were quick to distance themselves from the billion dollar eHealth boondoggle, as it was quickly labelled, but their distancing could not deflect reality. Karli Farrow left the Premier's Office to undertake a $10,646 contract for 32.5 hours of work over a three-week period.[48] Her work – taxpayer paid – included corresponding with Don Guy, McGuinty's former chief of staff and Liberal campaign director for the 2003 and 2007 elections.

Farrow was not just the former chief of staff to Health Minister George Smitherman. She also worked closely with McGuinty himself over a period of at least seven years: she was the Director of Policy and Research in the Premier's office, and was the person who crafted the health care portion of the Liberals' 2003 election platform. Then there was John Ronson: the co-chair of the 1995 Liberal election campaign – and also a Courtyard consultant. He billed a total of $1572 for spending a total of four hours working on "risk management" and "governance issues."[49] The registered lobbyist for Courtyard was Duncan Fulton – McGuinty's former press secretary who left that position for the same role in Jean Chretien's office.

The Auditor's Report

Auditor General Jim McCarter did not mince words about this failed government initiative: he said eHealth had wasted over $1 billion in taxpayer money.[50] He said eHealth Directors felt they could not control Kramer, since she was hired "with the support of the Premier." The Auditor General said any sort of strategic plan simply did not exist until after the program was launched – before they knew the specific needs of its users, how the needs would be met, who would be accountable for delivery, what the timelines would be, and how much each component of the system was expected to cost. In fact, it was not until 2009, just months before Kramer resigned, that eHealth actually finalized and approved its strategic plan. By that time, a total of $800 million had been spent on implementing eHealth without ever bothering to consider its strategic objectives.[51]

Furthermore, the McGuinty government did not establish eHealth Ontario with the proper oversight controls: while it was a good decision that the two agencies (EHA and SSHA) were merged into one, the Auditor General said the move lacked oversight of "sufficient rigour." This became glaringly obvious in Kramer's ability to unilaterally appoint senior consultants and advisors, "bypass[ing] standard procurement practices and mak[ing] the decisions and award[ing] the contracts that so captured public attention." Without such oversight, Kramer was free to sole-source those multi-million dollar contracts to high-paid consultants and advisors, many of whom had direct ties to the Liberal Party, the Premier's Office, or were former eHealth employees. In fact, according to the Auditor General, two thirds of the eHealth contracts were doled out by Kramer without ever being competed-for or subject to the normal procurement process.

So what exactly did those expensive consultants *do* for Ontario's tax money? The client registry, diagnostic imaging system, and clinical reports or immunization sections of eHealth were 95-100 percent complete. But the drug and laboratory information systems were only "partially complete," and the provider registry was still in the planning stages. This meant Ontario was left behind as provinces like Prince Edward Island and Alberta had already completed their electronic health records initiatives, and with British Columbia, Saskatchewan, and Newfoundland all being farther ahead than Ontario. Ontario was "near the back of the pack" according to Auditor General Jim McCarter.

As well, while Ontario was making progress on *some* of its promised initiatives, that progress came at an incredible price tag because eHealth was not properly planning or tracking its costs:

Projects were also typically started before all of the resources required to complete them had been identified and procured. For example, a complete analysis of staff and consultant hours and other input costs, such as the hardware or software acquisitions needed to complete the project, were often not determined. Once projects had started, project expenditures and deliverables were not being adequately tracked to give management assurance that the deliverables were being attained as the related costs were being incurred.[52]

This meant that even though the client registry, for example, was almost completed, it was completed over budget, beyond the projected time frame, and significantly delayed the other components of the eHealth project.

The picture of the McGuinty government's handling of the eHealth scandal is one of complete mismanagement, a lack of oversight and process, and an utter disrespect for taxpayers' money. "Ontario taxpayers have not received value for money for this $1 billion investment," the Auditor General summarized. Massive delays, the appointment of Liberal cronies with sole-sourced contracts, and the lack of even the most basic planning defined the eHealth boondoggle. Unfortunately for McGuinty, it also defines his competency in running the government and respecting taxpayers' money.

Liars

McGuinty knew his government's corruption and nepotism would not go over well with Ontario's residents. Just hours before the Auditor General released his report about eHealth, Health Minister David Caplan resigned and McGuinty appointed Deb Matthews as his replacement.[53] But McGuinty insisted all the rules were followed, and responded by complaining this was a case of the "private sector" contractors not being careful enough as public sector employees would have been. McGuinty was actually complaining that his own government had outsourced jobs without the proper oversight – and that was the private sector's fault. In a final twist of irony, McGuinty appointed a consulting firm – PricewaterhouseCoopers – to audit eHealth Ontario's use of consultants. That audit was cancelled, with the Liberals claiming it would only duplicate the work the Auditor General had already done.[54]

Scandal at Cancer Care Ontario

As if the eHealth scandal wasn't enough to get the McGuinty government's act together, another scandal was about to hit Queen's Park. In the wake of the lavish spending for Liberal cronies at eHealth Ontario came the Auditor General's report that the same was happening at Cancer Care Ontario, another health agency whose mandate was to provide research into cancer prevention. Over two years, Cancer Care Ontario gave one consulting firm a total of $18.7 million in contracts – many of them as "follow on agreements" which meant the contract price was being increased without having to re-compete for the contract.[55] Over two years, the more than $18 million in contracts handed out by Cancer Care Ontario were given to just three firms: two of them were the Courtyard Group and Accenture, and the third was not publicly named.

The Auditor General said at least 26 of these follow on agreements were handed out, which he called excessive. "The procurement processes, file organization, and consistency of documentation require[s] substantial improvement," said the Auditor General. If these deficiencies sound strikingly similar to those found at eHealth Ontario, they should. And if you think you remember reading about the Courtyard Group and Accenture just a few pages ago, you did. So what's the common link? *Sarah Kramer, then as Chief Information Technology Officer for Cancer Care Ontario, personally approved 22 of those 26 follow-on agreements.*[56]

Is the rot inside the entire McGuinty health care industrial complex becoming apparent enough yet? Kramer gave her buddies – consulting companies with known Liberal ties – over $18 million of taxpayers' money without engaging the competitive procurement process at all. And when her friends were all plump and wealthy, she left Cancer Care Ontario to head eHealth, where she gave away millions *more* of taxpayers' dollars to those same Liberal consulting companies.

eHealth Ontario is at it Again

As if the scathing Auditor General's report and massive public outrage weren't enough as the result of the first eHealth scandal, the lavish eHealth salaries and bonuses came back into the public's eyes in May 2011. Only five months before the October 2011 election, and in light of the ongoing delays and failures the organization was facing in implementing its mandate, the McGuinty government decided it was giving eHealth employees a 1.9 percent "merit-based" raise and an additional bonus equating to 7.8 percent of the employee's annual salary.[57] eHealth explained that the bonuses were required to keep the highly-trained and highly-specialized IT experts from being recruited into private firms; this was despite the Finance Minister's 2011/2012 freeze on public salaries for two years.

One anonymous "high-ranking Liberal" was quoted in the *Toronto Star* as saying "these guys just don't get it." Premier McGuinty, too, was angry. With an election just months away, McGuinty and his Liberals were overly cautious about any story that could appear as if the unionized employees were (once again) living a caviar lifestyle on the public's dime. He was so angry that he unilaterally cancelled the raises and bonuses (only after the scandal came into the public light),[58] so the union responded by filing an $11 million lawsuit. A judge negotiated a $7.16 million settlement to be shared between 738 employees, or an average of $9,702 per employee. The settlement would include the incentive bonus, but not the pay increase.

The second eHealth scandal was just another example of how the McGuinty government was being penny-wise, but dollar-foolish: Ontario taxpayers paid $115,000 in legal fees to have a settlement reached between the eHealth employees and the Ontario government. This despite the fact that eHealth blatantly ignored the direction of the Finance Minister to freeze all salaries, and promised its employees a bonus and raise anyway. Health Minister Deb Mathews tried to spin the settlement as the "smart" way to "avert costly litigation," reasoning that the lawyers' bills could have been much higher if the case actually went to trial.[59] The agreement meant the government was standing by its original wage freeze while still awarding bonuses to the same employees who were responsible for wasting over $1 billion less than two years ago.

Less than one month later, eHealth chief executive Greg Reed said he was resigning six months earlier than his contracted end date, on October 1, 2011, conveniently just 10 days before the 2011 election. His severance

Liars

package for voluntarily resigning? *Over $406,000*, almost double the Premier's salary.[60] Unlike the union lawsuit, Health Minister Deb Matthews would not even venture to try and defend the ludicrous severance package. In fact, Matthews said the severance payment was part of his employment contract whether he completed the contract or not.[61]

Another Severance Jackpot

The implementation of the HST was about to make Ontario's tax collectors very wealthy – unsurprisingly, again, on the backs of Ontario taxpayers. Only months before the HST was to come into effect, Ontario's provincial tax collectors were given $45,000 severance packages. The reasoning? Because collecting HST was a federal responsibility rather than a provincial one, the tax collectors were being "fired" from the Ontario Ministry of Revenue and instantly "hired" for the federal Canada Revenue Agency.[62]

On Education

One of the proudest legacies McGuinty wanted to leave was that of a compassionate and strong educator. He failed at being "the health care Premier," so he wanted to be "the education Premier." Premier Dad wanted to be Premier Teacher - the Premier whose government helped create the best education system in the world, the best students with the highest-ranking test scores.

Unfortunately, McGuinty never lived up to his dream. Kathleen Wynne, his Education Minister for four years of McGuinty government, had a direct role in crafting and implementing the government's education policy. The Fraser Institute annually compiles school testing data administered through the province's Education Quality and Accountability Office (EQAO).[63] In February 2014, that testing data showed disturbing results: the number of students who were improving in math by the time they reached grade 6 provincial testing "decreased from 28 percent to 17 percent." Furthermore, from 2010 to 2013 math testing revealed "merely 52 percent of grade 3 and 6 students met the provincial standard of 75 percent, or a B grade."[64]

It shouldn't have been a surprise to the McGuinty government, however. The 2009 Programme for International Student Assessment (PISA, released in 2010)[65] said 15 year-olds' performance in math had declined. Furthermore, students' decline in science was "statistically significant," dipping from an average score of 534 in 2006 to 529 in 2009. EQAO Chief Executive Officer Bruce Rodrigues said the PISA results "reinforce what EQAO's provincial assessments have been demonstrating for the past few years – that Ontario student math achievement is an area that needs urgent attention."[66]

Indeed, for the 2012-2013 budget to have spent $21 billion on education, Ontarians should rightly assume that their students are receiving a high quality of education. The 2013-2014 budget increased the previous budget by $3.1 billion – that's $8.5 billion more being spent on education since 2003, yet the Ontario education system has 250,000 fewer students.[67]

The problem, according to education experts, is that the Ontario government has strayed from teaching the basics. Doretta Wilson of the Society for Quality Education complained students were being pushed onto the next level of building blocks without ever having the chance to first master the important skills: "it's mostly because of how the curriculum is structured. You can't have complex thinking without having the tools at hand to do that more complicated higher-order thinking with. It's running without learning to crawl."

Anna Stokke, an associate professor of mathematics at the University of Winnipeg, agreed. She said the shift away from "memorizing timestables and doing basic tasks like adding in columns and long division" was part of a "radical curriculum." The provinces that implemented these "radical" and untested ideas typically had lower test scores.[68]

One of the most radical and unprofessional policy changes under the Mc-Guinty government also had to do with education. Beginning in 2009 under then-Education Minister Kathleen Wynne and continuing in 2010, the McGuinty Liberals began "updating" their sexual education policy. The new Liberal indoctrination would start in grade one, with children being able to identify sexual genitalia using the correct words. By the time they were eight years-old, they would learn about same-sex marriage and "gender identity," and by the sixth grade they would learn about using vaginal lubrication to ensure more pleasurable masturbation. By the time they were 12 year-old, they would know about oral sex and anal intercourse. Finally, grade seven would be about having safe sex by avoiding "unintended pregnancies" and sexually transmitted diseases.[69]

It was a completely inappropriate and unacceptable curriculum. There was simply no way to justify teaching children at such a young age about such mature subjects meant to be discussed between a parent and a child years down the road. The Liberals also released a school board-level policy booklet (see chapter seven) that would combine this new sex education agenda with teachings about how it was okay to cross-dress in class, or how students showed their true "homophobic" natures if they refused to go into a dark "kissing booth."

The massive outcries from parents, teachers, religious leaders, and early childhood educators caused the McGuinty government to abandon its sex education liberalization. These radically inappropriate and untested teachings to young children were a central election issue in the 2011 election, yet the McGuinty Liberals were never held to account. In fact, when the Progressive Conservatives dared question the education reforms, they were labelled as homophobic!

You Can't Eat Alphabet Soup

Under Dalton McGuinty's Ontario, the number of government agencies, boards, organizations, departments, and commissions has exploded. At the time of writing, the Ontario government employed over 560 organizations between 25 ministries, many of them bureaucracies with scarce details known about their cost or mandate.[70] There's the Committee to Evaluate Drugs. The Civil Rules Committee. The Death Investigation Oversight Council. The Deputy Judges Council, and a separate Deputy Judges Remuneration Commission. But there's also the Provincial Judges Remuneration Commission and the Provincial Judges Pension Board.

There's the Family Rules Committee and the Friends of the Greenbelt Foundation. The Office of the Employer Advisor. And don't forget the Office of the Worker Advisor, too, or else the Fairness Commissioner might get involved. There's the Soldiers' Aid Commission, which is quite puzzling, considering taking care of Canada's soldiers is a federal responsibility, not a provincial one.

There's the Source Protection Committee and the Training Completion and Assurance Fund Advisory Board. Ontario's provincial government has become an alphabet soup so large that you could probably throw any few letters together and it would turn out to be a McGuinty government agency!

The ballooning bureaucracy showed all too well where the priorities of the McGuinty government laid. While Ontarians were in deep economic and financial trouble, the Sunshine List grew exponentially. In 2003, when Conservative Premier Ernie Eves left office, the Sunshine List of government employees making over $100,00 per year consisted of just 12,000 people. By 2009, it had grew exponentially to a whopping 63,371 names – a 528 percent growth in just six years!

The McGuinty government never understood the real priorities on which Ontarians expected their elected representatives to focus. While McGuinty was busy tinkering with his wind turbine fantasy and growing the public service to unmanageable levels, Ontario was in deep trouble. Ontario's unemployment rate hit nine percent in 2009, its highest since 1996.[71] Ontario's tuition fees were the highest in Canada.[72] From 2004 to 2008, almost 200,000 manufacturing jobs were lost in Ontario.[73] In fact, in 2009, of

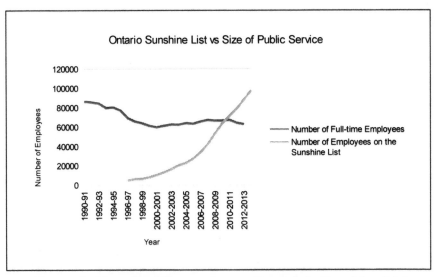

Figure 8: Size of public service vs. Growth in Sunshine List

all the job losses Canada-wide, 58 percent were in Ontario – a staggering 161,200 jobs wiped out. As the Drummond Report would later highlight, this was a government so obsessed with its pet projects – its incessant tax hikes and green energy investments – that it failed to properly manage the government and our economy.

McGuinty responded in true Liberal fashion: in 2009, he introduced the largest deficit in Ontario's history, a whopping $14.1 billion.[74] And be followed that up with even larger deficit budgets: $16.3 billion in 2010 and $16.1 billion in 2011. To be fair, he preceded his outrageous record-breaking budgets with three modest surplus budgets – in 2006, 2007, and 2008 – but those were largely premised on the massive tax increases implemented by McGuinty. Total government spending exploded under the McGuinty Liberals, so even if they were balancing the budget with a small surplus, they were doing so by taxing more to stay ahead of their spending.

A Crumbling Province

After eight years of McGuinty government, Ontario was falling apart. The McGuinty government had introduced a record deficit in 2009 and was showing no signs of slowing down its massive spending. Small, medium, and large businesses were beginning to get tired of an unstable and unpredictable provincial government that kept everyone constantly guessing about where and when the next tax hike would come. Scandals were building as the Liberals could barely go a day without a new scandal about spending, salaries, bonuses, or failed programs emerging in the news. The

Liars

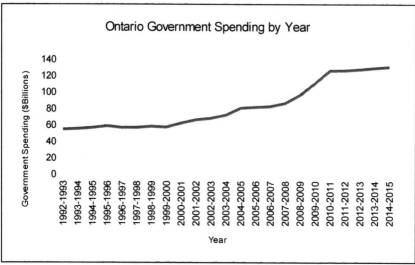

Figure 9: Ontario government spending

McGuinty government had seemingly raised taxes on *everything* despite his personal promises to the contrary.

Our once-great province had been hijacked, it was in trouble, and it needed desperate help. It had two new Opposition leaders, Tim Hudak and Andrea Horwath, who were eager, desperate for the chance to try to get our province back on track. Come October 2011, Ontarians had their second chance for change. Would they overtake the hijacker and get Ontario back on track?

1 Stephen Andrews, "Premier of Ontario, Dalton McGuinty, Announces New Cabinet," *Lexology*, October 31, 2007, http://www.lexology.com/library/detail.aspx?g=ad4acf0a-7b6c-418e-81fe-fefb441f5bf2.

2 Canadian Press, "McGuinty says Health Tax Review to go Ahead – but Tax to Stay," *CBC News*, last modified March 19, 2008, http://www.cbc.ca/news/canada/toronto/mcguinty-says-health-tax-review-to-go-ahead-but-tax-to-stay-1.734523.

3 Andrew Lehrer, "Andrea Horwath: Can a fresh face change the ONDP's fortunes?," *Rabble*, last modified February 26, 2009, http://rabble.ca/news/andrea-horwath-can-fresh-face-change-ondps-fortunes.

4 Office of the Auditor General of Ontario, *2011 Annual Report*, last modified 2011, http://www.auditor.on.ca/en/reports_en/en11/303en11.pdf.

5 "Power Data," Independent Electricity System Operator [Internet application], http://www.ieso.ca/.

6 Ontario pays wind turbines not to produce power, *Global News*, last modified September 11, 2013, http://globalnews.ca/news/832647/ontario-pays-wind-turbines-not-to-produce-power/.

7 "Ont. Electricity rates to rise 46% over 5 years," *CBC News*, last modified November 18, 2010, http://www.cbc.ca/news/canada/toronto/ont-electricity-rates-to-rise-46-over-5-years-1.948369.

8 Benjamin Dachis and Jan Carr, "Zapped: the high cost of Ontario's renewable electricity subsidies," *Essential Policy Intelligence*, May 31, 2011, http://cdhowe.org/pdf/ebrief_117.pdf.

9 Scott Stinson, "Kathleen Wynne backing away from McGuinty's Ontario Green Energy Act,"

National Post, last modified June 24, 2013, http://fullcomment.nationalpost.com/2013/06/24/kathleen-wynne-backing-away-from-mcguintys-ontario-green-energy-act/.

10 Blizzard, "Legacy of Dalton McGuinty…"

11 Parker Gallant, "Ontario's power trip: McGuinty's bigger debacle," *Financial Post,* last modified June 27, 2013, http://opinion.financialpost.com/2013/06/27/ontarios-power-trip-mcguintys-bigger-debacle/.

12 Claire Carter, "Councils waste millions on ineffective wind turbines that will take 190 years to repay," *The Telegraph,* last modified December 26, 2013, http://www.telegraph.co.uk/earth/energy/windpower/10524840/Councils-waste-millions-on-ineffective-wind-turbines-that-will-take-190-years-to-repay.html.

13 Gabriel Calzada Alvarez, "Study of the effects on employment of public aid to renewable energy sources," *Procesos de Mercados* 7, no. 1, http://www.juandemariana.org/pdf/090327-employment-public-aid-renewable.pdf.

14 Brad Molnar, "Renewable theology vs. economic reality, part 2," *Billings Outpost* (Billings, MT), November 24, 2012, http://www.billingsnews.com/index.php/commentary/3991-renewable-theology-vs-economic-reality-part-2.

15 Office of the Auditor General of Ontario, "News release: renewable energy requires cost-benefit evaluation," (Toronto, December 5, 2011), http://www.auditor.on.ca/en/news_en/11_newsreleases/2011news_3.03.pdf.

16 "What goes into my bill?," *Hydro One,* last modified 2013, http://www.hydroone.com/Regulatory-Affairs/RatesPrices/Pages/default.aspx.

17 "Historical RPP rates," *Ontario Hydro,* last modified November 1, 2013, http://www.ontario-hydro.com/index.php?page=historical_rpp_rates.

18 Keith Leslie, "Ontario electricity rates to rise 33% in three years under Liberals' long-term energy plan," *Financial Post,* last modified December 2, 2013, http://business.financialpost.com/2013/12/02/ontario-electricity-rates-to-keep-rising-as-long-term-energy-plan-released/.

19 Adrian Morrow and Shawn McCarthy, "Ontario projects steady rise in electricity costs for next 20 years," *Globe and Mail,* last modified December 2, 2013, http://www.theglobeandmail.com/news/politics/ontario-power-bills-expected-to-rise-14-per-month/article15717495/.

20 Adrian Morrow and Shawn McCarthy, "Ontario projects steady rise…"

21 Keith Leslie, Exporting surplus electricity cost Ontario $1 billion in 2013, NDP charges," *Hamilton Spectator,* last modified January 20, 2014, http://www.thespec.com/news-story/4325968-exporting-surplus-electricity-cost-ontario-1-billion-in-2013-ndp-charges/.

22 Dwight Duncan, "addendum: comprehensive integrated tax coordination agreement between the government of Canada and the government of Ontario," *Ontario's tax plan for jobs and growth,* (Ottawa: Ontario Ministry of Finance, 2009), http://www.fin.gov.on.ca/en/publications/2009/citca.pdf.

23 "HST fact sheet," *Certified General Accountants of Ontario,* accessed April 16, 2014, http://www.cga-ontario.org/assets/file/HST%20Fact%20Sheet.pdf.

24 Maria Babbage, "Who benefits when the HST takes effect in 2010," *City News,* last modified December 27, 2009, http://www.citynews.ca/2009/12/27/who-benefits-when-hst-takes-effect-in-2010/.

25 "Poll: 90% in B.C. and Ontario say HST is a government tax grab," *Vancouverite,* last modified December 5, 2009, http://www.vancouverite.com/2009/12/05/poll-90-in-b-c-and-ontario-say-hst-is-a-government-tax-grab/.

26 "HST will create jobs, not kill them, McGuinty says," *The Star,* last modified November 16, 2009, http://www.thestar.com/news/ontario/2009/11/16/hst_will_create_jobs_not_kill_them_mcguinty_says.html.

27 David Murrell, *Impact of HST on Ontario and British Columbia households by income quintiles,* (Ottawa: Canadian Centre for Policy Studies, 2010), http://www.carp.ca/o/pdf/impact_of_hst_implementation_on_bc.pdf.

28 "HST impact in Ontario difficult to gauge," *CBC News,* last modified June 30, 2011, http://www.cbc.ca/news/canada/toronto/hst-impact-in-ontario-difficult-to-gauge-1.1123653.

Liars

29 "HST impact in Ontario difficult to gauge," *CBC News.*

30 "Ontario eco fee model fell short: McGuinty," *CBC News,* last modified Jul 27. 2010. http://www.cbc.ca/news/canada/toronto/ontario-eco-fee-model-fell-short-mcguinty-1.890272.

31 Thomas Walkom, "The painful stupidity of McGuinty's eco fees," *The Star,* last modified July 21. 2010, http://www.thestar.com/news/ontario/2010/07/21/walkom_the_painful_stupidity_of_dalton_mc-guintys_eco_fees.html.

32 Brian Lilley, "Ontario eco-charges an illegal tax, say critics," *Canoe,* last modified September 6. 2011, http://cnews.canoe.ca/CNEWS/Politics/2011/09/06/18646576.html.

33 Ted Woloshyn, "Tired of all the taxes," *Toronto Sun,* last modified August 29, 2009. http://www.torontosun.com/comment/columnists/ted_woloshyn/2009/08/29/10661711-sun.html.

34 Woloshyn, "Tired of all the taxes"..

35 Candice Malcolm, "Liberals pass the buck on eco-fees," *Toronto Sun,* last modified November 20. 2013, http://www.torontosun.com/2013/11/20/liberals-pass-the-buck-on-eco-fees.

36 Office of the Auditor General of Ontario, *2010 Annual report,* (Toronto, 2010), http://www.auditor.on.ca/en/reports_en/en10/2010ar_en.pdf.

37 "Ottawa struggles with hip and knee wait-times," *CBC News,* last modified June 16, 2010. http://www.cbc.ca/news/canada/ottawa/story/2010/06/16/ott-wait-times-hip.html.

38 "Ontario cleans house at OLG," *CBC News,* last modified August 31, 2009, http://www.cbc.ca/news/canada/toronto/ontario-cleans-house-at-olg-1.777550.

39 Office of the Auditor General of Ontario, *Special report: OLG's employee expense practices.* (Toronto, 2010), http://www.auditor.on.ca/en/reports_en/OLGC_en_web.pdf.

40 "Fired lottery boss sues province for $9 million," *Hamilton Spectator,* last modified September 12. 2009, http://www.thespec.com/news-story/2178442-fired-lottery-boss-sues-province-for-9-million/.

41 Rob Ferguson, "Ex-OLG boss gets $750,000 payday," *The Star,* last modified December 26. 2009. http://www.thestar.com/news/ontario/2009/12/26/exolg_boss_gets_750000_payday.html.

42 "Examining eHealth Ontario," *CBC News,* last modified July 22, 2009, http://www.cbc.ca/news/canada/examining-ehealth-ontario-1.777661.

43 David Flaherty, *Report to the Information and Privacy Commissioner of Ontario on the Ontario Smart Systems for Health Agency's Compliance with the IPC's Privacy and Security Recommendations.* (Victoria, BC: Information and Privacy Commissioner of Ontario, 2007), http://www.ipc.on.ca/images/Findings/up-ssha_ipc_rpt.pdf.

44 "Ontario Health Agency scrutinized for contract tendering practices," *CBC News,* last modified May 27, 2009, http://www.cbc.ca/news/canada/ont-health-agency-scrutinized-for-contract-tendering-practices-1.819348.

45 "Ontario Health Agency scrutinized..." *CBC News.*

46 "Ontario Health Agency scrutinized..." *CBC News.*

47 "Head of eHealth Ontario is fired amid contracts scandal, gets big package," *CBC News,* last modified June 7, 2009, http://www.cbc.ca/news/canada/head-of-ehealth-ontario-is-fired-amid-contracts-scandal-gets-big-package-1.797216.

48 Tanya Talaga, "*eHealth scandal reaches Premier's inner circle,*" *Toronto Star,* last modified June 11, 2009, http://www.thestar.com/news/ontario/2009/06/11/ehealth_scandal_reaches_premiers_in-ner_circle.html.

49 Talaga, "*eHealth scandal reaches Premier's inner circle.*"

50 "eHealth scandal a $1 billion waste: auditor," *CBC News,* last modified October 7, 2009. http://www.cbc.ca/news/canada/toronto/ehealth-scandal-a-1b-waste-auditor-1.808640.

51 Office of the Auditor General of Ontario, *Special Report: Ontario's Electronic Health Records Initiative,* October 2009, http://www.auditor.on.ca/en/reports_en/ehealth_en.pdf.

52 Office of the Auditor General of Ontario, *Special Report: Ontario's Electronic Health Records Initiative.*

53 *CBC News*, supra note 50.

54 Keith Leslie, "McGuinty quietly drops eHealth review," *Globe and Mail*, last modified July 22, 2009, http://www.theglobeandmail.com/news/politics/mcguinty-quietly-drops-ehealth-review/article1227640/.

55 Amber Hildebrandt, "Cancer Care Ontario broke rules: audit," *CBC News*, last modified October 7, 2009, http://www.cbc.ca/news/canada/cancer-care-ontario-broke-rules-audit-1.853841.

56 Hildebrandt, "Cancer Care Ontario broke rules.

57 Robert Benzie, "Hundreds at eHealth Ontario get bonus despite call for wage freeze," *Toronto Star*, last modified May 18, 2011, http://www.thestar.com/news/canada/2011/05/18/hundreds_at_ehealth_ontario_get_bonus_raise_despite_call_for_wage_freeze.html.

58 Robert Benzie, "eHealth scraps raises and bonuses after Star story," *Toronto Star*, last modified May 20, 2011, http://www.thestar.com/news/canada/2011/05/20/ehealth_scraps_raises_and_bonuses_after_star_story.html.

59 Robert Benzie, "eHealth pays $7 million to settle employees' class action lawsuit," *Toronto Star*, last modified January 31, 2013, http://www.thestar.com/news/canada/2013/01/31/ehealth_pays_7_million_to_settle_employees_classaction_lawsuit.html

60 Rob Ferguson, "eHealth Ontario staff will share $2.3 million in performance bonuses," *Toronto Star*, last modified January 3, 2014, http://www.thestar.com/news/queenspark/2014/01/03/ehealth_ontario_staff_will_share_23_million_in_performance_bonuses.html.

61 Tanya Talaga, "NDP slams ludicrous payout to departing eHealth Ontario CEO," *Toronto Star*, last modified, June 11, 2013, http://www.thestar.com/news/queenspark/2013/06/11/ndp_slams_ludicrous_payout_to_departing_ehealth_ontario_ceo.print.html.

62 Tanya Talaga, "Taxman's double dip blasted," *Toronto Star*, last modified March 12, 2010, http://www.thestar.com/news/ontario/2010/03/12/taxmens_double_dip_blasted.html

63 Fraser Institute, *School Performance*, http://www.fraserinstitute.org/report-cards/school-performance/ontario.aspx.

64 Jenny Yuen, "Ontario subtracts on its math report: Fraser Report," *Toronto Sun*, last modified February 1, 2014, http://www.torontosun.com/2014/02/01/ontario-subtracts-on-its-math-scores-fraser-report

65 "Measuring up: Canadian results of the OECD PISA study," *Statistics Canada*, 2010, http://www.statcan.gc.ca/pub/81-590-x/81-590-x2010001-eng.pdf.

66 Jenny Yuen, "Ontario subtracts…," supra note 64.

67 Jenny Yuen, "Ontario subtracts…," supra note 64.

68 "Canadian students slipping in math and science," OECD Finds, *CBC News*, last modified December 3, 2013, http://www.cbc.ca/m/touch/canada/story/1.2448748.

69 "Sex ed opponents claim victory in Ontario," *CBC News*, last modified April 23, 2010, http://www.cbc.ca/news/canada/toronto/sex-ed-opponents-claim-victory-in-ontario-1.899830.

70 "All Agencies List," *Public Appointments Secretariat*, last modified April 16, 2014, https://www.pas.gov.on.ca/scripts/en/BoardsList.asp.

71 Ministry of Training, Colleges, and Universities, *The Ontario labour market in 2009*, July 2010, http://www.tcu.gov.on.ca/eng/labourmarket/currenttrends/docs/annual/annual2009.pdf.

72 "Ontario university students paying highest tuition fees in Canada," *Canadian Press*, last modified September 16, 2010, http://www.cp24.com/ontario-university-students-paying-highest-tuition-fees-in-canada-1.553366.

73 "Factory job losses hit Ontario hardest: study," *Toronto Star*, last modified February 20, 2009, http://www.thestar.com/business/2009/02/20/factory_job_losses_hit_ontario_hardest_study.html.

74 Richard Brennan, "$14.1 billion deficit is largest in history of Ontario," *Toronto Star*, last modified March 26, 2009, http://www.thestar.com/news/ontario/2009/03/26/141_billion_deficit_is_largest_in_the_history_of_ontario.html.

Chapter 7

The Chance for Change II
Ontario's Second Chance to Hold McGuinty Accountable

"McGuinty isn't just the friend of organized labour in the public sector. He's their pet, toothless, dog. And he hasn't just mortgaged out future with his out-of-control spending. He's done it by credit card, using taxpayers as his bank. And it's time we called in his loan."

-Sun News[1]

"Liberals are better campaigners than they are government."

-Laura Paquette, political science professor, Lakehead University[2]

The Lead-up to a Second Chance

Dalton McGuinty's first four years in office were filled with utter mismanagement and continuous scandals, and his next four years were not any better. His record of broken promises, increased taxes, and countless scandals continued. But hey, he had a majority mandate, right? And, being heavily backed by public sector unions and friends exempt from advertising laws, McGuinty operated without a care in the world for what the average Ontarian needed or wanted to see in their provincial government. From 2007 to 2011, Ontario's Liberal government was filled with scandal after scandal, tax after tax and a continual loop of reckless and expensive energy experiments.

Liars

In 2011, Ontarians had their second chance for change – their second opportunity to hold Dalton McGuinty's Liberals to account for their numerous scandals. The lead-up to the 2011 election was exciting. Ontario had two new provincial party leaders in The Ontario Progressive Conservatives' Tim Hudak and the New Democrats' Andrea Horwath. Both Hudak and Horwath were fresh faces to two tired political parties who needed new faces and new ideas if they ever hoped to form government. With two new leaders, both the PCs and the NDP were able to draw in fresh supporters and fresh donors who could keep their parties financially alive while the parties' leadership focused on generating new ideas.

They didn't have to look far. Dalton McGuinty's hijacking was causing Ontario to fail at every corner. The issues that would define the October 2011 election were laid out in chapter six: at every turn, Ontario was losing its position in Canada, and in the world. Seemingly every government announcement was becoming a new scandal, a new government department, a new tax, or a new announcement of another hit to Ontario's job market. Deficits were exploding, debt was through the roof. The Sunshine List was ballooning out of control and "smart meters" were being forced into people's homes – suddenly, it became more expensive to do laundry at 6:00pm instead of 7:00pm. The 2011 election was Ontario's second chance to reverse McGuinty's hijacking and get Ontario back on track.

McGuinty Breaks the Deficit Record

Figure 5 demonstrates the long-term deficit and surplus spending in Ontario, with clearly marked extremes under the Liberal and socialist NDP governments. From 2007-2011, Ontario saw just three surplus budgets: a modest $300 million surplus in 2005-2006, another $310 million surplus in 2006-2007, and $1.7 billion in 2007-2008. But those amounts were obliterated when McGuinty plunged the province into severe deficit spending in 2009, 2010, and 2011, with 2010's shortfall surpassing even NDP Premier Bob Rae's record deficit. Those three budgets took almost $50 billion from Ontario taxpayers, or, more accurately, from *future* Ontario taxpayers. That's *billion*. In just three years, Ontario's 13.2 million residents were billed $3,568 for every man, woman, and child just to sustain two years of McGuinty government spending. That does not even include the interest payments on the previously amassed debt.

The Golden Handshake – Generous Severance Payments

One of the largest mismanagements of Ontario taxpayers' money is the use of severance payments for just about everything. Dubbed "the golden handshake," generous severance packages for public employees and some contractors have cost taxpayers millions of dollars every year under the Liberal government. A severance payment, intrinsic in its title, is supposed to be for when the employer suddenly and without notice *severs* the employment of its employee. According to the Ontario government's own Ministry of Labour, severance pay "compensates an employee for loss of seniority and job-related benefits. It also recognizes an employee's long service."[3] Calculating severance pay is straightforward, and the Ministry of Labour provides several examples on its website. A full-time employee making $15 per hour, after working there for seven years, would receive a severance of roughly $4650, or just over 10 percent of her annual salary.

At some point in history, severance pay stopped being compensation for an imposed hardship and started being a golden handshake to say goodbye – regardless of why you were saying goodbye. Where else on Earth would a severance payment be provided to an employee who voluntarily resigned? These exceptions have made their way into the employment contracts of some very high-ranking public servants who are already drawing lavish salaries for their public service. Only a few instances of the outrage the McGuinty government faced over severance packages are included in the last chapter, including the packages of disgraced eHealth chiefs Greg Reed ($406,000) and Sarah Kramer ($317,000).

Frozen public sector wages… maybe

The 2008-2009 economic recession hit many people, companies, and governments hard, and Ontario was no exception. A public sector wage freeze was intended to help stabilize the economy; indeed, that is precisely what McGuinty promised,[4] but like many of his other promises, they were simply empty feel-good words flowing from his mouth but not backed by actions. Unions continued to receive generous pay raises, some of which remained secret until revealed by the media. Then there was the 8.5 percent pay increase for Ontario Provincial Police Officers. They first received a five percent increase in 2011. Then, due to legislation requiring they remain the "highest paid officers in Ontario," they were given another 8.5 percent increase in 2014.[5]

A Campaign Begins Early

It was with this disastrous record that Ontario came to the beginning of the 2011 election. Polling was incredibly high in favour of Tim Hudak's Progressive Conservatives. Ontarians told McGuinty time and time again that his time was over – that they had finally had enough. A Nanos Research poll on February 3 showed the Conservatives at 43 percent and Liberals at 39. That gap more than doubled in the March 11 Nanos poll, which showed

Liars

the Conservatives at 44 percent and Liberals at 35. It widened even further when the Liberals dipped to their lowest support, with just 26 percent, compared to the Conservatives' 41, in a June 22 Forum Research poll. These poll numbers indicated led that Hudak's Conservatives were in majority territory, that it was, indeed, the Conservatives' election to lose.[6]

McGuinty's platform put out the same message as his first campaign ad titled "Leadership," in which he explained his government was bad, but at least he wasn't as bad as the other guys! His platform said that voting for anyone other than the Liberals was a vote to "go off track and backwards."[7] The 2011 election was Ontario's second chance to defeat the McGuinty government, but the sure-win for the Conservatives slipped through the cracks due both to Liberal strong points as well as Conservative weakness. How did such a sure-win for the Conservatives fall through the cracks?

Involvement of Special Interests

McGuinty has had special interest groups working for him and the Liberal Party since being elected into government in 2003. Some of the most powerful special interests are the unions and the Working Families Coalition.

Unions & Massive Pay Raises

Unions have clung to McGuinty since he took office in 2003. They were upset that under Mike Harris' government they had a significantly smaller voice, and they were not allowed into the inner workings of Ontario's government in order to abuse public money and use influence for pay increases. Unions remained behind their true representatives, the NDP, but they also hitched onto the McGuinty government. McGuinty has all but repaid them for their support with numerous pay hikes, sometimes done behind closed doors and only revealed by chance. In 2009, McGuinty gave teachers a 10.4 percent pay increase over four years. That brought the maximum teacher's salary to $92,700 – plus benefits![8] They also adjusted the pay scale so teachers with as little as four years' experience could be making the maximum salary, all this during a time when McGuinty had frozen public sector wages – or so he said.)

Another union that received taxpayers' money for supporting the Liberals was the Ontario Public Service Employees' Union (OPSEU). In May 2011 it was revealed McGuinty had negotiated a secret deal with the union back in 2008. McGuinty said that giving them a modest two percent pay raise was victory for Ontario taxpayers, since the union was asking for three percent. But what was not revealed in the documents originally released to the media was that McGuinty would give them an extra percentage point – a three percent pay raise – in 2012.[9] The timing was not a surprise: the

Liberals were conveniently shutting-up the union until after the 2011 election – and they were doing it with taxpayers' money.

Taking it Easy on the McGuinty Government

The result of such a pay-off was the dramatic use of sensationalism against the former Harris government while taking it easy on McGuinty when it came to public servant layoffs. In July 2011 the Liberal government announced layoffs, "the biggest wave since the Mike Harris era" according to the Ontario Public Service Employees Union.[10] Yet McGuinty was mysteriously immune from any public outrage: OPSEU simply announced that McGuinty was making cuts, they were bad, and that was the end of it. It was very minimalist behaviour for a union that had just been told its members were being laid off. OPSEU even noted that McGuinty's cuts included layoffs in the Ministry of the Environment: layoffs which will "cut technical expertise in water safety and air quality."[11] Why was the same union which lambasted the Harris government for cutting environment staff and supposedly causing the Walkerton tragedy not holding the McGuinty government to account for doing the same? Considering the pay hike they had just received months earlier, you know the answer to that question.

The Working Families Coalition

Then there's the Working Families Coalition. They have an innocent sounding name – who could be against working families? - but they're really nothing more than a lobbying group for Dalton McGuinty and the Liberal Party. Their official mandate is to "advocate, educate, and create public awareness around public issues on behalf of working families."[12] They have happily discharged their mandate in the past several elections by mercilessly fear-mongering, lying, and distorting the truth about the Progressive Conservative Party. Since they're not "officially" connected to the Liberal Party of Ontario, they can be as venomous and deceitful as they please without any elected Liberals having to answer for it.

Who sponsors this group endlessly lobbying for McGuinty? Unions and more unions; their 13 sponsors are all unions![13] From the Elementary Teachers' Federation of Ontario to the Service Employees International Union, WFC receives 100 percent of its support from unions. They have been rightly labeled "a controversial, union-backed group that's funded attack ads targeting every PC leader since Ernie Eves."[14]

Despite the source of their financing, you may wonder if they are still capable of producing produce good advocacy work pertaining to issues important to Ontario's working families? As you can probably guess by now, this crooked organization cannot be given such a benefit of the doubt. Their website contains nothing more than sensationalist attack pieces targeted squarely at the Ontario PC Party. These were just a few of the articles on their website during the 2011 election:

- "Hudak fights against backward momentum in Ontario election"
- "Hudak's attack on gay-positive education"
- "Tim Hudak defends 'homophobic' ads"
- "Hudak plays blame game, fires shots at unions"
- "Ontario Conservative Platform has $10 Billion Hole"

Did you notice a trend? What about the issues that are important to working families yet are not addressed by the Liberals or NDP? Apparently they don't exist – which Canadian Autoworkers Union President Buzz Hargrove happily confirmed when he acknowledged the sole purpose of the WFC was to stop the conservatives from being elected. The WFC was never about advocating for working families: far from advocating and educating the public on issues important to "working families," WFC is really nothing more than an anti-Conservative lobby group.

The WFC is backed by unions, but who works for them? Elections Ontario answered that question in 2007 after months of calls for an inquiry due to such blatant interference in that election by a third party lobby group.[15] The ties between the Liberal Party and the WFC are staggering. Just a few employees include:

- Don Guy is McGuinty's former Chief of Staff and a current pollster at Pollara. He was the campaign chair for the Liberals' 2003, 2007, and 2011 election campaigns. He worked for the WFC in 2003 while also doing $293,549 in polling work for the Liberals. Following the election, Pollara was paid $1.07 million to do work for several provincial ministries. They have also received $541,147 to poll for Liberal MPP's and $1.05 million for Liberal caucus services.[16] You may also recognize Guy's name from chapter six, where he was involved in the eHealth scandal, and you will read his name again in chapter nine for his involvement in the ORNGE scandal.

- "WFC chair Gary O'Neill is also president of International Union Of Operating Engineers Local 793, which held a Liberal fundraiser at the union hall attended by McGuinty on June 22, 2006. Local 793 has donated $66,389 to the Liberals between 2003 and 2006. Two months ago, the government gave Local 793 a $1.98 million grant for its training centre."[17]

- "Marcel Wieder's firm, Arrow Communications Group, the coalition's ad agency in 2003 and this year, received $28,395 for ad services to the Liberals in the last election. Through his other company,

Policomm, Wieder was paid $165,500 by the Liberals for printing and communications work in the 2003 campaign. In addition, Policomm was paid $56,570 for helping 12 Liberal candidates in 2003. Since the Liberals took office, Arrow has been paid $1.15 million in various contracts for "caucus support" and other services."[18]

These connections are overwhelming. Elections Ontario concluded that, although the WFC was not being outright *controlled* by McGuinty's Liberals:

[...] the WFC's use of consultants with known Liberal connections who were simultaneously providing services both to the WFC and the [Ontario Liberal Party] and, where the very person running the OLP campaign, Don Guy, is president of the polling research firm hired by the WFC, certainly constitutes, in our view, grounds for concern which warranted this investigation.[19]

It took far too long for the WFC to be exposed. Only as of early 2014 is their secretive organization finally beginning to come to light.[20] Beyond those named by the Elections Ontario investigation, Patrick Dillon, the new head of the WFC, has enjoyed appointments to numerous provincial boards, including Kathleen Wynne's appointment to the transit panel. The WFC is anything but a coalition of working families. They're a group of unions with close ties to McGuinty, releasing attack ads against Conservatives without having to report their activities to Elections Ontario.

WFC is responsible for McGuinty's most visceral, untrue and unfair advertisements, outside of Ontario election and advertising laws, and McGuinty rewards them with steep government grants, contracts, and pay raises. The WFC has become "a super PAC [Political Action Committee]," the Big Labour kingmakers who have "hijacked the electoral process."[21] Elections Ontario's laws cap donations to a political party from any person, business, or union at $9300 per year, but there is no specific law that prohibits a third-party lobby group from targeting one political party with slander, libel, and twisted half-truths.

The WFC's budget simply cannot be matched. In 2011, the NDP spent $1.7 million on advertising; the Liberals, $5.07 million; and the Conservatives, $5.09 million. The WFC spent an estimated *$10 million* – eclipsing the other political parties while focusing solely on attacking the Conservatives. Unlike Canada's federal politics, Big Labour's money has a direct influence in Ontario politics. It's time to put an end to this loophole in election financing laws, and get Big Labour and Big Business' money out of provincial politics.

Liars

An Un-Motivated Conservative Base

Another reason for the disappointing turnout was that the Ontario PCs conservative base was unmotivated by *Changebook*, a platform many conservatives saw as being "Liberal-lite." The platform was devoid of the real meat which defines a conservative platform, instead opting to choose a platform which did not show a drastic enough change from McGuinty's Liberal policies (see below for a list of PC platform promises the other parties copied). When it came time to choose, voters felt it was better to stick with the devil they knew (McGuinty) instead of changing course and choosing the untested Hudak.

Even the *Toronto Sun*, a known conservative newspaper, commented on the unimpressive PC platform. Michael Den Tandt said *Changebook* was a "collection of vague bromides stitched together with a smattering of weakly stated promises."[22] He noted that they have the same balanced budget target (not until 2017-2018) and both promised to eliminate "red tape." For Den Tandt, *Changebook* should have been titled *Statusquobook*. His criticisms were echoed in the *Sun's* later announcement that they were not endorsing any political party.[23]

The *National Post*'s Kelly McParland opined that McGuinty's destructive record spoke for itself, but Hudak's ambitious platform was taking the focus off McGuinty's record:

> Income tax cuts. Income splitting. A break on HST. No more charges to pay off Hydro's "stranded" debt. Lower corporate taxes. More money for health care, more money for education — whatever McGuinty spends on education, the Tories will match it. $35 billion in infrastructure spending. Fewer civil servants. A tough line on pay increases."[24]

Even Randall Denley, the PC candidate in Ottawa West-Nepean and an *Ottawa Citizen* columnist, admitted the platform fell short, saying "people were looking for a little more of a sense of what the PC party will do exactly, what's our plan. I don't think they saw enough to satisfy them."[25]

The result of an unimpressive platform that failed to appeal to social or fiscal conservatives was an unmotivated conservative base that stayed home or, worse yet, threw their vote away by voting for a fringe party.

Irrational Voters

Voters are arguably never wrong, but they too hold responsibility for McGuinty's Liberals being re-elected in 2011. The old adage, "fool me once, shame on you. Fool me twice, shame on me." should have applied in 2011.

Ontarians were fooled twice – in 2003 and 2007 – and they let themselves be fooled again by someone whose career was based on making promises, then breaking them. Voters should have held the Liberals to account, but they did not and, for whatever reason, voters felt McGuinty's tax hikes were better than the PC or NDP platforms. That voters chose the Liberals while understanding full well the record of McGuinty's Liberals should speak volumes to the PCs and NDP about where voters' minds lay regarding the perception of their parties and promises.

Duplicate campaign promises

The release of any party's platform is essential in crafting an image to present to the voters while also strategically timing the release to gain the most attention. The federal Conservative Party has preferred to release their platforms later in the campaign, so as to avoid the duplication issues discussed below. A later platform release also allows the leader to tour the nation or province with a fresh new platform promise every day. On the other hand, if the platform is already released, the leader risks running out of things to say, and has to resort to repeating the same promises over and over.

Hudak's Progressive Conservatives, however, had to release their platform early to dispel any accusations of a "hidden agenda" and set the record straight that this platform would not be another Common Sense Revolution (even though, as we've seen, the CSR was incredibly positive). *Changebook,* released on May 29, 2011, was the complete platform, on the table for all to see. It was Hudak's way of saying "there's our plan for Ontario, right there" with no hidden agenda or possible accusations of the platform being another CSR (McGuinty repeatedly tried to claim the PCs had a hidden agenda somewhere, and the Liberal campaign was replete with comparisons of Tim Hudak to Mike Harris).

Unfortunately, releasing their platform first also meant that the other parties were free to copy the PCs' ideas. The NDP's platform was released a month later, on June 25, and the Liberals waited until the day before the writ dropped, September 5, to release theirs. The NDP had a month's head start to cherry pick the most "progressive" of the Conservatives' ideas or least craft a strikingly similar policy for their own platform. The Liberals had all summer, so they were probably carefully watching the parties announce their platforms and gauging support for those various policies. The best ones, they copied.

Paul Braczek of Fasken Martineau, a law firm practicing in major cities across the world, published an exhaustive comparison of the three major parties' platforms.[26] Just a few of the interesting similarities include:

Liars

- Both the Liberals and PCs would lower the tax rate to 10 percent by 2013
- Both the Liberals and PCs proposed "measures to reduce barriers to the hiring of foreign-trained skilled immigrants"
- Both the Liberals and PCs promised to balance the budget by 2017-2018
- Both the Liberals and PCs would implement full-day kindergarten by 2014
- Both the Liberals and PCs promised to create 60,000 more spaces in colleges and universities
- Both the PCs and NDP would remove the HST from home hydro bills
- Both the PCs and NDP would remove the HST from home heating bills
- Both the PCs and NDP would implement the Buy Ontario program to increase the market for Ontario's wines
- Both the PCs and NDP would eliminate Local Health Integration Networks (LHINs)

Save for a party operative blatantly admitting to plagiarizing another party's platform, we will never know for sure whether any party really copied the first-released PC platform. But one thing's for sure: the Conservatives released their complete platform first, leaving the other parties with ample time to cherry-pick the best ideas, including: the appealing promises of taking the HST off home heating and hydro bills. Once the PCs decided to released their platform first, they had no option but to accept this possibility.

Conservative Mini-scandals Distracted Focus from Liberals

The most obvious inconvenience to the Conservative campaign was the constant evocation of Mike Harris' name, as if Harris' time in office was bad news. According to both the Liberals and NDP, it was, even though chapter two of this book disproved that myth. The media joined in too, desperate to portray Tim Hudak's Conservatives as reckless Harris wanna-bes who would destroy Ontario if elected to government. Several times throughout the campaign, McGuinty referred to the "Harris-Hudak Conservatives,"[27] as if Harris' years as Premier were bad (and, of course, Harris' time ended over a decade ago).

Although there was no one scandal that doomed the PCs from victory, there were enough mini-scandals to distract the media's focus from Dalton McGuinty's track record in favour of criticizing Tim Hudak.

Homosexual education... for five year-olds

The largest and perhaps the most damaging scandal took place in the final days of the campaign, when PC campaign literature was labelled "homophobic" by the Liberals and the media. At least two Brampton-area Conservatives were canvassing with flyers pertaining to the Toronto District School Board's recently released *Challenging Homophobia and Heterosexism: A K – 12 Resource Guide*.[28] The flyer gave several quotes from the TDSB guide, accurately portraying the radical sex education agenda that was being implemented by Premier McGuinty and then-Education Minister Kathleen Wynne. It left parents out of the loop of what was happening at their child's school, and gave the schools direction to teach sensitive sexual topics to children as young as five years-old.

The topic is certainly a sensitive one, and the PCs certainly considered that if they were going to attack McGuinty on his promotion of sex education to five year-olds, they would have to do it carefully and without appearing to purposely spin the document to their own advantage. That's why every statement made in the Conservative flyer pertaining to the TDSB's document was sourced to a specific page in the document. It was a transparent plan to ensure that anyone could look up the quotes in the actual policy document, which is available online and footnoted below.

Many citizens, if not all, are also weary of political attack ads and feel the ads are inherently misleading or deviously spun. They're attack ads after all. But attack ads work incredibly well when used properly. The Conservative Party of Canada was enormously successful in exposing Liberal Opposition leader Michael Ignatieff as a self-entitled professor from the United States who was "just visiting" – coming back to his native Canada to opportunistically lead the Liberal Party and desperately grab for the title of Prime Minister. They were successful because they used Ignatieff's words against him. And when the country went to the polls after months of hearing Ignatieff's own words, he was defeated in his own riding and the Liberal Party was relegated to the third-place status in the House of Commons – their worst performance since Confederation![29]

The PC flyer was created with the intention of using McGuinty's and Wynne's own words against them. It was to show what kind of outrageous policies were being implemented under McGuinty's government – policies that included teaching cross-dressing and sex education to children in kindergarten.

But, typical of McGuinty, his spin team went to work, and by the end of it they successfully portrayed the flyer – completely rooted in quotes from

Liars

a policy implemented under *McGuinty's* government – as a homophobic attack. Liberal campaigners flatly called them "Hudak's homophobic flyers," while McGuinty claimed this was another instance of Hudak playing "divisive" politics.[30]

Here is what the flyer claimed, as well as the evidence backing it up:

- "McGuinty of purposefully (sic) keeping parents in the dark' about what is being taught in schools. – CTV, September 23, 2011."

The quote is properly sourced – we know where it was said and when. The quote is from Tim Hudak, which is not mentioned in the flyer, but this is irrelevant as the purpose of using it was to highlight media coverage of the issue. We clearly know that CTV News has reported upon Hudak's quote.

- "[The TDSB platform recommends] cross-dressing for six year olds. (p. 19)"

Indeed it does, although page 19 is a misquote. Page 19 contains a list of "significant international lesbian, gay, bisexual, transgendered, and queer individuals." But page 37 tells schools to "encourage girls and boys to role-play opposite roles, or to role-play animals or objects, or even parts of nature." Encouraging boys to role-play girls and girls to role-play boys could easily be extrapolated to include cross-dressing as a way of educating young children about the opposite gender.

- "[The TDSB platform recommends] reclaim[ing] Valentine's Day and celebrat[ing] sexual diversity with a kissing booth. (p. 143)"

Another true statement. The Liberals' policy recommends setting up a tent or "other structure" in a central location which teachers and students can enter. Upon entering, students are greeted with a stamp of a kiss on their cheek, as if the child has just been kissed on the cheek by someone wearing lipstick. No, the children are not literally being kissed, but the "structure" is set up to hide what's going on inside and is decorated as if it really is a kissing booth.

The real problem with these kissing booths is not that they're suggesting students get to "kiss" one another inside the tent. It's that the structure itself was being used as a bait-and-switch to measure the "climate" of the school - the degree of homophobia seen and heard in that particular school. Students are asked to enter the tent, which is bright with flamboyant decorations and anti-homophobia messages. Students are only told "don't worry, your experience in the kissing booth will be enjoyable."[31] When students (naturally) object to entering this mysterious tent with no one telling them what awaits on the inside, the "climate" of that school is said to be homophobic. After all, so the TDSB's line of thinking seems to be, who would object to entering a dark tent decorated with anti-homophobic messages if *not* for the fact that they must be homophobic?

- "Read some traditional folk tales and fairy tales with the class. Have students write/illustrate their own gender-bending versions. (p. 44)"

Yet another plank actually found in the TDSB policy. Are you noticing a pattern? Another recommendation in this section is to "share stories, articles, and illustrations of people in the media and communities who break gender barriers (e.g. female hockey player, male teacher who likes to cook or sew)." Did you miss the blatant hypocrisy in that sentence? The TDSB, in its document about combating homophobia, is suggesting that female hockey players and men who like to cook are operating outside of their "gender barrier." Outrageous!

- "Read Gloria Goes to Gay Pride. Additionally, students could have their own Pride Parade in their school and invite the local media. (p. 56)"

Also true. This recommendation to read *Gloria Goes to Gay Pride* and create their own pride parade comes from the section of recommended activities to partake in with children from kindergarten to grade three.

- "The 219-page guide, titled "Challenging Homophobia and Heterosexism," recommends schools not to (sic) inform parents. – CTV, September 23, 2011"

This final quote on the flyer is, of course, also true.

There you have it. A PC flyer accurately portrayed a policy implemented by the TDSB under *McGuinty's* Premiership and his Education Minister Kathleen Wynne. If voters in the two Brampton ridings where this flyer was used were outraged about the Liberal government's sex education reforms, as they should have been, the flyer, finally, encouraged to "vote against the McGuinty agenda" on October 6. The quotes were pulled from the TDSB platform and painted a disturbing picture: McGuinty's government was forcing a radical sex education platform on young children, and the PCs suggested response to voters was to vote against this policy on Election Day.

That McGuinty and his spin team were able to turn this flyer into a statement of how the PCs were supposedly "homophobic" is shocking. Somehow, accurately reporting upon policies implemented under McGuinty's government made the PCs homophobic. But the public's belief that Hudak's Conservatives really were homophobic, instead of reading the facts, should speak volumes that his reputation is broken and biased from the outset in the minds of voters.

Liars

"Foreign workers"

Just a few days into the campaign, the Liberal Party pledged to give "highly skilled newcomers the Canadian work experience they need." Although it took them several days to explain precisely what this meant, they eventually clarified that it would be a $10,000 tax credit to new Canadian citizens residing in Ontario for less than five years.[32]

It was bald-faced Liberal appeasement towards new Canadian citizens – those perhaps seeking direction or already heavily supportive of the McGuinty government for whatever reason. While we should all be disappointed in the long turnaround time in recognizing the credentials of new Canadians, Hudak's team played it as a move to benefit "foreign workers." But they were not foreign workers; they were Canadian citizens, residing in the province for at least a few years. The perceived fear – that "foreigners" would come to Ontario, receive this $10,000 in taxpayer money, and put Ontarians out of work – was moot. Even in the face of evidence that this credit was not for "foreign workers," the PCs persisted.

These three issues – the continued use of Harris' name, the rightful concerns about McGuinty's sex education policy, and questions about why foreign-educated workers were to be given preferential treatment over native Ontarians – were just enough to paint Hudak's Conservatives in an unfavourable light.

Scandals that should have doomed McGuinty

That McGuinty was not defeated and did not fall on his own sword with his numerous scandals means he truly did earn the "Teflon McGuinty" title. These were not small issues, yet voters failed to respond by voting him out of office. They just shrugged their shoulders and returned the guy to office with a minority. Instead, with much of the media focus on Tim Hudak's record, McGuinty was allowed to skate by with barely a peep about his own scandals. McGuinty's Liberals were running on their record, which made *his* scandals during the campaign all the more reason they should have been given more attention.

Broken Promises - Again

In 2003 McGuinty promised he would not raise taxes – and he did anyway. He did the same thing in 2007. McGuinty's promises versus reality paint a telling picture: McGuinty, even more than Bob Rae, has become known for his incessant tax hikes on *everything* in order to finance his endless union deals and expensive energy experiments.[33] Every single time McGuinty promised *not* to raise taxes, he raised taxes!

In 2011, McGuinty again promised he would "hold the line" on taxes. Voters were rightly skeptical, of course, considering the last two elections worth of promising not to raises taxes resulted with a swift slap in their faces barely before the election results were in. Five days before the election, two third of Ontarians surveyed in the lead up to the 2011 election said they distrusted McGuinty's 2011 claim that he would not raise taxes.[34]

Indeed, Ontarians were ever-more taxed while the McGuinty Liberals were tripling the size of the Sunshine List. In 2010 every man, woman, and child that resided in Ontario owed about $17,000 in order to pay off Ontario's debt – *a 50 percent increase* from when McGuinty took office in 2003, when the debt-per-person worked out to about $11,340.[35] Meanwhile McGuinty was stacking every possible Liberal-friendly crony or consultant onto the Sunshine List in a bid to spend even more money on Ontario's public service. As of 2013 almost 89,000 public servants were making more than $100,000 – *a 39 percent increase* under McGuinty's government since 2009.[36] Once again, this was during a supposed period of austerity, a time when the public service was supposedly under a "wage freeze" to help balance the budget.

Contempt for Northern Ontario and His Own Riding

Highlighting his continued contempt for Northern Ontario, McGuinty refused to attend the leaders' debates in Timmins[37] and Thunder Bay.[38] Somehow, both Andrea Horwath and Tim Hudak made the trek to the debate, but apparently McGuinty had a "scheduling conflict." He was actually found campaigning that day in Toronto and Hamilton. This should come as no surprise, however; the Liberals were simply avoiding the Conservative vote-rich parts of Ontario in favour of the Liberal-rich areas.

If McGuinty did not have the respect or courtesy to justify his government's decisions anywhere outside of the Liberal-friendly South, surely he could at least show up and campaign in his own riding of Ottawa South, right? Wrong! There, too, McGuinty failed to attend the all-candidates' debate, despite his impressive standing in his own riding. It would be reasonable to think, following the swift defeat of Michael Ignatieff in his own riding for the federal election just months earlier that party leaders - particularly one as unpopular as McGuinty - would put a bit of effort into campaigning at home. But no. McGuinty simply assumed his family would take care of the riding for him; he was completely disconnected as the riding's MPP, completely failing to answer even a few simple common questions.

McGuinty is well-rooted in his riding, and harnesses an impressive turnout of volunteers whenever needed. His father, Dalton McGuinty Senior, first captured the riding in 1987 when Peterson's Liberal government came to

Liars

power. Just three years later, McGuinty Senior tragically passed away, and McGuinty Junior took the seat in the 1990 election. Before that, Ottawa South, like the rest of Ontario, had been awash in Conservative blue for an impressive 61 years.

McGuinty grew up with nine brothers and sisters, each of whom have grown the family substantially with their own children. The result is an army of volunteers, just based upon family and associates of the family. Add in Liberal Party volunteers, shipped in from Toronto, who strategically spring up throughout Ottawa South, and we could easily estimate 300-400 volunteers on the McGuinty campaign. Any campaigning politician or serious candidate would love to see this many active volunteers working on the campaign trail. His younger brother, David, is the federal Member of Parliament for Ottawa South, and the family has strong personal connections with former Ottawa city mayor and current Wynne government minister Bob Chiarelli. In the quest to replace Michael Ignatieff, both David and Dalton mulled the possibility of running for the leadership of the federal Liberal Party.[39] (Ultimately, neither would enter the race.)

Despite such power in numbers, McGuinty's office was completely unresponsive and unwilling to work with constituents. It was obvious McGuinty's office was assuming they had the election in the bag – why actually campaign in his riding when it was already assumed he would win? As a resident of Ottawa South, I asked his office how many days of the 30-day campaign he was planning to spend campaigning in the riding. No response.

A while later, as a Riding Correspondent for the *Toronto Star*, I sent out an all-parties interview questionnaire, asking every candidate in the riding a few basic questions about their party, where it stood on the issues of the campaign, and how they could personally best serve Ottawa South. The only responses I received were from the Progressive Conservative's Jason MacDonald and the Green Party's James Mihaychuk. It was a sad testament to how much McGuinty either, at best, took his own Liberal votes at home for granted, or, at worst, simply did not care about the outcome.

A Carbon Tax

Late in the campaign it was revealed that McGuinty's green energy plan could be used to tax carbon. It was the bombshell that could have decided the election: it was the same plan which doomed the federal Liberal Party under Stephane Dion in the 2008 federal election.[40] In fact, even Liberal MPP Dave Levac repeated twice in one interview that his party was considering a carbon tax.

When this was revealed, McGuinty attempted to deflect blame and claim that Levac simply misspoke. Levac also claimed that he mistook "carbon tax" for "cap and trade" – a less controversial system already in place in multiple jurisdictions around the world. But Levac was not just any ordinary MPP who could possibly be excused for using the wrong terminology. Levac was the Parliamentary Assistant to the Minister of Energy, so it's awfully hard to believe that he did not understand the difference between the two macro systems of handling carbon and energy policy.

Such a revelation so late in the campaign should have doomed the Liberals, just as it did when the federal Liberals introduced the same policy. Yet the Conservatives and NDP, by that time sliding in the polls, could not effectively respond to what McGuinty brushed off as an unfortunate slip of the tongue.

Smokes-for-Votes

Another scandal hit the Liberals in the final days of the campaign. Nikki Holland, Vice President of the Liberal Party and Director of Political Operations was caught on tape telling a group of supporters "I have done crazy things, like...and if anyone repeats this I'll deny it until the cows come home...I have gone to a shelter in the riding of St. Pauls with a carton of smokes and said, 'I'll give you them after you vote.' I have done that."[41]

It was an incredible statement: here was the senior political Director of the Ontario Liberals flat-out admitting to vote-buying and election corruption! Of course, the Liberal spin team went to work and insisted that Holland was just joking around – telling a story to a group of fellow Liberals to get them fired up and eager to campaign. But Holland's degree of specificity tells another story: if she were "just joking" she would not have referenced a specific shelter in a specific riding to commit a specific act of vote buying. Liberal MPP Eric Hoskins would win that riding with over 58 percent of the vote, so it was not as if the Liberals scraped by with an illegitimate victory based on paying homeless people with cigarettes to vote. Why then pay the homeless people of St. Paul's for their votes at all? Was St. Paul's the Liberal training ground, the safe testing site where they could see how much voter fraud they could get away with?

I personally contacted Elections Ontario to request that they immediately investigate. If Holland was speaking of vote buying in a previous election, what corrupt ways to win were they conjuring up this time? Where and when were these tactics used before? Who gave the direction to use these tactics? Melanie Martin-Griem, writing on behalf of the Chief Electoral Officer, wrote back (after the election was over) to say that the allegations were based on media reports. Of course they were. The media had a record-

Liars

ing of Holland making these statements. And Holland and the Liberal Party did not deny the claims, since Holland resigned and Dalton McGuinty apologized for her "completely unacceptable" statements.[42] Perhaps we will never know how many other elections McGuinty has bought by rounding up desperate people and bribing them with gifts for they voting Liberal.

The ease with which the scandal was brushed off and thrown away – by Elections Ontario, by voters, and by the media – is troubling. Compare, for example, the federal controversy surrounding the use of automated telephone calls during the 2011 election. Now dubbed the "robocalls scandal," the investigation has been going on for over three years, cost more than $1 million, and has resulted in a grand total of one person being criminally charged. And why? Because one riding (Guelph) was subjected to "robocalls" that were against Canadian Radio and Telecommunications Commission (CRTC) rules. And we already know who was at fault: the Liberals! Yet the "controversy" persists and Elections Canada keeps investigating in the remote chance there is something else out there.

Why isn't the same ruthless investigative standard being applied to the provincial Liberals by Elections Ontario? Why aren't we asking questions like: is it standard operating procedure for Liberals to bribe homeless people to vote? Has this occurred in other ridings? If so, when and why? Which ridings were won or lost on the basis of the Liberals' bribery?

The Gas Plants Scandal

Just days before the election came the controversy that would plague the McGuinty-Wynne government for years to come. It would also plague Ontarians' electricity bills for *decades* to come. On September 28, Dalton McGuinty announced that a re-elected Liberal government would "relocate" two gas plants already being built in Oakville and Mississauga.[43] The cost, McGuinty said, was a paltry $190 million – which sounded like a drop in the bucket compared to what the actual cost turned out to be.[44] This decision was personally signed off by future premier Kathleen Wynne as the Liberal's campaign chair in the 2011 election.[45]

There was absolutely no legitimate reason to relocate the gas plants, which had already broken ground and were being built. Those gas plants were desperately needed in the locations in which they were being built for a simple reason: to produce electricity where it was needed in the rapidly growing parts of Ontario. But McGuinty did not even try to deny that the real reason for cancelling the gas plants was because his Liberal seats in Oakville and Mississauga were in danger of being lost over opposition to the plants. McGuinty was lambasted for playing politics with Ontario's electricity, as well as for his callous underplaying the issue by saying that it would "only" cost $190 million.

As will be discussed in chapter nine, the gas plants cancellation would come back to haunt the McGuinty-Wynne government, resulting in allegations of corruption, cover up, abuse of taxpayers' money, and an Auditor General's investigation that found the real price tag was far beyond that $190 million.

The Missed Opportunity

It was incredibly unfortunate that McGuinty was able to scrape together enough of a victory to form a minority government, but that is the reality with which Ontario was faced. A combination of the union juggernaut rallying for McGuinty and the media focus on minor Progressive Conservative scandals meant McGuinty was able to hold on with a sad campaign that boiled down to "hey, I'm bad, but not as bad as those guys!"

But even if Ontario voters were not completely ready to boot McGuinty from office, they were ready to teach him a lesson by reducing his majority to a minority. Dalton McGuinty lost almost 25 percent of the seats he had before the election: he lost 17 Liberal seats while Hudak's Conservatives gained 12 and Horwath's NDP gained seven. Voters also taught McGuinty a lesson by staying home: the 2011 election saw the worst voter turnout in Ontario's history. Less than 50 percent (49.2 percent) turned out to vote. If McGuinty was going to govern as he pleased without consulting Ontarians, what was the point of going to the polls to vote?

Faced with a minority government, McGuinty knew for his first time that he would have to work with both the Conservatives and New Democrats in order to have any chance of the Liberals staying in power. For the first time in eight years, McGuinty had to take a long, hard look at the way his government was operating. Nothing was on or off the table if McGuinty was to work with socialists on the left demanding more spending and more regulations, and conservatives on the right demanding debt and deficit reduction and less regulation. McGuinty commissioned the Drummond Report to provide a non-partisan view of Ontario's state of affairs – everything from health care to the economy to public service wages.

Liars

1   "McGuinty loves debt and taxes," *Toronto Sun*, last modified September 23, 2011, http://www.torontosun.com/2011/09/23/mcguinty-loves-debt-and-taxes.

2   Laura Paquette, "Ontario election results: McGuinty wins Liberal minority," *Huffington Post Canada*, last modified October 6, 2011, http://www.huffingtonpost.ca/2011/10/06/ontario-election-results-2011-live-coverage_n_999249.html.

3   "Severance pay," *Ontario Ministry of Labour*, https://www.labour.gov.on.ca/english/es/pubs/guide/severance.php.

4   John Snobelen, "Ontario's debt problem for McGuinty," *Toronto Sun*, last modified August 12, 2011, http://www.torontosun.com/2011/08/12/ontarios-debt-problem-for-mcguinty.

5   Keith Leslie, "McGuinty defends 8.5 percent pay hike for OPP in 2014," *Globe and Mail*, last modified May 17, 2011, http://www.theglobeandmail.com/news/politics/mcguinty-defends-85-per-cent-pay-hike-for-opp-in-2014/article2025822/.

6   "Hudak widens lead on McGuinty: poll," *National Post*, last modified June 12, 2011, http://news.nationalpost.com/2011/06/12/hudak-widens-lead-on-mcguinty-in-ontario-poll/.

7   "Forward together, http://issuu.com/ontarioliberalparty/docs/the_ontario_liberal_plan__2011_2015

8   Antonella Artuso, *Teachers get "Last Shot" at $700 Million Deal*, Canoe, February 11, 2009, http://cnews.canoe.ca/CNEWS/Canada/2009/02/11/8346801-sun.html

9   Matt Gurney, "No Excuse for Secret OPSEU Pay Hike," *National Post*, last modified May 5, 2011, http://news.nationalpost.com/2011/05/05/matt-gurney-no-excuse-for-secret-opseu-pay-hike/

10   "McGuinty begins biggest wave of layoffs since the Mike Harris Era," *Ontario Public Service Employees Union*, last modified July 14, 2011, http://www.opseu.org/news/press2011/july-14-2011.htm

11   "McGuinty begins biggest wave of layoffs..."

12   "Who is Working Families?" *Working Families Coalition*, http://www.workingfamilies.ca/about/

13   "Who is Working Families?"

14   Christina Blizzard, "Working Families Coalition meddling spells trouble for Hudak," *Toronto Sun*, last modified August 31, 2013, http://www.torontosun.com/2013/08/31/working-families-coalition-meddling-spells-trouble-for-hudak.

15   "Unions in Ontario have bought and sold McGuinty again," *National Citizens Coalition*, last modified September 16, 2011, http://nationalcitizens.ca/blog/2011/09/16/unions-in-ontario-have-bought-and-sold-mcguinty-again/.

16   Robert Benzie, "Conservatives seek probe of Liberals, "Families" Ties," *Toronto Star*, last modified August 24, 2007, http://www.thestar.com/news/ontario/2007/08/24/conservatives_seek_probe_of_liberals_families_ties.html.

17   Benzie, "Conservatives seek probe of Liberals..."

18   Benzie, "Conservatives seek probe of Liberals..."

19   Christina Blizzard, "Dalton McGuinty avoids penalty box," *Toronto Sun*, last modified April 13, 2011, http://www.torontosun.com/comment/columnists/christina_blizzard/2011/04/13/17984491.html.

20   *Working Families Exposed*, http://workingfamiliesexposed.ca

21   Tom Flanagan, "Organized Labour is now a super PAC," *Globe and Mail*, July 16, 2012,

http://www.theglobeandmail.com/globe-debate/organized-labour-is-now-a-super-pac/article4415926.

22   Michael Den Tandt, *PC's Changebook is Mamby Pamby, Toronto Sun*, last modified May 30, 2011, http://www.torontosun.com/2011/05/30/pcs-changebook-is-mambypamby

23   "Ontario deserves better," *Toronto Sun*, last modified September 30, 2011, http://www.torontosun.com/2011/09/30/ontario-deserves-better.

24   Kelly McParland, "Hudak warns the fat that it's about to be cut again," *National Post*, May 30, 2011, http://fullcomment.nationalpost.com/2011/05/30/kelly-mcparland-hudak-warns-the-fat-that-its-about-to-be-cut-again/.

25   Mohammed Adam, "Longtime Ottawa rivals Chiarelli, Denley agree Tory platform fell short," *Ottawa Citizen*, last modified October 7, 2011, http://www2.canada.com/life/denley+returns+writing+position+citizen/5520426/story.html?id=5520545.

26   Daniel Brock, "Ontario Provincial election 2011: comparison of party platforms," *Fasken Martineau*, last modified September 21, 2011, http://www.fasken.com/ontario-provincial-election-2011-comparison-of-party-platforms/.

27   "Building a stronger Ottawa together," *Ontario Liberal Party*, last modified 2011, http://www.ontarioliberal.ca/NewsBlog/NewsDetails.aspx?id=Building+A+Stronger+Ottawa%2C+Together.

28   "Challenging homophobia and heterosexism: K-12 curriculum resource guide," Toronto District School Board, 2011, http://www.tdsb.on.ca/wwwdocuments/programs/Equity_in_Education/docs/Challenging%20Homophobia%20and%20Heterosexism%20Final%202011.pdf.

29   Andrew Coyne, "Ignatieff, from both sides now," *Maclean's*, May 21, 2009, http://www2.macleans.ca/2009/05/21/ignatieff-from-both-sides-now/.

30   Patrick Maloney and Jonathan Jenkins, "Ontario grits rip Hudak over 'homophobic flyers,'" *Canoe*, last modified October 4, 2011, http://cnews.canoe.ca/CNEWS/Canada/OntarioVotes/News/2011/10/03/18776051.html.

31   *Toronto District School Board*, supra note 28, p. 145.

32   "Stop calling newcomers foreign workers," *National Post*, last modified September 12, 2011, http://fullcomment.nationalpost.com/2011/09/12/national-post-editorial-board-stop-calling-newcomers-foreign-workers/.

33   *Toronto Sun*, supra note 1.

34   Ian Robertson, "Ontarians distrust McGuinty's tax pledges: poll," *Ottawa Sun*, October 1, 2011, http://www.ottawasun.com/2011/10/01/ontarians-distrust-mcguintys-tax-pledges-poll.

35   "Ontario population and selected characteristics, 2001–2036," *Ontario Ministry of Finance*, 2012, http://www.fin.gov.on.ca/en/economy/demographics/projections/table3.html.

36   "Ontario's Sunshine List sees double digit growth," *CBC News*, last modified March 28, 2013, http://www.cbc.ca/news/canada/toronto/ontario-s-sunshine-list-sees-double-digit-growth-1.1372270.

37   "McGuinty mocked for missing northern debate," *Timmins Times*, last modified September 23, 2011, http://www.timminstimes.com/2011/09/23/mcguinty-mocked-for-missing-northern-debate-8.

38   Erin Criger and Shawne McKeown, "McGuinty misses debate on northern issues," *City News*, last modified September 23, 2011, http://www.citynews.ca/2011/09/23/cityvote-day-

Liars

17-mcguinty-misses-debate-on-northern-issues/.

39   Jane Taber, "David McGuinty mulls Liberal leadership bid at convention," *Globe and Mail*, last modified January 14, 2012, http://www.theglobeandmail.com/news/politics/david-mcguinty-mulls-liberal-leadership-bid-at-convention/article2302861/.

40   Lorrie Goldstein, "McGuinty will tax carbon," *Toronto Sun*, September 23, 2011, http://www.torontosun.com/2011/09/23/mcguinty-will-tax-carbon.

41   Matthew Coutts, "Liberal staffer resigns after 'inappropriate jokes,'" *CTV Toronto*, September 30, 2011, http://www.ctv.ca/CTVNews/Politics/20110930/week-remaining-in-ontario-provincial-election-110930/.

42   Jonathan Jenkins, Antonella Artuso, and Patrick Maloney, "Liberal campaign official quits," *Toronto Sun*, last modified September 30, 2011, http://www.torontosun.com/2011/09/30/smokes-for-votes-comment-completely-unacceptable-mcguinty.

43   Tom Adams, "Politicians should stop playing politics with Ontario's electricity," *National Post*, last modified September 29, 2011, http://fullcomment.nationalpost.com/2011/09/29/tom-adams-politicians-should-stop-playing-with-ontario%E2%80%99s-electricity/.

44   "Ontario Liberals found in contempt of Parliament over documents related to cancelled generating stations," *National Post*, last modified September 13, 2012, http://news.nationalpost.com/2012/09/13/ontario-liberals-found-in-contempt-of-parliament-over-documents-related-to-cancelled-generating-stations/.

45   Christina Blizzard, "Just how dumb do Liberals think we are?" *Toronto Sun*, last modified March 27, 2014, http://www.sunnewsnetwork.ca/sunnews/straighttalk/archives/2014/03/20140327-213934.html

Chapter 8

The Drummond Report

"The Drummond bombshell is dropped at last."

-Hamilton Spectator[1]

"The Drummond report is scathing, frightening, a grim portrait, an indictment of Ontario's fiscal management during the last eight years of McGuinty government."

-Rex Murphy[2]

"The Liberals' record as outlined by Mr. Drummond's painfully honest assessment is abysmal. The future is bleak (when the best the apologists can come up with is: "We're nowhere near as bad as Greece," you know you're in trouble). The premier's most cherished programs are unaffordable. His economic projections are fantasy. His spending record is irresponsible, his balanced budget deadline implausible, his claim we can afford it all is unsupportable."

-Kelly McParland[3]

The Drummond Report

The bombshell that perfectly summarized so much of what was wrong with the eight years of McGuinty government was the Drummond Report. The report, formally known as *The Commission on the Reform of*

Liars

Ontario's Public Services,[4] was chaired and written by Don Drummond. Drummond held an extensive track record of public and private sector finance experience. This included his work at Finance Canada, 10 years as the Senior Vice President and chief economist for TD Bank, and a fellowship at Queen's University, including a co-chairmanship of the C.D. Howe Institute's Fiscal and Tax Competitiveness Council. Drummond was joined by three highly qualified commission members: Dominic Giroux, the President and Vice Chancellor of Laurentian University and former Assistant Deputy Minister at the Ministries of Education and Training, Colleges, and Universities; Susan Pigott, a professionally trained nurse with a Masters Degree in social work and international health care experience; and Carol Stephenson, the Dean of the Richard Ivey School of Business at the University of Western Ontario with advisory experience in car companies, financial services, public research funding, and the 2010 Vancouver Olympic Games. All told, the four-person commission covered an incredible breadth of experience in the areas with which Ontario needed the most help: education, health care, finance, the economy, and public services.

Drummond was appointed as the chair of the Commission by Premier McGuinty in his 2011 budget. McGuinty mandated Drummond to:

> [...] examine long-term, fundamental changes to the way government works. The commission's work will include exploring which areas of service delivery are core to the Ontario government's mandate, which areas could be delivered more efficiently by another entity and how to get better value for taxpayers' money in delivering public services.[5]

The McGuinty budget charged Drummond with undertaking the analysis and providing recommendations for the future of Ontario's public service. However, McGuinty specifically limited Drummond's findings to those that would not increase taxes or recommend the privatization of health care of education. Drummond was handicapped by McGuinty from the beginning because McGuinty made it clear what he did *not* want to see recommended in Drummond's report, even if it were for the better management of taxpayers' money.

For nearly a year, the Drummond Commission conducted in-depth research and analysis, interviewed the very best expert witnesses, and studied the policies and actions (and lack thereof) of the McGuinty government. The 562 page report was a scathing indictment of the McGuinty government's management of just about every aspect of the Ontario government: from the economy to the health care system; from the education system to the social safety net; from natural resources to the justice sector. Drummond left no stone unturned.

McGuinty thought he could count on Drummond for a supportive report. McGuinty thought he could influence the report by steering him towards the right answers and ensuring he strayed clear of the conservative ones, resulting in a report that showered praise upon the Liberal government for their smart and progressive investments and fiscal management. Instead, Drummond's findings would rock the McGuinty government to its core by shining a light on the true record of its governance, management, knowledge, and experience in running Canada's largest province for the past eight years.

Debt and Deficits

Ontario's ballooning debt and persistent deficit spending were a problem central to McGuinty's financial management. From 1986 to 1990, Ontario's debt averaged 14.1 percent of gross domestic product (GDP), which was "easily carried by a province as wealthy as Ontario." That changed, however, in the 1990s with the recession and the election of Bob Rae's New Democrats. There, large deficits were the status quo, and cuts came in the form of reduced public spending rather than reducing the debt. Fast forward to 2007-2008 and the McGuinty government had almost doubled the debt ratio to 27 percent. By 2010-2011, the debt-to-GDP ratio topped 35 percent.

The government lacked a "clear plan" with "bold actions taken early and advanced steadily" to combat the deficit and reduce the level of debt Ontario was carrying. The 2010-2011 fiscal year ran a record-shattering $16.3 billion deficit, which meant the Ontario government spent $1235 from every man, woman, and child living in Ontario *more* than what they collected from those same people.

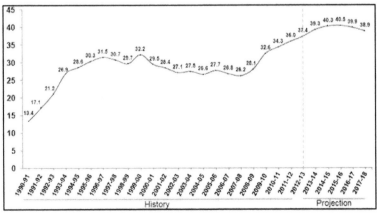

Figure 10: Ontario's debt-to-GDP ratio

Liars

By 2017-2018, Ontario would be spending $16.3 billion every year just to cover the *interest* on the ballooning debt. At 2.3 percent of the province's GDP, it was "the largest deficit relative to GDP of any province." And when the McGuinty government did set a goal to eliminate the deficit by 2017-2018, it was "at least three years behind that of any other province." Ontario was lucky that interest rates were being held so low following the 2008-2009 recession: as soon as interest rates rise, the cost of carrying that debt will skyrocket.

To balance the budget by 2017-2018, Drummond said, would require Ontario to cut $23.9 billion in program spending, a "wrenching reduction" of 17 percent. Mike Harris, by comparison, reduced spending by 3.9 percent. Those critics who demonized Harris to no end for his measly 3.9 percent spending reduction were in for a wakeup call. Harris would seem like a refreshing breeze by comparison. "If you lived through the Mike Harris years, you ain't seen nothing yet" said the *Toronto Star's* Martin Cohn.[6] Such an enormous reduction would be incredibly painful for Ontario families: at that rate, there would be no pick-and-choose public programs; the McGuinty government would be forced to engage in a slash-and-burn exercise of monumental proportions not seen since the decade of federal governance under Jean Chretien's Liberals in the 1990s (it was called the Decade of Darkness for a reason).

Ontario's failure to get its debt and deficit spending under control made it the outcast compared to every other Canadian province. Alberta, Saskatchewan, British Columbia, and Newfoundland ran surpluses and reduced their debt loads. While Manitoba had a "similar debt load between 2000 and 2005, Manitoba's debt has since fallen to about 25 percent of GDP while Ontario's has risen." The only province worse off than Ontario was Quebec, with its debt at 50 percent of GDP.

The Health Care System

Health care is the Ontario government's single largest budget item, and one of the most fundamental programs the provincial government needs to administer. In the 2010-2011 budget, the McGuinty government spent $44.77 billion on health care, but was spending too much time pondering its institutions and doctors and not enough time thinking about what mattered – the patients. "Better care delivered smoothly and briskly across a range of needs" would refocus Ontario's health care system into one that takes care of patients with both acute as well as chronic problems. It would also save money.

Health care costs are growing at an average rate of 6.4 percent per year, and they are only expected to increase as Ontarians get older, new technologies are developed, inflation increases, and hospital operations become more expensive. By 2017-2018, health care spending could reach $62.46 billion.

Drummond was prohibited by McGuinty from making any suggestions to increase taxes or privatize the health care system, so Drummond opted to mostly discuss public opinion polls regarding whether Ontarians would accept higher taxes for a better health care system, or whether they would prefer instead lower taxes and a more minimalist health care system. The merits of public versus private health care is one of the most visceral political debates, especially considering the recent implementation of the *Affordable Care Act* ("Obamacare") in the United States. The best Drummond could muster was to say that Ontario's health care system was "not as public as most people think" since Canadian public spending on health care only accounts for 70.6 percent of the total; we still pay for certain private services, medications, surgeries, and treatments.

Primary and Secondary Education

While Drummond may have spared McGuinty the brunt of his criticisms when it came to health care, he was blunt and honest when it came to education: the guy who fancied himself "the education Premier" was in for a rude awakening. At $21.9 billion, education is another provincial portfolio in which Ontarians believe the government should play a large role. Yet, "over 76 percent of ministry spending goes to salaries and benefits for teaching and non-teaching staff," inverting the education ministry away from its purpose of providing an education. Since 2002, Ontario schools have also seen 120,000 fewer students enroll, yet 24,000 *more* teachers and "non-teaching staff" have been added to the payroll. If student-teacher ratios had been kept in line with student declines since 2002, Ontario would actually have 35,000 *fewer* teachers and non-teaching staff by 2010-2011. By 2011, per-student funding had grown by 56 percent.

With *increased* budgets, *more* teachers, and *fewer* students to teach, had Ontario's education system become one of the best in the world? Actually, the money had been poured into what Drummond called "sustained labour peace and stability." Teachers were given more preparation time before classes; classes were smaller; and wages and benefits were better. *Half* of all teachers were making the maximum salary of $95,000 per year.

In the midst of the recession and its recovery, the McGuinty government thought it would be a great idea to implement full-day kindergarten. They appointed Charles Pascal as the Premier's special advisor on early-learning who was to provide the government with recommendations on implementing a full-day early-learning program. (Implementing a full-day kindergarten program was not part of the Liberal Party's 2007 re-election platform. It was, however, an NDP policy proposal for that same election.[7])

By 2010 it became a reality, and a new $1.5 billion program was added to Ontario's books. While Drummond appreciated "the research and analysis performed by Dr. Pascal," the timing was not right to introduce such an expensive program at such a fiscally uncertain time. "Not enough restraint," Drummond said, was balanced against the new cost of full-day kindergarten while still meeting deficit elimination targets. It was a transparent ploy to keep teachers occupied and "peaceful" on the public dole rather than laying them off.

While the McGuinty government was focused on keeping its core Liberal voters happy, Aboriginal students were suffering. Drummond implored the government, while refocusing its education strategy, to "significantly improve the provision of on-reserve First Nations education in the province." This was one area in which the McGuinty government failed miserably. It could have approached the federal government with the objective of obtaining a long-term strategic education plan for Ontario's aboriginal students, whose high school completion rates were 36 percentage points *lower* than the general population's average. Instead, the needs of aboriginal students were secondary to the needs of sustaining "labour peace."

Post-Secondary Education (PSE)

If the primary and secondary education system was broken, the post-secondary education system was a whole different story of fairly positive accomplishments. Sixty three percent of Ontarians had completed some form of post-secondary education, 79 percent attained university degrees, and 65 percent held college diplomas. These figures made Ontario the leader of the Organization for Economic Co-operation and Development (OECD). An educated workforce is essential because over two thirds of all jobs in Ontario require some form of post-secondary education.

"However," Drummond noted, "there is no coherent, purposeful plan that extends beyond attainment or addressing the parts as opposed to the whole system." The McGuinty government was spending $6.2 billion on improving access to and quality of Ontario's post-secondary education, yet it could not craft a plan that clearly identified for what that money was intended.

In 2003, when McGuinty was still leader of the Official Opposition, he proposed freezing tuition and paying 50 percent of tuition for students in financial need.[8] When he took office he implemented a tuition freeze, until he cancelled it in 2005.[9] Drummond responded sharply that a tuition freeze was not in the students' best interests: "Freezing tuition now reduces revenues at a time of constrained government funding; institutions will find other ways to make up for lost potential revenues, resulting in lower-quality PSE."

Social Programs

Social programs are another fundamental part of the provincial government's responsibility to its citizens. In Ontario's social programs we take care of our most vulnerable members of society: those with disabilities, the elderly, and our children. But are the programs affordable? Between 2000 and 2010 their costs increased six percent per year. "Social assistance," meaning Ontario Works (welfare) and the Ontario Disability Support Program (ODSP), account for 51 percent of the total $13.8 billion budget.

Much of the money wasted (although Drummond did not say how much) was due to bureaucratic duplication; he called upon the McGuinty government to "transform" its benefits programs so they were better coordinated, and gaps and duplications of effort were minimized. Furthermore, those who needed the benefits programs were left with a non-user friendly, bureaucratic web of numerous departments, agencies, and sections that often dealt with the same issues but offered a slightly different benefit.

The delivery of many social programs was done with a focus on the process rather than the client. Fewer agencies operating through a single-desk service model with better coordination between departments in the background would offer social assistance based on helping the person requiring it. An electronic benefits directory was a good start; believe it or not, *this was only launched in March 2011.* A single-desk service point for developmental benefits was a good start, but Drummond called upon the government to implement the same single-desk option for all benefits programs. Finally, maintaining Ontario Works and ODSP as separate benefits administered by separate departments was also leading to duplicated work.

Discretionary social programs were still seeing long wait lists that only seemed to continue to grow. Family and children services, and children's mental health services needed to be better integrated or aligned with the relevant government agencies. By creating better, more formal links between these related agencies, the provincial government would provide better customer service. They would also find efficiencies in figuring out that a single-desk service point would eliminate much of the work being duplicated in separate offices.

Liars

Employment and Training Services

Employment and training services solidify a person's skills and education. However, this assumes that there are jobs out there available for these people to fill. The recession typified the struggles of many people to find work, but it was a long-coming issue. Eighteen percent of recent immigrants were unemployed, and the aboriginal unemployment rate topped 20 percent in 2010. Over 141,500 workers were laid off in 2009. What use was the McGuinty government's 30 percent discount on post-secondary tuition if the students were completing their post-secondary education with debt and no job prospects? Employment Ontario was supposed to answer this problem.

"Still in its relative infancy," Employment Ontario is intended to be the umbrella department responsible for delivering employment- and training-related services offered by the Training, Colleges, and Universities; Citizenship and Immigration; and Community and Social Services ministries. With its $1 billion per year, Employment Ontario did a relatively good job of offering bridge training programs and language training to new immigrants, and providing support to youth, unemployed, and laid off employees. Much like Ontario's social programs, however, Ontario's employment and training services needed to be better streamlined and the organizations behind the services needed better coordination. Even as Employment Ontario operated, other ministries offered their own, separate programs, for youth for example. "Streamline and integrate other employment and training services with Employment Ontario," Drummond recommended.

There were also large gaps in how Ontario gathered and tracked labour market and employment statistics: "data gaps limit Ontario's ability to effectively target investments in labour-market programming at a strategic level." Without this information, the McGuinty government did not have the information it needed to determine which programs were getting more Ontarians into work and which ones needed to be refocused or eliminated.

Immigration

Ontario's immigration policy is directly related to its economic policy. "If immigration averaged about 70,000 per year (which is about half the population projection reference scenario of 139,000 per year), Ontario would have 1.4 million fewer people in the 15–64 working-age group by 2036 available to contribute to the economy and pay taxes," reported the Ontario Ministry of Finance. Furthermore, immigrants cannot fully contribute their skills and experience to Ontario's economy if their foreign qualifications are not recognized as equivalent to Ontario credentials.

The McGuinty government had failed to influence the federal government to give Ontario its "considerable weight" in determining its position on immigration policy that best served the province. The implication was obvious: 1) the McGuinty government had no immigration policy; and 2) the Liberal government could not articulate its unknown immigration policy to federal officials. Ontario needed to develop its own policy and "catalyze national discussions on immigration policy" according to Drummond.

Without a clear immigration policy, McGuinty was also unable to accommodate refugee claimants. In 2010, 56.3 percent of all refugees accepted into Canada came to Ontario. And once in Ontario, "the incidence of social assistance attachment for refugees" was substantial: they experienced much higher rates of unemployment, part-time employment, and temporary employment; and they were less likely to have their foreign credentials recognized in Canada.

Immigrants were unable to integrate into the labour market, which further proliferated an increased draw on social programs while failing to contribute adequate tax revenues. The unemployment rate of very recent immigrants was the second highest in Canada, at 15.7 percent, only behind Quebec, at 18.6 percent. There was a stagnant gap between landed immigrant employment growth and provincial population growth: while their share of population growth was 36.7 percent, their share of employment growth was only 15.6 percent, the largest gap in Canada's provinces.

Landed immigrants are, on average, better educated than their Canadian-born equivalents, yet they are more likely to live in poverty. As of 2010, the average weekly wage of a recent immigrant was 23.9 percent lower than the Canadian-born employee. By 2005, the earnings gap between the two groups was over $27,000. Failing to recognize foreign credentials was a major barrier to integration - the proverbial doctor driving a cab while waiting for his medical degree to be recognized. Other barriers were fluency in English or French, which was beginning to be addressed by language programs through Employment Ontario (see above), but for those already here and ready to work, it was not enough.

Immigrants settling in Ontario were faced with a bleak future. Immigrants must wait for months, if not years, as their credentials are run through the bureaucratic gauntlet. In that time they are taking from Ontario's social programs without recontributing in the form of taxes. Or, they might take a job wherever one presents itself. It's no wonder more immigrants are choosing to settle out west - in Alberta, Saskatchewan, or Manitoba - instead of Ontario.[10]

Liars

Business Support (The Economy)

Business support, also known as business subsidies, corporate welfare, and corporate tax breaks, is an essential piece of the overall package that lures businesses to set up shops in some jurisdictions while avoiding others. While the government can only create jobs by employing public servants, the government *can* play a much larger role in the economy by supporting businesses that create and maintain the right kinds of jobs. Traditionally it's a convenient punching bag for Liberals and New Democrats as they both race to outdo the other in slandering and scandalizing some of our best job creators. Indeed, despite its enormous potential and real impact on the economy, business support programs were "not in the same league as spending on education and health care – nor [were they] at the same level of priority" to the McGuinty government.

The government provides two types of business support: in 2010-2011, it provided businesses with over $1.3 billion in direct support (loans and grants) and over $2.3 billion in indirect support (tax credits and the subsidy of certain industries). It's "a hodgepodge of direct and indirect programs scattered across a variety of ministries with various economic development mandates," Drummond said. Furthermore, these "programs can distort business decisions to the point that they are no longer based on sound economic criteria or require a reasonable degree of private risk." Moreover, "business support" should not equate to government bailouts of private companies:

> [...] while they can achieve short-term objectives such as job retention, over the long term they can impede structural shifts and allocation of resources that would improve productivity in the overall economy. Bailouts entail a potential political risk, provoking questions of fairness and the creation of an "un-level" playing field among business competitors. The record of such interventions has generally featured more failures than successes.

In other words, the Canadian and Ontario governments' decision to bail out General Motors and Chrysler to the tune of $13.7 billion in 2009-2010[11] was a monumentally stupid and short-sighted decision.

Much of Drummond's focus in this chapter is not on literally *supporting* businesses, but on the provincial government *creating the right conditions* so businesses can survive and flourish. Governments need to understand the challenges currently facing Ontario's businesses, and the challenges they will face in coming years and generations. The government can create the right conditions for businesses to thrive through its understanding of, and action on: inflation; internal and external free trade; lower taxes on capital; removal of barriers to firm growth; the removal of work disincentives; lower marginal personal income tax rates; and a shift away from taxing income to taxing consumption. Furthermore, they can encourage the growth of certain businesses while discouraging the growth of other businesses. They do this through increasing or decreasing taxes, regulations, duties, tariffs, exceptions, and a whole host of other conditions that can make Ontario a more attractive place to set up business than, say, Wisconsin or Quebec.

According to Drummond, the key to successful and appropriate support of the private sector was a government that had a plan on where it wanted to see the economy go over time. It is not surprising, then, that Drummond had to call on the McGuinty government to create such a plan, since there was no evidence that one existed. That policy, should the Ontario Liberals choose to create one, should have "nine key ingredients: a top-quality labour force; effective integration of immigrants into the workforce; world-class infrastructure, including transit; a reliable electricity system; being a leader in the environment; a competitive tax system; enhanced trade; shift from dependence (social assistance) to labour-force participation; and supportive federal policy." The provincial government would be flying in the dark if they did not know the economic vision they were seeking to accomplish. Therefore, it "needs to present a strategy that aligns with efforts to realize the economic objectives of the government — one that uses increased productivity as a keystone."

The good news, however, is that Ontario is "poised for growth" *if it understands and sets the right conditions for businesses to thrive.* As noted earlier, about 64 percent of Ontario's population between 25 and 64 years-old have a post-secondary education, making Ontario a highly skilled and educated workforce. Furthermore, the tax reforms created in the 2010-2011 budgets "will save business about $4.4 billion per year from the removal of the embedded sales tax, $2.5 billion per year from the corporate income tax rate (CIT) reductions, and more than $1.8 billion per year from elimination of the capital tax." All told, that's more than $8 billion in annual tax savings for businesses – tax savings that can be invested into hiring new employees, increasing warehouse stock, or purchasing new, more efficient equipment. By 2018, "Ontario's marginal effective tax rate on new business investment" will be cut in half, Drummond said, "making Ontario one of the most attractive jurisdictions in the industrialized world in which to invest and create jobs."

Liars

Infrastructure, Real Estate, and Electricity

As infrastructure ages, its costs grow. Since 2003, the McGuinty government had spent $62 billion on it, with another $12.8 billion planned in the 2011-2012 budget. Transportation was another big part of it: at 82 minutes for a round-trip Toronto commute, it's the longest in North America. The lack of infrastructure and demanding commute was estimated to cost Ontario about $6 billion in lost productivity each year. The issue was only bound to get worse, especially in the Greater Toronto Area as Ontario's capital and Canada's largest city. However, "public discourse on the actions needed to meet this challenge — or the consequences of not acting — has simply not materialized with any degree of province-wide prominence." Drummond was prohibited from suggesting tax increases, so the best he could muster was to suggest the McGuinty government "engage citizens in an open, public dialogue on how best to create new revenue sources for future transportation capital needs."

Drummond's recommendations on electricity are where the McGuinty government was in for another reality check. In 2011, the McGuinty government implemented the Ontario Clean Energy Benefit (OCEB), a 10 percent rebate on monthly hydro bills "to help with the transition to higher prices associated with the shift to cleaner energy supply." That equates to over $1 billion in lost revenue and "distorts [the] true cost of electricity and discourages conservation." When the benefit is completed, since it's only a five-year "transition program," it can be expected to "create a considerable price shock to ratepayers." Much larger, "direct savings" could be accomplished by reducing the $1.35 billion spent on the over 80 local distribution companies which provide operations, maintenance, and administrative support. An integrated power support plan (IPSP) "would provide producers, consumers, utilities and other sector participants with a detailed, 20-year blueprint for the electricity sector." The Ontario Power Authority submitted one to the McGuinty government – in 2007 – but the minister never responded. (The McGuinty government very quickly refused Drummond's suggestion.[12])

The feed-in tariff (FIT) program was launched by the McGuinty government in 2009 "to facilitate the increased development of renewable generating facilities of varying sizes, technologies and configurations via a standardized, open and fair process."[13] In sum, a company wishing to build a "green" electricity facility would be subsidized by the McGuinty government, and, once completed, would receive a 20- or 40-year contract at a fixed-rate for providing electricity to Ontario.[14] The buy-in for this program was huge: the private sector was building enormous power-generating facilities and the public sector was returning the favour by paying a long-term fixed rate for electricity. Drummond said the government should lower "the initial prices offered in the FIT contract" and introduce "degression rates that reduce the tariff over time to encourage innovation and discourage any reliance on public subsidies." Ontario also needed "larger generation facilities," and it should procure them "through a request for proposal (RFP) process." This was a direct shot at the McGuinty government's decision to cancel the Mississauga and Oakville gas plants in the midst of the 2011 election – a decision that ended up costing over $1.1 billion.

The Environment and Natural Resources

Two of the most important ministries to the economy – Environment and Natural Resources – were bleeding money through lost revenues. The McGuinty government was spending $15 million a year through several ministries that were responsible to "manage water quantity and encourage its efficient use." Yet the government was charging a paltry $3.71 for every *million* litres of water taken from Ontario's rivers, lakes, and streams by beverage companies, concrete factories, and canning and pickling factories. In fact, the Ontario Auditor General found the two ministries were recovering less than 40 percent of the actual program costs. Drummond was forbidden from recommending tax increases, but he could recommend that the government at least recover the cost of the benefits it was offering to businesses and manufacturers. A much more effective program would have recovered the costs up front, then rebated businesses for meeting goals such as better efficiencies or reduced water consumption.

Much of what the Ontario environment and natural resources ministries were doing was overlapping with what other ministries – provincial and federal – were already doing. Municipal Affairs and Housing was responsible for planning requirements, including the planned use of land. The Ministry of Energy "sets goals for the province's energy plans, including conservation and fuel standards." Local municipalities are the ones that "make local planning decisions to operate in areas that are currently regulated by the province, such as local air standards and waste." On the federal front, the provincial government could better liaise with the federal government in areas such as lakes and rivers, since the federal Department of Fisheries and Oceans has a role to play there. There are also 36 "conservation authorities." Such "jurisdictional crowding," as Drummond called it, was resulting "in inefficient use of government resources and creates uncertainty and confusion for industry, developers, and citizens."

There was some good news, however. Coming into effect just days after the October 2011 election, the new environmental project approvals process was based upon risk and provided more of the certainty businesses and industry needed. It replaced the previous system that required a Certificate of Approval, which was "relatively inflexible" in requiring all projects to go through the same process regardless of the potential risk. This distracted the Environment Ministry "from focusing on potentially unique or more complex applicants that posed more significant environmental risks." More needed to be done, but it was a good start.

Back to water, the Ontario Clean Water Agency (OCWA)[15] was a confusing provincial Crown corporation. It was initially established under Bob Rae's New Democrats in 1993 as a Crown corporation that would manage the province's water treatment and waste water treatment facilities. Over 10 years it made the province $11.7 million, but its operations were running deficits every year. Their business model was "neither sustainable nor competitive." It mandate needed to be reviewed to determine precisely what the agency was doing and what it needed to be doing.

Finally, development in the Ring of Fire "represents a significant opportunity to both realize major mineral development in the region and improve socio-economic opportunity and quality of life for Aboriginal People and other residents of the north. Managed properly, the project will provide benefits over several decades." It was a precautionary warning that, as will be discussed in chapter ten, was unfortunately missed by the McGuinty government.

Justice Sector

Since 2001, spending on the justice portfolio had increased an average of 5.6 percent per year. Much of the spending increases came from "the high rate of spending on special initiatives in recent years" – "special initiatives" that could not be afforded if they came at the expense of the fundamental parts of the justice portfolio (courts, police, public safety, and so forth). However, "the primary cost driver" for the growth in justice spending was actually the salaries and benefits for Ontario's police, judges, and other sector employees. In 2012, the McGuinty government gave the Ontario Provincial Police (OPP) a whopping 8.5 percent pay increase to come into effect in 2014. Remember, Finance Minister Dwight Duncan had already imposed a wage freeze on public sector servants, yet that was openly defied by executives at Ontario Power Generation and the Ontario Lottery and Gaming Corporation. Why should the police be any different?

One of the most gaping flaws in the McGuinty government was exposed: it wasn't using "evidence-based data collection" to analyze the outcomes of its justice programs! As just one example, Drummond noted the province pays municipal governments for court security and the transportation of offenders through a self-reported honour system. If a municipality says it needs $1 million, the province pays $1 million without ever tracking the outcomes of how much money is being spent on court security and offender transportation. Part of the issue, too, was the standard *collection* of data that could be analyzed by justice officials. Correctional services, standard policing costs, public safety training programs, the impact of federal legislation on provincial jurisdiction, tracking court cases, and family mediation services – all of these fields collected *some* form of data, yet they failed to report that data in a simple, standardized format so it could be analyzed by justice officials. Yet again, the McGuinty government was flying blind because it didn't know what it didn't know.

Policing was becoming more expensive, especially thanks to McGuinty's 8.5 percent pay hike. But the broader issue was that the core responsibilities of police officers had not been defined. It is not uncommon, for example, to see an on-duty police officer directing traffic around a construction site. Nor is it uncommon to see an officer hired in his non-scheduled hours to provide security at a public or private event. In each of these cases, because the core responsibilities of police officers have not been defined, police departments cannot properly train their officers or allocate resources. Special constables could be hired for the former and private security guards could be hired for the latter – both are much cheaper to afford and would allow police officers to focus on the fundamental duties of actual policing.

Labour Relations and Compensation

Much of the McGuinty record on labour relations and compensation has already been laid out in earlier chapters: lavish bonuses and wage increases for public employees during a time wages were supposedly "frozen." An 8.5 percent pay increase for the Ontario Provincial Police. A lucrative $95,000 salary cap for teachers. And so on. But Drummond added a new perspective on the matter, including more startling statistics. Seventy percent of Ontario's public sector is unionized – a very high percentage compared to other governments and private sector employers. The sector with the highest unionization rate was also, unsurprisingly, the sector with an incredible pay and benefits package, and also one of the closest sectors to McGuinty's inner circle: the teachers. The education sector grew by 34 percent between 2000 and 2011. The other sectors with very high unionization rates are also the sectors that saw their employment rates explode under the McGuinty government. In the same 11 years, public sector employment in health care and social services increased by 39 percent. By 2011, over 17 percent of total employment in Ontario was provincial public service jobs.

Liars

Not only was the Ontario public service ballooning, so were their salaries. Since 2003 the average public sector wage had increased 28 percent, compared to the consumer price index, which increased by 17 percent. The wage freezes announced by Finance Minister Dwight Duncan were thought to be actual wage freezes, although, as you have already seen and will see again, those freezes were commonly ignored. However, contracted agreements that already contained annual wage increases in them (for example, doctors and full-time equivalent employees) had *not* been renegotiated, meaning these groups were still seeing annual pay increases. These accounted for almost 225,000 public servants.

Drummond also noted "history shows that wage freezes are often followed by wage catch-up periods." In other words, take a wage freeze this year, and we'll overpay you next year. This is what the McGuinty government did with the Ontario Provincial Police, who technically agreed to a one-year wage freeze in exchange for an 8.5 percent increase the following year. These periods "would undermine our longer-term fiscal mandate and damage labour relations."

Furthermore, how bonuses were decided upon was done in a non-transparent manner. At the time of the report, 70 percent of managers were given an "automatic bonus" that became part of their base pay. There was little incentive to become better leaders, actually *lead,* or provide better results for one's department if their bonus (for doing just that) was automatic. With such an arbitrary system, internal politics could manipulate the bonus system from being about excellent work to being about rewarding one's personal lackeys. At the very least, Drummond said, a "tough-but-fair" approach should divide bonus levels into three categories: full bonus for excellent work; a partial bonus for above average work; and no bonus at all. Employees falling in the third category "would clearly be on notice that dismissal will follow if their performance does not soon improve."

Operating and Back-Office Expenditures

Almost half (48 percent) of Ontario's $10 billion budget for our public service goes towards wages. Twenty six percent was for the provision of services, and 20 percent was for employee benefits. "Transportation, communication, and supplies" represented the last six percent. As noted above, the incredible cost of Ontario's overly-unionized public service was the "driving force" behind being able to budget for the overall operation of Ontario's public service. Since 2003, the cost of operating Ontario's public service has increased by $2 billion, or 20 percent over nine years.

"Back-office expenditures" accounted for another large portion of the overall operation of the public service. As has already been discussed from earlier chapters in the Drummond Report, there are considerable opportunities for finding efficiencies and thus reducing costs by combining similar offices, reducing overhead expenses, eliminating redundancies, and offering single-desk service windows through agencies such as Employment Ontario and Service Ontario. One of the best areas for growth, Drummond said, was through Service Ontario, which could expand its mandate by "pursuing additional partnerships for service delivery within the Ontario Public Service, and furthering service delivery partnerships with municipal and federal levels of government." They could also push more people to online services for services such as birth certificate registration and driver's licence renewal.

Information and information technology was another major opportunity: Ontario spent $987 million on these services in 2010-2011. Although "significant leaps" had been made in this field over the past decade, much more could be done through alternative service delivery or outsourcing the jobs to private contractors. "Blending" service delivery between public servants and private contractors could "make the difference between the continuation and the end of some services."

Supply chains and "back-office" services were also well overdue for a makeover. Both included working "horizontally" to provide services across the whole provincial public service rather than specialized silos that only work within their departments. Opportunities in cleaning up the back office administration included human resources services like payroll; financial transactions such as accounts payable and accounts receivable; collections; forms, printing, and distribution; risk management and insurance services; and high-volume mail services such as government mail-outs.

Final Chapters

The final chapters mainly dealt with the more minor details about Ontario's governance. Most of the juicy Drummond recommendations were contained in those summarized above. However, the final chapters of his report did highlight some of the scandals to be discussed later in this book: on government business enterprises, Drummond explored fully or partially privatizing the Liquor Control Board (LCBO), the Lottery and Gaming Corporation (OLG), Ontario Power Generation (OPG), and Hydro One. Privatizing the LCBO became a central policy of Tim Hudak's bid for the Premiership, and the latter three organizations would give McGuinty constant headaches in the coming months and years. But while Drummond vaguely explored the three scenarios (retain ownership or full or partial

Liars

privatization), he did not consider in principle whether the government should continue to be in the lottery and alcohol business, for example. His suggestions were mostly limited to finding efficiencies in current operations, assuming the government would retain ownership, or only privatizing the businesses if "the net, long-term benefit to Ontario is considerable and can be clearly demonstrated through comprehensive analysis."

In "revenue integrity" it was determined that Ontario was owed a staggering $1 billion in fines not yet paid by provincial offenders. Furthermore, user fees had rarely been increased since 2003, leaving the government on the losing end of recovering the costs associated with providing services in the first place (for drivers' licences, for example). In his chapter on "liability management," Drummond identified pension funds as a major liability that would increasingly require the government's attention considering Ontario's aging population. "One of the biggest questions from a liability management perspective is who is ultimately responsible should a plan or plans get into serious financial difficulty." The health of the pension plans, it turned out, was not something the public was entitled to know, despite shortfalls due to the 2008-2009 recession. The answer to the underfunded pension plans, Drummond said, was to reduce benefits rather than increase contribution rates.

Finally, on "intergovernmental relations," Drummond found several issues with the way the McGuinty government was working with other provincial governments and the federal government. The McGuinty government did a poor job of liaising with the federal government to determine the costs of implementing new *Criminal Code* offences, for example. They did not advocate for the $220 million that the federal government did not provide the province under the Canada-Ontario Immigration Agreement. This meant "the success of immigrants could be impaired without adequate services to help newcomers settle, integrate, receive language training and find work." Yet the McGuinty government did nothing to correct the issue or uphold the federal government's funding commitment for new immigrants.

Even as a "have-not" or "losing" province (compared to the "have" or "winning" provinces), Ontarians contributed almost $45 billion *more* to the provincial-federal Equalization Program than we received back from the federal government through equalization payments. This highlights the inadequacies of the calculations to determine equalization payments, Drummond said, yet the McGuinty government did nothing to advocate for reforms that would better account for resource revenues and prices differences between provinces. Employment insurance, too, needed reforms, but McGuinty was silent.

The final chapters of the Drummond Report offered fewer recommendations and less juicy policy recommendations than the other chapters, but they highlighted the growing narrative of a McGuinty government plagued with scandals, incompetence, mismanagement, and expensive experiments. His government failed to collaborate and consult with other provinces and the federal government. They failed to keep pace with the changing demographics of the province. They did not take action when action needed to be taken, leaving the government falling behind in several portfolios fundamental to the provincial government's core mandate. They overspent on keeping unions happy and underspent on aboriginal education and infrastructure demands.

The Bombshell that Rocked Ontario

When the Drummond Report was released it sent shockwaves through Ontario's political, academic, business, and government circles. The articulate and relentless report meticulously catalogued every aspect of the McGuinty Liberals' failed policies. To be clear, there were reports of positive provincial accomplishments. On education, for example, the question was how to make a good system even better while keeping salaries in check. On social assistance programs, the question was how to take multiple benefits offered by multiple government agencies and transform those agencies into single-desk services.

The overwhelming tone of the Drummond Report was one of abject failure throughout a near-decade of McGuinty government. As Kelly McParland summarized:

The Liberals' record as outlined by Mr. Drummond's painfully honest assessment is abysmal. The future is bleak (when the best the apologists can come up with is: "We're nowhere near as bad as Greece," you know you're in trouble). The premier's most cherished programs are unaffordable. His economic projections are fantasy. His spending record is irresponsible, his balanced budget deadline implausible, his claim we can afford it all is unsupportable.[16]

But if you're a Liberal apologist, perhaps it's easy to find solace in any one of several excuses. For one, McGuinty *did* call upon Drummond to write the report. That has to count for something. Secondly, much of the report took aim at broad shifts in the public sector, not necessarily the responsibility of any *one* McGuinty cabinet minister. Thirdly, governance is a slow-moving, constantly evolving process that McGuinty could not have countered without the facts found in the Drummond Report. Fourthly, maybe the McGuinty government is completely free from any of the criticism found in the Drummond Report. Maybe the Drummond Report was written and targeted towards criticizing the public service, but not towards the individual ministers who held ultimate ministerial responsibility. Maybe. All of these are convenient excuses, so if they help you sleep at night, feel free to indulge!

However, the question, I believe, is whether the McGuinty government *did* know, *could have* known, or *ought to have* known about many of the issues plaguing the government in advance of the Drummond Report being commissioned or released. Why was such an analysis not readily available or being conducted internally by the public sector already? The answer to this question, considering the multiple public sector unions in bed with the McGuinty government, should be fairly obvious. If you believe in ministerial responsibility, each minister and their ministries named in the Drummond Report should bear full liability for what they did know, could have known, and ought to have known. Collective responsibility belongs to Dalton McGuinty, both for failing to know and for failing to take action before, during, and after the issues highlighted in the Drummond Report.

Drummond did exactly what McGuinty asked of him: he presented a thorough report on the "long-term, fundamental changes to the way government works." Drummond's 362 recommendations over 562 pages just weren't what McGuinty wanted to hear. Instead of independent confirmation that his Liberal government was doing the right things for Ontario, he received a sobering report that lambasted most of the McGuinty legacy. Instead of a leading Canadian economist singing praise for the Liberal record, the Liberal record was exposed as a partisan, ideological, incomplete, untested, unconfirmed, expensive, reckless experiment led by a government that could rarely comprehend what it was trying to do.

How did McGuinty respond? He minimized the report, saying it was only "advice" that his government would consider in making the "tough choices."[17] Two years later, the Ontario government is no closer to being back on track. Two years later, Ontario's debt has only increased, we're still investing in expensive and untested energy experiments, taxpayers' money is still being thrown into lavish public servant benefits, and the McGuinty government had still failed to get Ontario's economy back on track. This trend has only continued under Kathleen Wynne, who also seems to be taking zero interest in implementing anything Drummond recommended.

1   "Drummond bombshell is dropped at last," *Hamilton Spectator*, last modified February 16, 2012, http://www.thespec.com/opinion-story/2237112-drummond-bombshell-is-dropped-at-last/.

2   Rex Murphy, "The Drummond report and Ontario's sham election," *National Post*, last modified February 18, 2012, http://fullcomment.nationalpost.com/2012/02/18/rex-murphy-the-drummond-report-and-ontarios-sham-election/.

3   Kelly McParland, "Don Drummond catalogues the McGuinty mess in meticulous detail," *National Post*, last modified February 16, 2012, http://fullcomment.nationalpost.com/2012/02/16/don-drummond-catalogues-the-mcguinty-mess-in-meticulous-detail/.

4   Commission on the reform of Ontario's public services, *Public services for Ontarians: a path to sustainability and excellence.* (Toronto: Ontario Ministry of Finance, 2013), http://www.fin.gov.on.ca/en/reformcommission/.

5   *2011 Ontario Budget: Managing Responsibly,* Ontario Ministry of Finance, 2011, http://www.fin.gov.on.ca/en/budget/ontariobudgets/2011/bk2.html.

6   Martin Cohn, "Drummond report merely the end of the beginning," *Toronto Star*, last modified February 15, 2012, http://www.thestar.com/news/canada/2012/02/15/cohn_drummond_report_merely_the_end_of_the_beginning.html

7   City Manager's Office, *2007 Ontario General Election...*"

8   Christine Roulston, "McGuinty proposes tuition freeze," *Western News*, last modified January 31, 2003, http://communications.uwo.ca/western_news/stories/2003/January/mcguinty_proposes_tuition_freeze.html

9   "Students slam McGuinty for breaking tuition freeze promise," *CBC News,* last modified September 25, 2007, http://www.cbc.ca/news/canada/students-slam-mcguinty-for-breaking-tuition-freeze-promise-1.645881.

10   Tobi Cohen, "Immigration shifts westward, raising concerns about settlement funding in Ontario," *Postmedia News*, last modified May 8, 2013, http://www.canada.com/Immigration+shifts+westward+raising+concerns+about+settlement+funding+Ontario/8354111/story.html.

11   Mark Milke, "The government auto bailout: $474,000 per GM employee," *Fraser Institute*, 2012, http://www.fraserinstitute.org/uploadedFiles/fraser-ca/Content/research-news/research/articles/government-auot-bailout-CSR-spring-2012.pdf.

12   "Drummond report cuts: electricity rebates to stay, McGuinty says," *Huffington Post Canada*, last modified February 23, 2012, http://www.huffingtonpost.ca/2012/02/23/drummond-report-cuts-electricity-rebates_n_1296291.html.

13   "FIT program," *Ontario Power Authority,* last modified 2014, http://fit.powerauthority.on.ca/fit-program.

14   "FIT program pricing," *Ontario Power Authority,* last modified 2014, http://fit.powerauthority.on.ca/fit-program/fit-program-pricing.

15   See Ontario Clean Water Agency, http://www.ocwa.com.

16   Kelly McParland, supra note 3.

17   Robert Benzie, "Drummond report: sweeping education reforms only advice, McGuinty says," *Toronto Star*, last modified February 14, 2012, http://www.thestar.com/news/canada/2012/02/14/drummond_report_sweeping_education_reforms_only_advice_mcguinty_says.html.

Chapter 9

Minority Government, Same Mistakes
The Fall of the McGuinty Minority (2011-2012)

"Dalton McGuinty is lucky he's the Premier of Ontario and not the President of the United States. If he were the President, we'd all be calling for his head and Congress would be preparing Articles of Impeachment."

-The Kingston Whig[1]

"The Liberals have lost the moral authority to govern."

-Northumberland View[2]

McGuinty's Fall Begins Early

It had only been a short time since the 2011 election, and the McGuinty government was already in free-fall mode. For the first time in eight years, McGuinty, who had become accustomed to listening and answering only to his union buddies and Liberal Party advisors, suddenly had two political parties he had to work with in order to get anything done. One party, Andrea Horwath's New Democrats, would attempt to pull McGuinty to the left, with more government spending, even higher deficits, and ruthless government regulation. The other party, Tim Hudak's Progressive Conservatives, stood alone as the sole party demanding the government undergo a thorough reality check to reduce its spending, balance its budget, eliminate useless red tape, and save any hope of getting Ontario back on track.

147

Liars

McGuinty said he would work with both the NDP and Progressive Conservatives, but he would not do business with "those who seek to divide Ontarians at a time when we need to be strong."[3] As it would turn out, the McGuinty government rarely needed to worry about the Opposition parties attempting to divide Ontarians: the Liberals' policies would do that on their own.

McGuinty commissioned the Drummond Report in his 2011 budget and the report was tabled in 2012, when the Liberals had already been reduced to a minority. That report should have been the wakeup call Ontario needed. It was thorough, desperate, and honest: Ontario was in trouble and needed decisive government action to get it back on track. But instead of following Drummond's report, McGuinty dismissed it as "just advice" and continued the same reckless indifference to anyone but his Liberal advisors and his union buddies.

The ORNGE Scandal

The election had barely settled when the ORNGE scandal broke. ORNGE is Ontario's $150 million per-year air ambulance service, overseen by the Minister of Health and Long-term Care. When the scandal broke, this was Deb Matthews. At the time of writing, Matthews is still Minister, meaning she had the full support of Dalton McGuinty and continues to enjoy the confidence of Kathleen Wynne.

President and CEO Chris Mazza had been disclosing his annual salary up to and including 2007, as was required under the Sunshine Law. In 2007, Mazza was on the Sunshine List as making $298,000, but every year after that his salary was never declared. The *Toronto Star* revealed that at least five senior ORNGE executives were not reporting their salaries for the Sunshine List.[4] he issue wasn't new: as far back as 2010, the NDP and Conservatives had been asking Matthews for disclosure of the salaries at ORNGE. Each time she said she would look into it.[5] This time, she pleaded ignorance: "It's not clear to me. I can't say that I have seen this arrangement before. I need some help understanding why some executives are not on the sunshine list." ORNGE responded that it only needed to disclose the salaries of its operations and maintenance staff, since the rest of the staff belonged to those separate private consulting firms, which conveniently included Mazza. Mazza was, presumably, having an out-of-body experience: he was the President and CEO of ORNGE but apparently didn't work there! Ten days later, the Auditor General announced its investigation.[6]

The scandal quickly went from bad to full-blown crisis. ORNGE was plagued with staffing issues: over 10 months there were a total of 237 occurrences where the ORNGE helicopters sat idle with pilots but without paramedics.[7] That equated to a total of 1300 hours the helicopters sat grounded without any paramedics; sometimes up to 28 hours straight before paramedics could be found. On August 18, 2011, when it came time for the ambulance to respond to a critically injured cyclist, it was delayed by 44 minutes, quite possibly costing the life of 21 year-old Lindsey Sanders. ORNGE said it would update its policies to reduce delays.' Sanders death was, arguably, a direct result of the McGuinty government's incompetence, just like the Liberals claimed Kimberley Rogers' death belonged to Mike Harris.

That same day, Mazza's salary was revealed to be a whopping $1.4 million per year – making him the highest paid civil servant in Ontario.[8] Auditors and insiders were beginning to reveal what was really going on at ORNGE: ORNGE's headquarters was dubbed "the crystal palace" by its employees for the lavish renovations and upgrades it undertook upon moving into its Mississauga office facility. Mazza took full advantage of his palace's amenities, all paid for with taxpayers' money, including his demand that he be brought an ice-cold smoothie at precisely 3:00pm while exercising in the Palace's executive gym. (There was a separate gym for executives and another for the lowly employees.) That same day, Mazza took "indefinite medical leave."

The scandal continued to grow. Mazza's girlfriend (who was also the Associate Vice President of ORNGE) and the ORNGE Chairman's daughter (who was also a junior ORNGE executive) had been hired by Mazza to work on a small "market research" binder that was presented to the Italian helicopter firm AgustaWestland. That binder cost $6.7 million, which was conveniently paid only weeks after ORNGE agreed to purchase 12 Agusta helicopters at a cost to taxpayers of $144 million.[9] Most of this multi-million dollar "report" was done using simple Google searches.[10]

Finally, on February 2, Mazza and two other executives were fired without severance pay.[11] It seemed the Liberals had finally learned something from their multiple dealings with public servants taking lavish bonuses and severance packages, although they could have wasted millions less in taxpayers' money if McGuinty and his Minister of Health had established and enforced the proper controls of ORNGE in the first place.

A month after Mazza was fired, the Ontario Provincial Police were called in to investigate the financial irregularities behind a $24 million loan against ORNGE's head office, which included $5.6 million that was paid out to former ORNGE officers.[12] One year into the investigation, the OPP said it could take until March 2014 to conclude the investigation and determine if charges could or would be laid.[13]

The Auditor General's Report

But while the police would take some time longer to investigate the criminal allegations, the Auditor General was able to conclude more quickly. The Auditor General had already been working on deciphering the complex web Mazza was attempting to weave in order to avoid being accountable.[14]

ORNGE's claim they did not need to disclose salaries since they were paid through private subsidiaries of ORNGE was false according to the Auditor General. He determined ORNGE's top five executives made a total of $2.5 million in 2010. ORNGE's six board members made a total of $643,000 in 2010-2011 as "retainers," with over $200,000 of that total going to just one board member. The Auditor General noted this "did not include reimbursement for any other expenses incurred by board members." Much of what ORNGE was doing simply "didn't pass the smell test," according to the Auditor.[15]

The Liberal Connection

Just like the multiple other McGuinty government scandals with eHealth, the Lottery and Gaming Corporation and the Power Authority, the fact remains that the ORNGE scandal is a question of competence, ethics, and proper oversight. The simple truth is that Health Minister Deb Matthews should have been fired on the spot when the story first broke of ORNGE's $1.4 million CEO salary going unreported, contrary to the law. Instead, both McGuinty and Wynne stood beside Matthews as her incompetence and responsibility in wasting millions of dollars of the public's money was exposed to the world without any punishment.

Perhaps a few Liberal sympathizers will complain the ORNGE operations had nothing to do with the Health Minister, and the McGuinty government was in no way connected to the ORNGE scandal. That isn't true. Like the eHealth scandal, the Liberal Party has direct ties to ORNGE: in January 2011, former Liberal Party President Alfred Apps sat down with ORNGE and Ministry of Health officials "to outline plans to create a for-profit division that would expand air ambulance services into new markets."[16] The Liberal Party was directly involved in the expansion plans of ORNGE; it is absurd to believe no one thought to ask about the legality of turning a division of a taxpayer-owned entity into numerous smaller for-profit private entities – supposedly without any input from the government. Apps, after all, was there to serve as legal advisor.

But the connections to the McGuinty government go deeper than the former Liberal President who served as legal counsel during a meeting. McGuinty personally met Mazza at a Liberal Party fundraiser after being introduced by Apps.[17] Over nine years of McGuinty government, law firm Fasken Martineau received $9.5 million for its services to ORNGE. Don Guy – McGuinty's former chief of staff, Liberal campaign manager in 2003, 2007, and 2011, and Working Families Coalition director – received a piece of that money. Guy was personally picked by Apps and paid just shy of $108,000 to "advise on the ORNGE file."[18] The *Toronto Star* called it "the gift that kept on giving," to the "Who's Who of the political-industrial complex."[19]

The Result

In June 2012, Mazza was issued a rarely-used Speaker's Warrant to compel him to appear before a committee and explain himself. In November 2013, Mazza reappeared in the public spotlight as a "temporary" doctor working at the Thunder Bay Regional Health Science Centre.[20] At the time of writing, Mazza was still employed at the Centre and is also the subject of an investigation by the Ontario College of Physicians and Surgeons.

The result of the ORNGE scandal is that – once again – Ontario taxpayers lost millions of dollars to public employees thanks to poor government oversight and control. There can only be so many government scandals, so many wastes of the public's money, so many transparent conflicts of interest and cases of blatant nepotism before we say enough is enough. People have died because of this Liberal government's incompetence. This was not just a story about a rogue public department not following government policies, but of a government that abjectly failed to implement the proper policies that would respect taxpayers' money and enforce those policies in the first place. Matthews' continuation as Health Minister when Premier Wynne took office shows that Wynne is satisfied with Matthews' work, including her oversight of the ORNGE file.

The Conservatives pressed the Liberal government on the ORNGE scandal for months. In fact, they were ready to spring a summer 2013 election over the Liberals' rampant abuse of taxpayers' money, among the other scandals up to that point thanks to the McGuinty and Wynne governments. But, in the final moments, Andrea Horwath's NDP sided with the Liberal government, passing that year's budget and killing Parliament for the summer.[21] Horwath's NDP stood with the McGuinty-Wynne Liberals to accept the ORNGE scandal and deny Ontarians the right to know more about it. The NDP accepted the building scandals as okay, and passed the budget; only the Conservatives opposed the budget and thought Ontarians deserved a bit of clarity and resolution as to how the ORNGE scandal began and how the Wynne government planned to end it.

Recruiting the youth vote... through deception

One of McGuinty's attempts to court the youth vote in the 2011 election was to promise a 30 percent rebate on post-secondary school tuition. "A 30% across-the-board postsecondary undergraduate tuition grant," promised the Liberal platform.[22] That's it, that's all - what student would not love such a promise? In an age where the youth unemployment rate is over 16 percent[23] and students constantly complain about not being able to find work after completing their degree, a government-funded reimbursement of 30 percent of tuition costs was a welcome promise. Considering the average annual cost of tuition in Ontario is $5,138 for university[24] and $2,400 for college,[25] that meant an average annual savings of $1,541 and $720 respectively. A university student could save over $6,000 on their four-year degree; a college student: over $2,100 on a three-year diploma.[26] What a great promise, so they thought. Young adults, usually the most likely demographic to avoid voting unless the issues specifically cater to their needs, turned out to vote for the guy who would put up to $6000 in their pockets if they voted for him.[27]

But wait! These naïve students did not read the fine print coming from a political party that had grown fond of promising one thing then doing another. The fine print released on the Ontario Student Assistance Plan (OSAP) website – months after the Liberals were re-elected – stated:

"You could be eligible for 30% off your student tuition if:

- You're a full-time student at a public college or university in Ontario
- It's been less than four years since you left high school
- You're in a program that you can apply to directly from high school
- Your parents' gross income is $160,000 or less"[28]

These were qualifications conveniently left out of the initial Liberal promise. McGuinty clearly left out that his promise would only apply to a select few students, at the expense of cancelling valuable government grants which benefitted all students. The *Toronto Star* broke the news that mature students (defined as students who have been out of high school for more than four years) were not eligible for the rebate.[29] Neither are part-time students, which is defined as any student taking less than 60 percent of a full course load. For thousands of parents, mature students, and people who needed to work after high school, this unnecessary and unfair exclusion bars them from having the Ontario government rebate their tuition as McGuinty promised they would.

You also must be attending college or university in Ontario, even though other student assistance rules state you must only be *residing* in Ontario to receive OSAP. Furthermore, graduate students are not eligible for this program. Considering their education is not one which can be applied for "directly from high school," and considering it takes more than four years after high school to enter a graduate program, some of Ontario's brightest and most educated students were abandoned by McGuinty's Liberals; students pursuing advanced education desperately needed in some fields were left in the cold, only after voting McGuinty back into power.

These ridiculous rules disqualify hundreds of thousands of students – over 100,000 mature students alone, according to the Ontario Undergraduates' Student Association[30] – but it gets one layer worse. This expensive $420 million program, which we now know only applies to a select few students, is going to be paid for by cancelling grants from which all students could benefit. The Textbook and Technology Grant; the Trust for Student Support; and the Queen Elizabeth II Aiming For the Top – grants and scholarships which aimed to help all students - were cancelled to pay for McGuinty's wasteful student rebate for the select few.[31] It was just another broken promise; just another example of the Liberals promising the world to a select group of society, then reversing that promise once being re-elected.

Unfulfilled Promises Continue

The Liberals were elected on a platform in 2003 that included promises to "introduce Internet voting and work to increase voter turnout by at least 10 percent." Eight years went by with absolutely no progress. It wasn't for a lack of cooperation: the Chief Electoral Officer of Ontario tabled a comprehensive report within the first year of McGuinty taking office.[32] That report advocates for further study into "non-paper" methods of voting, and compares the successes and challenges other governments have had around the world with studying or implementing internet voting. Yet the McGuinty government did nothing in over eight years to fulfill its campaign promise.

Furthermore, voter turnout has only plummeted under McGuinty's leadership. The 2011 election set a new record-low as the Liberals were re-elected with one seat shy of a majority and not even 50 percent of Ontario voters showed up to vote. In 2003, it was the McGuinty Liberals who complained the Eves government had no authority to lead since voter turnout had declined under that government. That was when the voter turnout had just dropped below 60 percent, so surely, using McGuinty's own logic, he had lost the authority to govern Ontario.

Harris evocations continue

But just because McGuinty had made no progress on his own agenda items did not mean his love affair with blaming things on Mike Harris or Ernie Eves had to stop. In 2012, then-Transportation Minister Bob Chiarelli blamed the tragic deaths of 10 people on Northern Ontario highways on Mike Harris' highway policies *from 1996!*[33]

Chiarelli's logic was incomplete and puzzling. *If* there were problems with the Conservatives' highway policies *from the 1990s,* then the McGuinty government had over two majority governments and 16 years to fix them! Harris' name was nothing more than a convenient excuse for an incompetent cabinet minister who either did not know or did not care enough to amend his own department's regulations – that is, assuming there were any issues with the Harris-era highway policies to begin with.

Abundant Perks Continue

The gravy train of Ontario public servants and hired contractors being paid lavishly for their work never ended just because McGuinty was in a minority government. Just three months after the 2011 election, the McGuinty government was caught giving several Toronto hospital executives $1 million severance packages, $75,000 travel allowances, and annual $100,000 pension top ups.[34] On top of this, many executives were given memberships to exclusive fitness and social clubs and offered tax preparation services. Once again, this was despite the McGuinty government's edict that salaries were frozen and perks such as gym memberships and social clubs were prohibited – even according to Health Minister Deb Matthews. What did the McGuinty Liberals do about it? Nothing!

Alcohol Price Raise

Not to worry about those lavish perks: they could be paid for by increasing taxes on alcohol! Celebrating (or mourning, depending on your perspective) the re-election of Dalton McGuinty's Liberals would cost you 6.7 percent more. Over the Christmas season, the McGuinty government raised taxes on alcohol, setting minimum prices on spirits, wine, and beer.[35] It was yet another tax hike from, you guessed it, the guy who promised only months earlier that his tax-raising days were done. Merry Christmas!

Ontario could cure world hunger in 3 short years

The McGuinty government's utter disrespect for taxpayers' money did not stop at giving hospital executives multi-million dollar perks or hiking alcohol prices at Christmas time. By the end of 2011, Ontario's debt reached a massive $257.9 billion.[36] On this amount Ontario pays a whopping $59 million in interest *per day.* Servicing our debt is now the third-most expensive budget item: behind only health care and education.

Just imagine if that money going towards interest – money going straight back to Ontario's creditors – could be used for something positive which benefits Ontario. Ontario's multi-billion dollar interest payments could be going towards community and social services, upgrading infrastructure, or further paying down the debt; all of these are provincial responsibilities that are taking a backseat while Ontario continues to spend more and more on debt servicing. Or what if that money could be used to serve the entire world? The United Nations has said world hunger could be cured for a minimal US$30 billion.[37] That's just shy of three years' worth of interest payments on the debt. Ontario could cure world hunger with its interest payments in just three short years! Surely that is a more noble example of how Ontarians' money could be used instead of experimenting with green energy or stuffing Liberal pockets with consulting contracts.

Other examples of what could be done with this money include eliminating half of the deficit; cutting income taxes by 44 percent; or reducing the HST by four percent. So why not get our debt repayments back on track and put our money towards something useful? At best Ontario could cure world hunger. At the very least, Ontario could pay down its debt and use the reduced interest payments to the benefit of Ontario residents by lowering taxes. Either way, this record-breaking debt requires that we do something to eliminate the tax imposed on future generations.

2012-2013 Budget "Consultations"

These are the ideas the Ontario government needs to hear if it wants to balance its books. I am not seriously considering that Ontario actually budget $30 billion towards curing world hunger. However, I am suggesting that each person needs to consider what Ontario is throwing away by choosing instead to spend massively on interest payments – and make their voices known to the Ontario government.

The Liberal government said they would be open and accountable by holding public consultations for the 2012-2013 budget. However, McGuinty reneged and instead gave the job to one consultant at the cost of $1,500 a day.[38] That consultant was Don Drummond – a puzzling choice considering that he was putting the final touches on the Drummond Report, which would be released at Queen's Park just weeks later. Why was McGuinty consulting an economist already working on distilling the cold truth about Ontario, and paying him to do the same thing again?

Millions for a Manitoba Museum?

January 2012 was a busy month for the McGuinty government. It had been barely three months since the last election and only days into the new year, and his government's scandals were beginning to come home to roost. To end that month it was revealed the McGuinty government was contributing $5 million to a Manitoba museum.[39] But there was no spending announcement – no press release from the Liberal government saying they were making this contribution to a museum in another province and the justification for doing so. Instead, it was discovered and reported on by the media, and only then did the government confirm that it was indeed investing $5 million into what would become the Canadian Museum for Human Rights.

It was a puzzling financial decision: at a time when the province was struggling with a $16 billion deficit, why was Ontario contributing *any* amount of money to another province's museum? The government reasoned Ontario students would visit there, thus making it a worthy investment for Ontario. However, the issue was not just that the Liberal government was sending $5 million to Winnipeg instead of spending that money at home. (And nothing against Winnipeg!) The real issue was that the McGuinty government attempted to cover up the amount being spent, and only admitted to it and later justified it after being exposed by the media. Yet again the McGuinty government was caught with their hand in the cookie jar, doling out the taxpayers' money to projects we never heard about or approved of – and we would have never known about it if it weren't for the media. Sadly, but not surprisingly, the total project cost for the museum has exploded out of control: over $351 million as of January 2012 when the total project was supposed to be $270 million.

The Future of Class Warfare: Public vs. Private Employees

Forget about the supposedly growing "rich-poor gap." True animosity will be driven by the growing public employee-private employee gap. Jealous neighbours who served in an honourable private sector career for their entire life are being continually eclipsed by their much younger and much wealthier public sector counterparts. The gap between public and private sectors wages and benefits has only grown under Dalton McGuinty and Kathleen Wynne's governments.

It used to be that the public sector's wages were significantly *lower* than the private sector because public employees were compensated by having a highly stable, reliable job in the government, whereas private sector employees were paid more because their jobs were more easily changed, moved, or eliminated. Somewhere in history, unions got involved and they drove wages and benefits through the roof while demanding the same job security terms as previously offered.

Even considering those McGuinty-ordered "wage freezes" that are frequently ignored, Ontario's public servants are incredibly well paid. The growing gap between public and private sector employees will drive an alarming wave of jealousy. Canadian Federation of Independent Business (CFIB) President Dan Kelly says he's concerned such "societal dislocation... will occur when private sector employees can't afford to retire at 65 but see their neighbours leaving the workforce at 57 and spending winters in Florida because they worked for the government."[40]

In its February 2013 Ontario Prosperity Initiative, the Fraser Institute found "on average, a 13.9 percent wage premium" for public sector employees "over their private sector counterparts."[41] Where it becomes even more alarming is when non-wage benefits are factored in: 76.5 percent of public employees have a registered pension plan, compared to only 26 percent of private sector employees. Furthermore, 97.3 percent of public employees have a defined benefit pension plan compared to only 53.5 percent of private employees.

Between 2007 and 2011, the average Ontario public sector worker retired at 60.7 years-old; the private sector worker at 62. Even during the recession and the much-vilified budget cutbacks, Ontario's public employees were still able to retire almost two years sooner than their private sector counterparts. In fact, even in the same recession period, more of Ontario's *private sector* employees lost their jobs (3.9 percent) compared to public employees (only 0.7 percent).

When better wages, fewer working hours, and lucrative non-wage benefits are factored in, an Ontario public servant is receiving a staggering 25 percent *more* than his or her private sector equivalent. The private sector simply can't keep up: it cannot increase the wage of a $40,000 employee to $50,000 just so it can remain competitive with the public sector – unless it eliminates other jobs to pay for the raise, or raises prices. It is simply impossible for the private sector to compete with the public sector when the public sector has free access and a monopoly to use taxpayers' money as they please.

Liars

Public service used to be about public service, not getting rich off the tax-payers' dime. Somewhere along the line, unions and special interests were given the powerful keys to threaten strikes and walk-outs whenever they didn't get their way. Such special access was given long before Dalton Mc-Guinty or Kathleen Wynne ever took office, but their governments have only exacerbated the divide between public and private employees. Public sector unions need to be outlawed if the government is to be allowed to govern without interference.

A Broken Government

The McGuinty Liberals were barely done their first quarter as a minor-ity government before Hudak's Conservatives and Horwath's NDP began making demands in exchange for their support of the 2012-2013 budget with its $9.2 billion deficit. For six months, McGuinty made some effort to work with the Opposition parties, usually the NDP, but that song-and-dance quickly got old. One apt and succinct observation said McGuinty's minority government had completely fallen apart, "resembl[ing] an aging, wonky, virus-infested computer, unable to take commands or perform even the simplest tasks without aggravating delays and strange hiccups."[42]

The PCs said there was no way they could support the budget, while the NDP said their support could be bought by increasing funding for child care and the Ontario Disability Support Program.[43] McGuinty agreed, so Hor-wath went further: she also wanted to hike taxes on the rich; invest more in home and community care; create a $250 million job creation tax credit; keep Ontario Northland as a public company; and subsidize "industries affected by the budget," specifically horse racing and tourism. McGuinty refused. In the end, the NDP abstained from voting and the Conservatives voted against it – allowing the budget to pass.[44]

The Deal of a Lifetime

All of this politicking and compromise was hard work for a Premier who spent eight years getting his way and answering to no one. Ontario voters left him just one seat shy of being able to return to his majority govern-ment, where the Opposition could kick and scream all they wanted but Mc-Guinty could still run things the way he pleased. In April 2012 McGuinty made his move: he made Elizabeth Witmer, the veteran Ontario PC MPP for Kitchener-Waterloo and former Deputy Premier, an offer she could not refuse. Witmer was appointed Chair of the Workplace Safety Insurance Board (WSIB), resigning as an MPP.[45] It was a $68,000 pay raise for the 65 year-old Witmer, and for McGuinty, a suddenly vacant seat could now be won in a byelection. With the other timely resignation of Vaughan Liberal

MPP Greg Sorbara, McGuinty was suddenly within reach of regaining his coveted majority.

As Premier, McGuinty could set the byelection date for the most opportunistic time of his choosing. He picked September 6, just two days after the Labour Day long weekend and the same week kids were returning to school. Voter turnout was unsurprising, at only 50.53 percent in Kitchener-Waterloo and a dismal 32 percent in Vaughan. Unfortunately McGuinty's plan failed: the safe Liberal seat in Vaughan remained, but Kitchener-Waterloo swung from Witmer's Conservatives to the NDP's Catherine Fife. McGuinty was still one seat short of his majority.[46]

Betraying Core Supporters

His minority government still as it was, McGuinty should have proceeded with the most careful and cautious agenda possible. Instead, McGuinty clumsily trudged along, not only forgetting that he was beholden to the Ontario legislature, but also disrespecting his core Liberal supporters: doctors and teachers.

In an effort to get them to play ball in a collective bargaining negotiation, McGuinty slashed 37 doctors' fees from Ontario health insurance coverage to save $338 million, meaning doctors would either have to live without collecting those fees or charge them to patients. The Ontario Medical Association was furious. President Doug Weir said the McGuinty government was "stomp[ing] on the rights of physicians" by using "a heavy-handed approach" to interfere with collective bargaining.[47] The OMA threatened to take the Ontario government to court, saying the cuts were really about pushing the doctors to make a deal with the government to accept lower wages.[48]

Then came the teachers. Throughout the summer the Liberal government had been attempting to negotiate new teachers' contracts with their unions. In July, Catholic school teachers reached a deal with the government, agreeing to a wage freeze, but others held out.[49] In an effort to speed up the bargaining process, the McGuinty government introduced Bill 115, the *Putting Students First Act,* which, among other policies, imposed a two-year wage freeze, a 1.5 percent pay cut by giving three unpaid professional development days (welcome back, Rae Days!), and restructured the terms of collective bargaining with the teachers so the terms and their legality could never be questioned in any court.

The bill quickly passed and received Royal Assent on September 11, 2012, with McGuinty saying it would save the province $2 billion and prevent $473 million in spending.[50] Needless to say, Ontario's teachers, those unionized and traditional Liberal supporters who had defended McGuinty for the past eight years, were furious. The teachers were used to a *quid pro quo* arrangement, where they supported McGuinty during election time in exchange for his support during bargaining time. They were blindsided. They organized a work-to-rule strike in which they refused to participate in any extra-curricular activities: environmental clubs, track and field, and sports clubs were all shutdown as teachers refused to participate in anything beyond the bare minimum conditions of their contract.[51] McGuinty had angered his base and he would pay for it: Elementary Teachers' Federation of Ontario President Sam Hammond said they were "outraged" and "betrayed" by McGuinty's government, and found it appalling that McGuinty had styled himself as "the education premier" yet proceeded to treat teachers in such a disrespectful fashion.[52]

A Tired Premier

By the time the fall arrived, McGuinty had been the MPP for Ottawa South for 22 years, the leader of the Ontario Liberal Party for 16 years, and the Premier of Ontario for nine years. Not even one year into his minority government, McGuinty simply could not adapt to having to work with the Opposition parties: he was used to having it his way, where he could abuse the public purse as he pleased in order to keep his Liberal supporters happy. Whenever something went wrong, he used to be able to pay one of his Liberal friends to "consult" on the issue and report back. Now, the Opposition controlled the agenda.

McGuinty had become so scandalized and so unwelcome throughout his nine years in power that his promises became sore jokes – he simply could not be taken seriously any longer. He promised not to raise taxes several times – and did anyway. His government gave lavish salary and bonus increases to public servants who were supposedly under a "wage freeze." They promised to balance the budget and pay down the debt. They said they would stop school closures – they didn't. They promised to govern "with honesty and integrity" –except, apparently, when there was money to be made by a Liberal "consultant" or "advisor" at eHealth, ORNGE, OLG, or OPA.[53] The summer, normally a relatively quiet time for politics, was filled with criticisms and questions surrounding his handling of the doctors' and teachers' portfolios.

In a September 2012 AngusReid poll, only 32 percent of Ontarians felt he was doing a good job, compared to 60 percent who thought he was not.[54] He was among the least popular Canadian Premiers, with only British Columbia's Liberal Christy Clark and Nova Scotia's New Democrat Darrell Dexter faring worse. That was followed by a September 28 Forum

Research poll that found only one in five voters intended on voting for McGuinty; they were either looking for tax breaks and siding with the Conservatives, or looking for better public services and siding with the NDP.[55]

On October 2, the NDP and Conservatives passed a motion at committee to hold Energy Minister Chris Bentley in contempt of Parliament for the Liberals' 2011 election decision to cancel the Oakville and Mississauga gas plants.[56] That motion meant Bentley would have to explain the government's actions to the finance committee before a vote would be taken in the legislature. The result of that unprecedented vote could have meant jail time for Bentley.[57]

On October 15, McGuinty called it quits, surprising everyone – even his own cabinet – announcing he was proroguing the legislature (thus killing the possibility of Bentley going to jail), resigning as Premier, and vacating his Ottawa South seat for an upcoming byelection. His stated reason was "it's time for renewal... it's time for the next set of ideas."[58] On his way out, he said Ontario's priorities would remain the economy and negotiating the public sector wage freeze, oblivious to the fact that the legislature would have to sit to actually work on those priorities. Ontario PC leader Tim Hudak said McGuinty should reconsider the decision to prorogue, saying there was still important work to be done.

Of course, the real reason for the prorogation was to give the Ontario Liberal Party a chance to hold a fast-and-furious leadership race and (hopefully) return to Queens Park, able to distance themselves from McGuinty's track record. NDP leader Andrea Horwath put it best: "the people who make this province work every day sent us here to do a job. That work shouldn't stop while the Liberal Party focuses on their leadership race."[59]

The prorogation eliminated any possibility of the Liberals being held accountable for the never-ending gas plant scandal, and it also prevented Ontario teachers, still angry and on rotating strikes as a result of Bill 115, from being able to seek any clarification or direction from the provincial government. Instead, they were left to hash out deals in private with public servants.

Even members of the left were upset and confused that their buddy and pal McGuinty was leaving. The *Toronto Star's* Rick Salutin lamented that the left-wing's golden ticket (McGuinty) "trashed" all he supposedly stood for: education and good government.[60] McGuinty had "torpedoed" all he stood for, both in his personal legacy and in what he and his government stood for. Laughably, however, Salutin said McGuinty had be-

Liars

come too *right-wing* on the advice of an American Barack Obama campaign consultant, when McGuinty had actually spent most of his time as a minority government pandering to the NDP.

The End of an Era

McGuinty's resignation as the Liberal Premier was the end of an era. McGuinty was off to join failed federal Liberal leader Michael Ignatieff as a senior fellow at Harvard University.

The McGuinty legacy was nothing any person or political party should be proud of. In an Innovative Research Poll, almost one quarter of the province – 23 percent – said Dalton McGuinty had made things "a lot worse" for people in Ontario.[61] This was compared to only three percent who said he made it "much better," the 21 percent who said McGuinty's Premiership made "no difference," and the 20 percent who said it was "somewhat worse." Interestingly, even 34 percent of Liberal supporters polled said the McGuinty government made no difference or made the province slightly or much worse. Obviously, these are the friendliest numbers compared to the responses from NDP and Ontario PC voters. Those few who said McGuinty made Ontario better said he did so by generally doing a "good job" by improving finances, the economy, health care, education, and environmental and energy programs. The overwhelming group who said McGuinty made Ontario worse said he did so by making the economy and employment worse; by not handling education well; by raising taxes; by increasing the deficit and spending recklessly; by being dishonest; and generally doing a bad job.

A month after McGuinty took office in 2003, his approval rating was a dismal nine percent. No one thought it could get any worse, but it did, with only *three* percent of Ontarians believing McGuinty made the province much better when he left office nine years later. When over one third of his own Liberal Party believed he was either doing nothing or making the province worse, it was a clear sign it was time for McGuinty to go.

Finally, after nine years of McGuinty rule in Queen's Park, a new leader would be chosen by the Ontario Liberal Party. This leader had the opportunity to set himself or herself apart from the McGuinty legacy, and choose to set Ontario back on track. This new Premier could undo McGuinty's hijacking and set the right policies in motion that would bring Ontario back to its former prosperity. Would the Liberals elect the leader who could do it?

1   Stephen Skyvington, "Mr. McGuinty: it's time to go," *The Kingston Whig*, last modified October 5, 2012, http://www.thewhig.com/2012/10/05/mr-mcguinty-its-time-to-go.

2   "Liberals have lost the moral authority to govern," *Northumberland View*, last modified May 1, 2013, http://www.northumberlandview.ca/index.php?module=news&type=user&func=display&sid=22012.

3   "Dalton McGuinty unveils Ontario cabinet: Premier pledges to work with other parties," *Huffington Post*, last modified October 20, 2011, http://www.huffingtonpost.ca/2011/10/20/ndp-disappointed-with-lack-of-change-dalton-mcguinty-unveils-new-ontario-cabiner_n_1021877.html.

4   Kevin Donovan, "Executive pay kept secret at airlift service," *Toronto Star*, last modified December 5, 2011, http://www.thestar.com/news/gta/2011/12/05/executive_pay_kept_secret_at_airlift_service.html.

5   Kevin Donovan, "Ontario auditor to dig deeper into air ambulance executive salaries," *Toronto Star*, last modified December 15, 2011, http://www.thestar.com/news/canada/2011/12/15/ontario_auditor_to_dig_deeper_into_air_ambulance_executive_salaries.html.

6   Donovan, "Ontario auditor to dig deeper…"

7   Kevin Donovan, "Shortage of paramedics leave ORNGE helicopters idle," *Toronto Star*, last modified December 20, 2011, http://www.thestar.com/news/canada/2011/12/20/shortage_of_paramedics_leaves_ornge_helicopter_idle.html.

8   Kevin Donovan, "ORNGE president was paid $1.4 million per year," *Toronto Star*, last modified December 22, 2011, http://www.thestar.com/news/canada/2011/12/22/ornge_president_was_paid_14_million_per_year.html.

9   "Girlfriend, daughter of ORNGE brass headed $6.7 million project, *TorStar News Service*, last modified April 25, 2012, http://metronews.ca/news/canada/118214/girlfriend-daughter-of-ornge-brass-headed-6-7m-project/.

10   Kevin Donovan, *ORNGE Exec's Girlfriend, Daughter did $6.7 Million Report Using Google*, Toronto Star, April 25, 2012, http://www.thestar.com/news/canada/2012/04/25/ornge_execs_girlfriend_daughter_did_67million_report_using_google.html

11   Kevin Donovan, "ORNGE founder Chris Mazza terminated," *Toronto Star*, last modified February 2, 2012, http://www.thestar.com/news/canada/2012/02/02/ornge_founder_chris_mazza_terminated.html.

12   Jacquie McNish and Karen Howlett, "OPP in the hunt for Ornge's missing millions," *Globe and Mail*, last modified March 13, 2012, http://www.theglobeandmail.com/news/politics/opp-in-the-hunt-for-ornges-missing-millions/article534709/.

13   "ORNGE investigation may take another year, says OPP," *CBC News*, last modified March 20, 2013, http://www.cbc.ca/news/canada/toronto/ornge-investigation-may-take-another-year-says-opp-1.1353565

14   Office of the Auditor General of Ontario, Special Report: Ornge Air Ambulance and Related Services, March 2012, http://www.auditor.on.ca/en/reports_en/ornge_web_en.pdf

15   Christina Blizzard, Disgraced ex-Ornge CEO Chris Mazza Lands ER Job in Thunder Bay, Toronto Sun, last modified November 26, 2013, http://www.torontosun.com/2013/11/26/disgraced-ex-ornge-ceo-chris-mazza-lands-er-job-in-thunder-bay

16   Jacquie McNish and Karen Howlett, supra note 13.

17   Karen Howlett, Ornge Founder Chris Mazza to Testify at Government Committee, *Globe and Mail*, last modified July 17, 2012, http://www.theglobeandmail.com/news/politics/ornge-founder-chris-mazza-to-testify-at-government-committee/article4424380/

18   Antonella Artuso, Ornge Paid Millions to Prominent Consultants, Toronto Sun, last modified April 25, 2012, http://www.torontosun.com/2012/04/25/ornge-paid-millions-to-prominent-consultants

19   Martin Cohn, Ornge Mess a Sorry Tale of Bad Judgement, Human Error, Toronto Star, last modified April 25, 2012, http://www.thestar.com/news/canada/2012/04/25/cohn_ornge_mess_a_sorry_tale_of_bad_judgment_human_error.html

20   "Ex-CEO Chris Mazza should be in jail, not ER, says MPP," *Toronto Star*, last modified November 26, 2013, http://www.thestar.com/news/queenspark/2013/11/26/tories_say_chris_mazza_should_be_in_

Liars

jail_not_working_in_hospital_er.html.

21 "Ontario NDP vote to pass budget, avoiding election, *CBC News*, last modified June 11, 2013, http://www.cbc.ca/news/canada/toronto/ontario-ndp-vote-to-pass-budget-avoiding-election-1.1327190

22 Ontario Liberal Party, Forward together, http://issuu.com/ontarioliberalparty/docs/the_ontario_liberal_plan__2011_2015.

23 "Ontario's youth unemployment among worst in Canada," *CBC News*, last modified September 30, 2013, http://www.cbc.ca/news/canada/kitchener-waterloo/ontario-s-youth-unemployment-among-worst-in-canada-1.1872206.

24 "University tuition fees," *Statistics Canada*, last modified 2011, http://www.statcan.gc.ca/daily-quotidien/100916/dq100916a-eng.htm.

25 "Paying for college: tuition and financial assistance," *Ontario Colleges*, http://www.ontariocolleges.ca/ontcol/home/confirm/money-matters/tuition-fees.html.

26 Rebates were capped at $1,600 per year for university students and $730 per year for college students.

27 Marion Menard, "Youth voter turnout in Canada – reasons for the decline and efforts to increase participation," *Parliament of Canada*, last modified April 20, 2010, http://www.parl.gc.ca/content/lop/researchpublications/2010-21-e.htm.

28 "30 percent off Ontario tuition," *Government of Ontario*, last modified 2013, http://www.ontario.ca/education-and-training/30-off-ontario-tuition.

29 Louise Brown, "Older students not eligible for Ontario tuition rebate," *Toronto Star*, last modified January 15, 2012, http://www.thestar.com/news/ontario/2012/01/15/older_students_not_eligible_for_ontario_tuition_rebate.html.

30 Brown, "Older students not eligible…"

31 James Bradshaw, "Tuition rebate to be funded by cutting expenditures, Ontario says," *Globe and Mail*, last modified January 5, 2012, http://www.theglobeandmail.com/news/national/education/universitynews/tuition-rebate-to-be-funded-by-cutting-expenditures-ontario-says/article2292979/.

32 "Access, integrity, and participation: towards responsive electoral processes for Ontario," *Elections Ontario*, September 2004, http://www.elections.on.ca/NR/rdonlyres/063715FC-A692-4473-A756-CC43663D27F0/0/election_report_2003_en.pdf.

33 "Liberals still blaming Harris," *Toronto Sun*, last modified January 13, 2012, http://www.torontosun.com/2012/01/13/liberals-still-blaming-harris.

34 Megan Ogilvie and Laura Stone, "Generous perks given to Ontario hospital executives, contracts reveal," *Toronto Star*, last modified January 4, 2012, http://www.thestar.com/news/gta/2012/01/04/generous_perks_given_to_ontario_hospital_executives_contracts_reveal.html.

35 Antonella Artuso and Jonathan Jenkins, "Tough news to swallow – booze prices to rise," *Toronto Sun*, last modified January 13, 2012, http://www.torontosun.com/2012/01/13/tough-news-to-swallow--booze-prices-to-rise.

36 "Ontario Debt Backgrounder," *Canadian Taxpayers Federation*, 2011, https://www.taxpayer.com/media/OntarioDebt_Backgrounder.pdf.

37 Food and Agriculture Organization, "The world only needs $30 billion to eradicate the scourge of world hunger," *United Nations*, last modified June 3, 2008, http://www.fao.org/newsroom/en/news/2008/1000853/index.html.

38 "That's no way to run a government Premier," *Toronto Sun*, last modified January 24, 2012, http://www.torontosun.com/2012/01/24/thats-no-way-to-run-a-government-premier.

39 Antonella Artuso, "Ontario puts $5 million toward Winnipeg museum," *Toronto Sun*, last modified January 25, 2012, http://www.torontosun.com/2012/01/25/ontario-pays-5-for-winnipeg-museum.

40 Sue-Ann Levy, "Private, public sector wage gap growing," *Winnipeg Sun*, last modified February 10, 2014, http://www.sunnewsnetwork.ca/sunnews/straighttalk/archives/2014/02/20140210-082600.html.

41 Amela Karabegović, Milagros Palacios, and Jason Clemens, *Comparing Public and Private Sector*

Compensation in Ontario, Fraser Institute, February 2013, http://www.fraserinstitute.org/uploadedFiles/fraser-ca/Content/research-news/research/publications/comparing-public-and-private-sector-compensation-in-ontario.pdf.

42   Kelly McParland, "Kathleen Wynne packs her Ontario team with rookies and rivals," *National Post*, last modified February 11, 2013, http://fullcomment.nationalpost.com/2013/02/11/kelly-mcparland-kathleen-wynne-packs-her-ontario-team-with-rookies-and-rivals/.

43   "Ontario budget 2012: Liberals agree to NDP demands on child care, disability support," *Huffington Post Canada*, last modified April 20, 2012, http://www.huffingtonpost.ca/2012/04/20/ontario-budget-2012-mcguinty-ndp-deal_n_1441653.html.

44   "Ontario snap election avoided as budget passes," *Student Vote Canada*, last modified June 20, 2012, http://studentvote.ca/news/2012/06/20/updated-ontario-snap-election-avoided-as-budget-passes/.

45   Robert Benzie and Rob Ferguson, "MPP Elizabeth Witmer leaves Tories for WSIB post," *Toronto Star*, last modified April 27, 2012, http://www.thestar.com/news/canada/2012/04/27/mpp_elizabeth_witmer_leaves_tories_for_wsib_post.html.

46   "Ontario Liberals fall one seat shy of majority after byelections," *CBC News*, last modified September 6, 2012, http://www.cbc.ca/news/canada/toronto/ontario-liberals-fall-1-seat-shy-of-majority-after-byelections-1.1247773.

47   Rob Ferguson, "OMA threatens to take provincial government to court," *Toronto Star*, last modified June 12, 2012, http://www.thestar.com/news/canada/2012/06/12/oma_threatens_to_take_provincial_government_to_court.html.

48   Ferguson, "OMA threatens…"

49   Kristin Rushowy and Robert Benzie, "Ontario Catholic teachers reach deal with provinces, agree to wage freeze," *Toronto Star*, last modified July 5, 2012, http://www.thestar.com/news/canada/2012/07/05/ontario_catholic_teachers_reach_deal_with_province_agree_to_wage_freeze.html.

50   "Putting Students First Act," Ontario Ministry of Education, , last modified August 27, 2012, http://www.edu.gov.on.ca/eng/document/nr/12.08/bg0827.html.

51   Louise Brown and Megan Ogilvie, "Ontario teachers' boycott of after-school programs creates confusion," *Toronto Star*, last modified September 11, 2012, http://www.thestar.com/yourtoronto/education/2012/09/11/ontario_teachers_boycott_of_afterschool_programs_creates_confusion.html.

52   "Wage freeze bill for teachers passes in Ontario Legislature," *CBC News*, last modified September 11, 2012, http://www.cbc.ca/news/canada/toronto/wage-freeze-bill-for-teachers-passes-in-ontario-legislature-1.1150207.

53   Christina Blizzard, "10-year anniversary of Ontario Liberals' broken promises," *Toronto Sun*, last modified October 1, 2013, http://www.sunnewsnetwork.ca/sunnews/straighttalk/archives/2013/10/20131001-183330.html.

54   Alex Boutilier, "Dalton McGuinty among the least popular Premiers in Canada: poll," *Metro News*, last modified September 10, 2012, http://metronews.ca/news/ottawa/364540/dalton-mcguinty-among-the-least-popular-remiers-in-canada-poll/.

55   Robert Benzie, "Ontario Liberals' support slumping, poll finds," *Toronto Star*, last modified September 27, 2012, http://www.thestar.com/news/canada/2012/09/27/ontario_liberals_support_slumping_poll_finds.html.

56   Jonathan Jenkins, "Contempt motion against energy minister Chris Bentley passes key vote," *Toronto Sun*, last modified October 2, 2012, http://www.torontosun.com/2012/10/02/contempt-motion-against-energy-minister-chris-bentley-passes-key-vote.

57   Robert Benzie and Rob Ferguson, "Chris Bentley could face jail time if found in contempt of Parliament," *Toronto Star*, last modified October 2, 2012, http://www.thestar.com/news/canada/2012/10/02/chris_bentley_could_face_jail_if_found_in_contempt_of_parliament.html.

58   "Ontario's McGuinty surprises with resignation, prorogation," *CBC News*, last modified October 15, 2012, http://www.cbc.ca/news/canada/toronto/ontario-s-mcguinty-surprises-with-resignation-prorogation-1.1156014.

59   "Ontario's McGuinty surprises…" *CBC News*.

Liars

60   Rick Salutin, "Premier Dalton McGuinty disappears into mystery," *Toronto Star*, last modified December 20, 2012, http://www.thestar.com/opinion/editorialopinion/2012/12/20/salutin_premier_dalton_mcguinty_disappears_into_mystery.html.

61   *Provincial Liberal leadership*, Innovative Research Group, October 17-22, 2012, http://www.innovativeresearch.ca/sites/default/files/pdf%2C%20doc%2C%20docx%2C%20jpg%2C%20png%2C%20xls%2C%20xlsx/OTM1210%20-%20In-Depth%20-%20vFINAL2.pdf.

Chapter 10

The Wynne Years – More of the Same

"New **revenue tools** to pay for upgrades to public transit in the Toronto-Hamilton corridor are just one of the policy ideas being debated by about 500 Liberals at a provincial council meeting this weekend, the first get-together since Wynne took over as premier last January."

CTV News[1]

"The premier's role, from signing the cabinet document (to cancel the Oakville plant) to her decisions as (Liberal) campaign chair, has finally caught up with her and the trail of bread crumbs led the OPP right to the premier's door. We're at the point where it takes a team of OPP officers with crowbars just to pry these secrets out of your scandal-plagued government."

-Conservative MPP Rob Leone speaking to Premier Kathleen Wynne regarding her involvement in the cancelled gas plants[2]

"Kathleen Wynne and the Liberals have lost the moral authority to govern."

Toronto Sun[3]

The fall of an empire, or more of the same?

For nearly a decade, Dalton McGuinty's Liberal government hijacked Ontario from its prosperous path and put us on a dangerous course to massive debt, deficits, expensive green energy experiments, numerous scandals and abuses of taxpayers' money, and reckless new taxes on everything at every corner. With the Liberal scandals mounting and the Ontario Provincial Police investigating the Premier's Office like the potential crime scene it was, McGuinty saw it a convenient time to call it quits and flee the country, joining fellow failed Liberal leader Michael Ignatieff as a professor at Harvard University in the United States.[4] Good riddance. As the senior fellow at the Weatherhead Centre for International Affairs, McGuinty specializes in "the re-emergence of manufacturing in Ontario and the Great Lake states post-recession." His phone number and email address are publicly available.[5]

Dalton McGuinty's departure was an opportune time for the Liberal Party. The Liberals would be the only ones voting to choose a new Premier for Ontario – Ontario citizens would have no say – so the Liberals had a great opportunity to elect a new leader and put a fresh face on their tired party and government. They had a chance to right all the wrongs of the McGuinty government and rebuild the Liberal government as one that would govern for all people, keep unions in their place, keep partisan Liberal hacks out of lucrative "consulting" jobs, and get to the bottom of the numerous scandals that plagued most of McGuinty's time in office.

The Race

With the leadership election set for January 26, 2013, candidates had barely three months to campaign to replace McGuinty as Liberal leader and become the next Premier.

A total of six candidates entered the race: Kathleen Wynne, Sandra Pupatello, Charles Sousa, Gerard Kennedy, Eric Hoskins, and Harinder Takhar. (Glen Murray, MPP for Toronto Centre, was the first to announce his campaign on November 4, but withdrew on January 10, 2013 and endorsed Wynne.)

Early opinion polling of all Canadians was in favour of the "big names" in Ontario politics. An Innovative Research Group poll conducted October 17-22, starting two days after Dalton McGuinty resigned, failed to show any significant preference for one person or another. Those with the biggest names were the "best recognized" but also carried the "most baggage," Innovative Research Group stated.[6] The best recognized was David McGuinty, Dalton's brother and the federal MP for Ottawa South, but he had just lashed out at Alberta MPs, telling them to "go home" because they "didn't belong" in Canada's national legislature. Twenty three percent of those interviewed said they "were a lot less likely" to vote for an Ontario

Liberal Party with him as leader. Sixteen percent said the same for Dwight Duncan, 17 percent for Deb Matthews, and 15 percent for Chris Bentley.

Enter Kathleen Wynne

Kathleen Wynne was among the top contenders, but regularly swapped places with Pupatello for second place while Kennedy remained the front-runner. A total of 1857 delegates attended the leadership election at Maple Leaf Gardens in Toronto, and on the third ballot they elected Kathleen Wynne over Sandra Pupatello with 57 percent of the vote. Three weeks later, Wynne was sworn in by the Lieutenant Governor in as Ontario's 25th Premier, the first female Premier, and the first openly gay Premier. As Ontario would quickly find out, just like Dalton McGuinty, Kathleen Wynne was also a fan of setting record firsts.

Business As Usual

Kathleen Wynne had the perfect opportunity to set herself apart from the scandal-plagued McGuinty government days. Of course, they were from the same Liberal Party, Wynne was a McGuinty cabinet minister, and Wynne was McGuinty's 2011 election campaign chair – the one who personally signed off on the $1.1 billion decision to cancel the gas plants – but it was the perfect moment and setting for Wynne to set herself apart from the McGuinty.

Instead, Wynne showed it was business as usual. The *National Post* noted over half of Wynne's first cabinet were "rookies and rivals."[7] Charles Sousa, who dropped off the leadership ballot after the second vote and endorsed Wynne, was given one of the most important roles considering Ontario's struggling economy as Minister of Finance. The *National Post* noted three of Wynne's new ministers had only just been elected as MPPs less than a year ago (Teresa Piruzza, Michael Coutu, and Tracy MacCharles).[8's] The Ontario Liberal Party President became Minister of Labour, another important cabinet post considering the provincial government's attempts to rein in public sector unions and the damage McGuinty did to the doctors and teachers on his way out.

Eric Hoskins, another leadership contestant, was named Wynne's Minister of Economic Development and Trade Minister. Glen Murray, who dropped out of the leadership race before the elections, became Minister of Transportation and Infrastructure. Harinder Takhar, who dropped out after the first ballot and endorsed Sandra Pupatello, was given two jobs: Minister of Government Services and Chair of the cabinet management board. In fact, the only Liberal leadership contestants who *didn't* get a cabinet post were

Liars

Wynne's main challengers, Pupatello and Gerard Kennedy, who is currently without a seat in any legislature despite being a popular provincial and federal Liberal leadership contender. Wynne reportedly offered the Minister of Finance job to Pupatello, but she refused and returned to working on Toronto's Bay Street. Wynne demoted Laurel Broten, the McGuinty education minister who took over when Wynne left the ministry and who was partially responsible for the government's controversial sex education reforms.[9] (A few months later, Broten resigned.)

The Mass Exodus

Just two weeks after Wynne became leader, three cabinet ministers resigned within 24 hours of each other. First was Dwight Duncan, McGuinty's right-hand man throughout most of his years in office as his Finance Minister. Duncan said he was leaving politics for a job on Bay Street, but would not say where.[10] (He's a Senior Strategic Advisor at MacMillan LLP, a law firm specializing in investment and financial laws.[11]) Next was Rick Bartolucci, the Minister of Northern Development and Mines, who took the same line as McGuinty, saying Wynne "needs a new team to lead the government."[12] Third was Chris Bentley, rivaling Duncan for the most disgraced of the three, as the Energy Minister who oversaw the partisan $1.1 billion decision to cancel the gas plants in Oakville and Mississauga. Bentley refused to say he was leaving because of the scandal, which included the potential of criminal charges and, instead, said he wanted to spend more time with his wife and daughters.[13]

OLG Gets Caught – For the Third Time

Kathleen Wynne would quickly have to begin damage control of a resurgent McGuinty scandal as the Ontario Lottery and Gaming (OLG) Corporation was caught a third time for its unacceptable practices. Between 2010 and 2012, wages for the 10 highest-paid OLG executives were increased by 49 percent – from $2.4 million to $3.6 million.[14] This– once again – despite the fact that the McGuinty government had ordered a wage freeze. President and CEO Rod Phillips made almost $673,000 in 2012, including a $298,000 bonus. Compare that to the British Columbia lottery boss, who made less than half of what Phillips did and received a $40,000 bonus; and the Quebec lottery boss who also made less than half, and only received a $21,000 bonus. Could the McGuinty government not be bothered to control its employees who broke the rules? Or did they assume some pay increases would be fine as long as they weren't made public? Why, after all, did it take nearly four years for Ontarians to learn about what the OLG bosses paid themselves *in 2010?* Once again it was up to the media to tell Ontarians what the Liberals didn't want them to know.

Those are just a few of the questions that need to be answered in an Auditor General's report that is being written but has not yet been released at the time of writing. It promises to ruffle more than a few feathers if it's anything like the 2010 report - especially considering that Phillips was dismissed as President and CEO in May 2013.[15]

The Wynne Legacy is McGuinty's Legacy

Since naming her cabinet in February 2013, Wynne's government has done nothing to set itself apart from the McGuinty legacy. The byelections that took place in August 2013 to replace the mass exodus of cabinet ministers only reaffirmed that the Liberals under Wynne had the same stale taste as the Liberals under McGuinty.[16] Wynne touted that it was her "job" to create more jobs in the same month Statistics Canada announced that Ontario had *lost* 60,200 jobs.[17] It was a tacit admission by Wynne herself that she wasn't doing her job – and the residents of five ridings knew it.

Of the five seats being decided – Scarborough-Guildwood, Etobicoke-Lakeshore, Ottawa South, Windsor-Tecumseh, and London West – *three of them* were lost by the Liberals. Broten, Duncan, and Bentley – the major players in the McGuinty government who personally wore so many of the scandals described in this book – were replaced by one Conservative and two New Democrats. The Liberals held onto Ottawa South, McGuinty's former seat, oddly enough by running McGuinty's right hand constituency aide, John Fraser – the guy who was there to sell every lie, every policy decision, and every deleted gas plant email to Ottawa South residents – as a candidate.[18] (As a resident of Ottawa South, I'm still trying to figure this out.) The Liberals also held onto Scarborough-Guildwood, but only narrowly, losing 13.1 percentage points while the Conservatives and NDP gained 2.14 and 8.95 respectively.

No, Wynne Can't Run the Economy

Wynne followed up her resounding rejection in the byelections and admission she wasn't doing her job with an article for the *Huffington Post,* where she proudly declared "Yes, I'm a woman who can manage the economy."[19] Reality, unfortunately, is not on Wynne's side, and being a woman does not change that.

Wynne proudly flaunted that she was Ontario's first gay female Premier. But she went beyond the absurd when she created her own controversy, saying she was surrounded by naysayers who insisted a gay female could not run the economy:

Liars

> We have to shatter the myths put forward by experts, strategists, consultants and talking heads - those who say *they* know who can win and how.

> [...] those people did not think *I* could win. Right from day one, they didn't want me. I wanted to run in my home riding, Don Valley West. Because I am gay, these experts did not think I could win in North Toronto. They wanted me to run in a more "downtown" riding. These same people will tell women that they need a lot of money, or a certain background, or the right connections. That they should cede the way to a "star candidate."[20]

Several questions arise about Wynne's pessimistic advisors. Firstly, who exactly gave her such a grim outlook? Who were these "experts, strategists, and consultants"? Were these Liberal staffers giving Wynne such advice? What was their hesitation in supporting their future boss? Perhaps most importantly of all, why was the future Liberal leader surrounding herself with such advisors and purported professionals? And what was missing from Wynne's empty declaration that she could manage the economy? Any policies lowering debt or taxes, killing those expensive McGuinty-era energy experiments, encouraging small businesses to start up, or helping to expand the large businesses that offer thousands of jobs to Ontario workers.

The True Cost of the Cancelled Gas Plants

But while Wynne was busy self-prophesizing about how great she was, she was about to be hit hard with the cost of her decision to cancel the Mississauga and Oakville gas plants in order to save Liberal seats. In the days following the cancellation announcement, the McGuinty Liberals and the Ontario Power Authority said the cost of cancelling the Oakville plant was "only" $40 million and the Mississauga plant "only" $180 million.[21] *Only* as if the Ontario taxpayers should have to pay even one penny to save Liberal seats.

Nearly a year later, the total cost became $230 million.[22] Six months later the total cost became $275 million. A month later the figure more than doubled to a whopping $585 million: $310 million for cancelling the Oakville plant and $275 million for the Mississauga plant. The true cost was finally revealed in a scathing report released by the Auditor General in the fall of 2013: a sickening $1.1 Billion.[23] That's Billion, with a 'B.'

Energy Minister Bob Chiarelli callously dismissed the cost to Ontario residents as being "less than the cup of Tim Horton's coffee a year."[24] The $1.1 billion cancellation means each man, woman, and child living in Ontario will be paying $81.42 so the Liberals could keep their seats in Mississauga and Oakville. It so perfectly summarized the attitude that started with the McGuinty Liberals and continued with Wynne: waste public money for partisan reasons? No big deal!

The Auditor General also said over half of that $1.1 billion could have been saved if the gas plants stayed in the Greater Toronto Area (GTA). Instead, the Liberals completely cancelled them and chose the new spot for one in Napanee, a Conservative riding that the Ontario Power Authority recommended *against*. [25] And by separating the plants by so much, it more than doubled the cost of cancelling the Oakville plant.

The question that has never been asked is why Ontario needed these gas plants in the first place. The Independent Electricity System Operator (IESO) noted the Liberal government was losing $1.2 billion by exporting power to neighbouring provinces and states.[26] At a time when Energy Minister Bob Chiarelli was proudly raising hydro rates, Ontarians were also each paying for $250-worth of electricity to be sent to another province or state! This is a government whose priorities have become so convoluted, so backwards, and so counter-intuitive that most Ontarians have simply taken to shaking their heads and – regretfully – paying up.

This wasn't just a bad decision: it was allegedly criminal. In November the Ontario Provincial Police anti-rackets division visited the Premier's office, searching for evidence related to why the Liberals chose to cancel the gas plants and why what they claimed the cancellation would cost was so far off.[27] (As if the Liberals would make an evidence-based policy decision!) But the absence of that evidence was also allegedly a crime: in her special investigation, Ontario Privacy Commissioner Ann Cavoukian said the Liberals broke the law by mysteriously deleting emails and memos - any trace of anything at all – from computers in the Premier's Office and in the Energy Minister's Office.[28] "It is difficult to accept that the routine deletion of emails was not in fact an attempt by staff... to avoid transparency and accountability," said Cavoukian in her appropriately titled report *Deleting Accountability: Records Management Practices of Political Staff*.[29]

At the time of writing, the OPP investigation was homing on one of the Premier's staffers being considered for criminal charges: Dalton McGuinty's former chief of staff David Livingston. The OPP allege that Livingston called in the boyfriend of a staffer in the Premier's Office who was, at the time, an information technology expert contracted to the Liberal Party caucus, to wipe clean any electronic evidence pertaining to the gas plants scandal.[30] [31] This was purposely done during the "transition period" between when McGuinty resigned and Wynne was elected Liberal leader and Premier, which raised legitimate questions as to who, exactly, ordered Livingston to get rid of the evidence. This was an inconvenient and inevitable question for Kathleen Wynne to answer, with her predecessor long gone to the United States, so when it was asked, she responded with a libel lawsuit! That's right, asking tough questions about how and why the Liberals spent $1.1 billion of taxpayers' money to save their seats in Oakville and Mississauga will get you sued in the McGuinty-Wynne Ontario![32]

Wynne Loves Running

The Premier's Office was being investigated by the police. The Wynne government's response was almost as amusing as Liberal cabinet minister Chiarelli's claims that it would *only* cost you the price of a cup of coffee every year: they released an ad in which Kathleen Wynne proudly admitted she loves running!

In an awkward ad released in November 2013, Wynne jogs along a rural road and says "there are things most people don't know about me. One, I love running. Two, I try to speak simply and get to the point. Three, I set goals. Really hard to accomplish goals. Four, I never stop until they're done."[33] It was one of the most bizarre political statements released since the Eves Conservatives' claim that McGuinty was an "evil reptilian kitten-eater." It was as if they were intentionally creating a pun on Wynne running from the issues and trying to make it humorous. But did Ontarians *want* a Premier who tried to drive straight to the point of Ontario's "simple" issues? Did the rest of Ontario consider our problems to be simple? Did Ontario need "hard to accomplish goals," or did we just need to start meeting goals, period?

The best exploitation of Wynne's own words came from the first point of her list: "I love running." At the time when the gas plants scandal had reached a boiling point and the Ontario Provincial Police were searching the Premier's office for evidence of fraud and breach of public trust, it was absurd that the Liberals were promoting their leader, the Premier *they* – not Ontario – elected, as *loving to run*. All it took was the Ontario PC's addition of a police siren over Wynne's words, and her own ad backfired. Suddenly, it looked as if Wynne was running away as the police chased her in the background 34– a tie-back to the ongoing gas plant scandal. Indeed, this was their intent according to Ontario PC MPP Lisa MacLeod. And it worked brilliantly. Looking back at how easily their own ad was tweaked to expose the real meaning behind it, one can only wonder what the Liberals were thinking.[35]

Massive Expense for Pan Am Games

Also in November, it was revealed that the cost of Ontario hosting the 2015 Pan Am Games was a staggering $2.5 Billion.[36] At a time when Ontario was seeing massive job losses and the closures of factories that had been a part of Ontario's heritage for generations, the Wynne government deemed it more fiscally prudent to spend $2.5 Billion hosting a games weekend. By comparison, when the federal government hosted the G8 and G20 summits (that's *two* summits featuring world leaders requiring significantly higher security costs) in Toronto and Huntsville in 2010, it came in under budget at $858 million, nearly a third of the cost of Wynne's Pan Am games. Comparing the costs of the previous Pan Am Games doesn't help either: the 2011 Games in Guadalajara, Mexico cost only $750 million, which seems like a bargain compared to Wynne's multi-billion dollar Toronto Games.

The actual cost of hosting the Games were only the tip of the iceberg. The Games' Chief Executive Officer (CEO) turned out to be raking in a staggering $477,260 for his work as lead organizer. (But that was a pay cut from the $552,065 he made in 2011 – budget cuts, people! We all need to do our part!) The Senior Vice President, a cool $292,744; the Chief Financial Officer, $307,115; another Senior Vice President, $309,530; yet another Senior Vice President, $297,583; a Vice President, $232,845. All told, *that's almost $2 million just on executive salaries.*[37]

If the salaries were not outrageous enough, their expense statements certainly were. The CEO billed taxpayers 80 cents for his parking chit while giving a media interview, and $6.45 for water while he visited Mexico. Business meetings, work "check-ins," and recruiting potential executives was frequently done over an evening of $100 steaks and fancy cocktails – all paid for by you and me. The Chief Financial Officer billed taxpayers for two $1.89 Starbucks teas and another $2.11 for a tea while visiting Guadalajara. But those were just drops in the bucket of her overall $37,072 expense reimbursement.

We also paid $27,000 to move Allen Vansen, the Senior Vice President making $309,530, from Vancouver to Toronto so he could take that job. Being the generous Ontarians we are, the Wynne government also gave him $110.25 to move his pet and $53.76 to have his mail forwarded from his Vancouver address. We also paid for the executives' laundry and $400 to cancel a Telus cell phone contract. Aren't we generous! Lavish dinners and private limousine rides complete with a private chauffeur– the Liberal government certainly wasn't going to spare any expense in making sure these executives were happy.[38] When the story broke, the Liberals did what they do best: they blamed it on the Game's Chief Executive Officer, Ian Troop, and sent him away with a $500,000 severance package.[39]

The Running Has to Stop Sometime

Regardless of how well Premier Wynne thinks she can run from the incredible cost of cancelling gas plants or the ballooning cost of hosting the Pan Am Games, she cannot run forever – she has to stop at some point and face the music. That music is becoming ever louder and harder to ignore (just look at the Drummond Report). By 2014-2015, Ontario's debt is set to become 40 percent of Ontario's GDP.[40] That is a *massive* expense that will cripple the Ontario government's ability to do *anything* else, since we will be spending so much on debt and interest charges. Education, health care, and infrastructure will be a far cry away with interest payments to be made and debt ballooning out of control. Jobs are an incredibly important concern. As noted in the introduction, small, medium, and large businesses are closing every day because they simply cannot take the immense costs of doing business in Ontario. They're moving to neighbouring provinces or the United States.

Hydro rates have been pushed through the roof thanks to McGuinty's *Green Energy Act* and the McGuinty cabinet decision (which included Wynne at the table) to squander $1.1 billion of taxpayers' money to cancel two gas plants. Investing in the Ring of Fire – with a potential of adding $60 billion to Ontario's economy – was a project completely mismanaged by the Wynne government. The main company backing development in the Ring of Fire, Cliffs Natural Resources, could no longer take it, and ceased its operations.[41][42] Another resource development company, Northern Superior Resources, is suing the Wynne government for $110 million for "absolutely failing" to develop a framework for resource development in which the developers could operate.[43] Ontario's future is bleak and it needs real leadership from a government that isn't afraid to make the tough calls to do what's right for Ontario families.

Apparently, though, this was a good time for celebration: in October 2013 the Wynne government gave public servants $21.1 million in bonuses.[44] But weren't public sector wages frozen to help combat the deficit? Nah, that wage freeze was just a guideline, didn't you read the fine print? Why *not* reward 4,800 public servants with bonuses?

New Taxes and New Fees
– The Wynne Legacy Continues the McGuinty Legacy

It's a destructive, ironic game where public servants are bought off for "labour peace" which is then paid-for through higher taxes and new fees for services that were previously free. Kathleen Wynne has continued the Liberals' love for raising taxes and imposing new fees – now they're called "revenue tools" instead of "taxes" or "fees."

Drive Clean

Drive Clean, for example, was a Harris government program introduced in 1999. Its purpose was to ensure vehicles on the road were performing within acceptable pollution levels. It was to be a revenue-neutral program, meaning the fees charged by the government were only to cover the cost of operating Drive Clean, and not to make a profit for the province. By 2013 only five percent of vehicles failed the Drive Clean exam, thanks to more fuel efficient vehicles and cleaner burning gasoline.[45]

The Ontario government profited $11 million from Drive Clean in 2011-2012, which the Ontario Auditor General said could be considered a *de facto* tax since the fees exceeded the costs.[46] But hey, why *not* make extra money when you *can* make extra money?

Increase the Gas Tax to Pay for Toronto Transit

Or what about the Premier's advisory panel's recommendation to raise Ontario's gas tax by 10 cents per litre in order to pay for Toronto's Metrolinx expansion?[47] If implemented, Wynne's gas tax would cost drivers at least $260 per year.[48] The panel's other, only slightly less repulsive recommendation, was to raise the gas tax by only 5 cents per litre, but also change the corporate income tax rate and potentially the HST rate. At the time of writing, the Wynne government has not announced whether it will raise gas taxes for all Ontarians in order to pay for Toronto's transit expansion.

An Ontario Pension Plan?

Or how about an entirely new tax that forces people to save for retirement? While public servants were taking home an average $4,400 bonus for happening to be public servants in 2013, and the Wynne government was musing about raising gas prices by 10 cents per litre, they were also focused on finding yet *another* bill to add to Ontarian's paycheques. In late 2013, the provincial Finance Ministers met with federal Finance Minister Jim Flaherty in Ottawa. Among the topics of discussion were pension plan reforms; the issue, apparently, that 23 percent of Canadians were not saving enough money for retirement, thus suffering a decrease in their standard of living once retiring. Some ministers felt the easiest solution was to double CPP deductions, forcibly taking more money from employees and employers and stuffing it into a government-controlled investment coffer. Flaherty rightly refused, saying he would prefer a "targeted approach" to deal with those segments of Canadians not saving enough rather than a "bazooka."[49] The media and Opposition response was swift: they tried to say the federal government was "leaving seniors poor."[50]

The scene was set for Wynne's tax grab: since the national pension plan was apparently insufficient, the Ontario government would go the way of Quebec and implement its own pension plan by spring 2014.[51] This would not be an optional pension plan: it needed to be mandatory in order for it to be successful, Wynne said. She hired former Liberal Prime Minister Paul Martin to assist her. [52] [53]

Just like that, the Wynne government had signalled their intention to add yet another tax to Ontarians' paycheques. But it wasn't a tax to pay for roads or improve transit – it was a forced retirement savings plan. Why should the government's coercive power be used to force Ontarians to save? Why can't we be responsible for our own savings, or lack thereof? Ontarians will have to watch the 2014-2015 budget closely for the truth about this new mandatory retirement savings plan: how much will it cost? How will it work on top of Canada Pension Plan deductions?

Changes to Green Energy Policy

The Wynne legacy hasn't been all negative: she has made *some* improvements to the reckless energy experiments that cost us billions under McGuinty's nine years as Premier. For example, in June 2013 the Wynne government announced it was cutting back on the $7 billion Samsung deal, reducing it to $6 billion.[54] That's a good improvement to the McGuinty *Green Energy Act* that has killed so many jobs and made so many others simply unaffordable. But there's a catch: Samsung will invest $2 billion less in the province, will create 1,369 megawatts of energy rather than 2,500, and will create "900 direct jobs" instead of the previously promised 16,000.

So, in return for Wynne saving us $1 billion, Ontario is receiving less power, fewer jobs, and less investment in the province. The Wynne government started out strong in its attempt to craft an energy policy distinct from the scandalized *Green Energy Act*, but it ended up only further hurting Ontario.

Wynne Government Sues Itself

The *Green Energy Act* has become so convoluted, so shrouded in mystery and scandal and unknowns that the only responsible thing the Liberal government could do is completely scrap it and start from scratch. Clean, renewable energy *does* have a place in the energy market, but only if that energy is affordable, reliable, safe, and placed on property that does not interfere with others' enjoyment of their own property. A novel concept, I know.

When the facts aren't clear and a government pursues ideology instead of well-researched policies, you get bizarre outcomes like the Wynne government suing itself. An environmental review tribunal rejected Gilead Power's Ostrander Point Project, a proposed wind farm in Prince Edward County, because the Ontario Ministry of Natural Resources says the area is home to the "threatened" Blanding's Turtle species.[55] Yet, the Ministry of the Environment disagreed with the Ministry of Natural Resources and backed Gilead's Power appeal to an Ontario divisional court. The company, backed by a Wynne government department, ended up winning and overturning a decision made by another Wynne government department![56]

Natural Disaster Hits Ontario

But sometimes governance isn't about turtles and wind farms – it's about far more important issues like the health and safety of Ontario's residents. Public safety is an important area of provincial responsibility. Just days before the 2013 Christmas, most of Ontario was hit with the worst freezing rain, ice, and snow since the 1998 ice storm. In the 1998 storm, then-Premier Mike Harris toured the damaged communities and served in a central role to ensure cleanup operations went smoothly. It affected Ontario, Eastern Canada, and the Eastern United States cost an estimated $5-7 billion as power lines were downed, trees fell, roads were damaged and blocked, traffic lights were broken, and hundreds of thousands of residents went without power for six cold January days.

Ontarians were rightly concerned about a repeat of the 1998 ice storm, and drew comparisons about the impact (and potential impact) it would have. The 2013 ice storm hit Ontario on December 21, 2013 and moved east into the Maritime provinces, crippling the infrastructure of southwestern and eastern Ontario cities. Woolwich Township declared a state of emergency, and approximately 53,000 Waterloo Region residents remained without power three days after the storm cleared. Residents were warned they could be spending Christmas in the dark, as power companies said they could not clear the entire backlog of repairs until at least December 28.[57][58]

Among the hardest hit was Toronto, which had a total of 115,000 residents still without power on Christmas Eve, three days after the storm first hit. Toronto, too, was warned they could suffer from a Christmas without power, and the city responded quickly to triage downed power lines and ensure warm shelters open to the public.[59] Toronto Mayor Rob Ford attempted to take a high-profile role in speaking to media about how Canada's largest city and Ontario's capital was dealing with the cleanup. The mayor, speaking on behalf of council, said the cleanup operations could be handled without declaring an emergency. Indeed, city council *was* divided on whether to do so, and the mayor was speaking on their behalf.[60] Notwithstanding Ford's personal demons, he was still the mayor of Toronto, he had done a great job of safeguarding the taxpayers' money, and he was leading the city's response to the storm but, in one of the most bizarre and disrespectful acts by a premier ever, Wynne went directly to Deputy Mayor Norm Kelly to discuss Toronto's cleanup efforts. But in one of the most bizarre and disrespectful acts by a Premier ever, Wynne castrated Ford and went directly to Deputy Mayor Norm Kelly to discuss Toronto's cleanup efforts.[61]

After a 40-minute meeting with the deputy mayor, Wynne was questioned why she bypassed the mayor in favour of the mayor's deputy. Wynne responded that the deputy mayor was "the representative of Toronto city council," seemingly forgetting that the mayor *is* the senior-ranking and elected official from city council. (The deputy mayor, too, is elected but only serves in the Mayor's absence and is certainly not *the* representative of city council.) Wynne repeated "the ongoing relationship [and] ongoing discussion will be with the representative of city council, who is the deputy mayor."[62]

Wynne's decision was mind-boggling, an incredible demonstration of disrespect for a Mayor who happens to be conservative in favour of his deputy who happens to be Liberal. Just imagine, for example, if Canada's Conservative Prime Minister bypassed Premier Wynne and said he would only work with the Conservative Official Opposition (who is also elected). There would be outrage that the disrespectful Prime Minister was ignoring the democratic representatives of Ontario! As I asked at the beginning of this book: why don't we hold provincial Liberals to the same standards as federal Conservatives?

It didn't help highlight Wynne's good judgment when it turned out that her self-selected Toronto Council representative left the damaged city in the middle of the blackout so he could celebrate Christmas in Florida.[63] Nor did it help when Wynne threw together a sloppy public relations stunt that didn't add up: she went door-to-door in a bright Liberal red jacket, offering residents bins of food from Loblaws or gift cards for Loblaws, Shoppers Drug Mart, Sobeys, or Metro (because gift cards work in blackouts?). The Wynne government couldn't do basic math: they were short $14.8 million between what they were pledging to offer to residents and what they were promising to pay. The cards were also incredibly illusive and hard to come by.[64] [65]

It was all, Wynne said, to encourage Ontarians to pull together and help their neighbours in a difficult time. Families and neighbours with power should take in those living in the cold and dark, she said. Except that Wynne was exposed as a hypocrite: her own neighbours were left to tough it out in the cold for several days after Wynne's power was restored.[66] It was the reliable "Do as I say, not as I do" Liberal brand that served Dalton McGuinty's decade in office so well.

More Expensive Services, Outrageous Bonuses

The exploding energy costs were another burden on Ontario's residents – to them, it was another government rate hike when our families could least afford it. Ontarians received an even bigger slap in the face when it turned out the Wynne government was *rewarding* Ontario Power Generation (OPG) with enormous bonuses, sometimes exceeding their annual salary.[67] In her report, the Ontario Auditor General called OPG's salaries "significantly more generous" than similar public sector salaries, with many OPG executives making more than deputy ministers. Furthermore, the Auditor General said "about two-thirds of OPG's operating costs are human resource related. Not only has the size of its executive and senior management group grown disproportionately, but 67 percent of people in this group received high annual incentive awards in the period from 2010 to 2012." This led to a "top-heavy organization," said the Auditor General, which, despite reducing its overall staff by 8.5 percent, had actually increased the size of its executive and senior management group by almost 60 percent since 2005.

Approximately 8000 employees, or 62 percent of the staff, made the 2012 Ontario Sunshine List by making more than $100,000. The incentive program for non-unionized employees, depending on the person's job, performance, and base salary, could equal a maximum bonus of $1.3 million. That's $1.3 million on top of the employee's base salary during – don't forget – a "wage freeze."

The "pension plan is generous by any standard," declared the Auditor General. Since 2005, for every $1 an OPG employee put into his or her pension, the employer (i.e. the taxpayer) put in between $4 and $5. This is far more lucrative than the Ontario Public Service, which uses an equal, 1:1 ratio for its employees. At age 65, annual pensions for the top five OPG executives would range between $180,000 and $760,000. Even at the low end, $180,000 is more than a federal MP or Ontario MPP makes in a year. Even the salaries of the Ontario Premier, at $209,000, and Canada's Prime Minister, at $318,000, pale in comparison to the pensions these OPG executives would be collecting upon their 65th birthdays – and we'll be paying for it.

Ontario Power Generation was an organization out of control, spending beyond its means, yet it was rewarded for its performance by the Ontario government or, perhaps more accurately, by the Ontario taxpayer. When the Auditor General's report was released, Chiarelli responded with shock, as if he had never before heard anything about the generous salaries and bonuses being doled out in a Crown corporation under his portfolio. Chiarelli fired three people – the Chief Financial Officer, the Executive Vice President for Strategic Initiatives, and the Vice President for Internal Audit – as an obvious after-the-fact attempt at damage control.[68] The cost of firing these three individuals was an amazing $3.4 million.[69]

OPG, in their own attempt at damage control, released a statement from the Chairman of the OPG Board of Directors, saying they were "disappointed in the findings," but "strongly believe[d] the report [would] serve as a catalyst for further positive changes at OPG that will allow us to serve Ontarians better."[70] The President and CEO of OPG, Tom Mitchell, wrote an open letter to all OPG employees, admitting there were instances "where we have not met expectations as caretakers of the public's money, or have not exhibited the best judgement possible."[71] (Mitchell is Ontario's highest paid public servant, at $1.7 million per year.)

The most interesting reaction came from Premier Wynne herself. She said the "culture" of the organization had necessitated a requirement for the government to "take unprecedented control of the salaries, benefits, and pensions of public sector executives."[72] It was an obvious attempt to woo the New Democrats, who has generally continued to support the Wynne Liberals' minority government throughout the preceding year of endless scandals. The NDP had long been pushing the Liberals for a cap on public sector salaries, and they finally had the perfect scandal which could make it a reality. The NDP wanted to set the cap at $418,000, or double the Premier's annual salary. At the time of writing, Wynne's "unprecedented" bill that would cap salaries, straight out of the NDP's playbook, had not yet been introduced in the legislature.[73]

New Year, New ~~Fees~~ "Revenue Tools," Same Scandals

Ontarians were shaken following the December ice storm. Millions went without power for various periods, from as little as a few hours up to almost a week. Residents of Toronto, one of the hardest hit cities, looked to their mayor for advice and leadership, just as Ontario residents looked to their Premier. Kathleen Wynne had the opportunity to use the ice storm to her advantage, just like Ernie Eves used the 2003 blackout to his advantage to show leadership, courage, organization, control, and a presence during a difficult crisis. Instead, Wynne let the opportunity pass.

With a new year, though, Wynne's Liberals yet again had the opportunity to set the record straight, to define 2014 as a new year that would not be marred by scandal and outrage, but instead by the good government Ontario needed to get back on track. Instead, they blew it within two weeks of the new year: openly musing about increasing fees on seniors' drivers licences; playing politics with wine and hospitals; blatantly pledging to only hire black females for public service jobs; and shutting down an Opposition proposal to create one million jobs. From the beginning of 2014, it was clear it was business as usual for Wynne's Liberals.

eHealth Comes Back - Again

Considering the ongoing eHealth Ontario expense scandals which were described in chapter six, one could safely assume that the Wynne government would do everything possible to keep the Crown corporation out of the media. But that wasn't the case. Barely 72 hours into the New Year, they announced $2.3 million in lavish bonuses for eHealth Ontario employees, doled out to a total of 704 workers, most of whom were information technology experts; each person would receive between $500 and $7000 for their performance in the 2012/2013 year.[74]

But why the bonuses? Wasn't there a provincial government wage freeze? Not for eHealth employees! (Are you noticing a pattern yet?) The justification for these bonuses remained the same as the 2011 bonuses, which was the same excuse the Auditor General had criticized just years earlier: apparently eHealth required top-notch, highly specialized IT experts, and the bonuses were required to keep them from being poached by private employers.

Increasing Fees on Seniors

In one of the latest quests for "revenue tools," Kathleen Wynne's government, it was revealed in early 2014, was considering new driver's licence charges for any senior above age 65 who had been convicted of a driving offence, and for any person over age 80 seeking a commercial driver's licence. The $85 fee was just one of many proposals submitted to Wynne's cabinet through the Ministry of Transportation, a way of increasing revenues through specific service charges against seniors rather than raising taxes. Yet Liberal Transportation Minister Glen Murray categorically ruled out any "new fees for senior drivers."

Liars

One Million Jobs

While the Wynne Liberals were busy seeking new ways to find "revenue tools" to pay for their energy experiments and cancelled gas plants, there was at least one party releasing new ideas and desperately attempting to restore lost hope to Ontario. Indeed, with another 39,000 Ontario jobs lost in December 2013, Ontario needed hope. This was only compounded through the numerous company announcements throughout 2013 that they would be shutting their Ontario doors and opening plants in the United States or another province. As mentioned earlier, the closure of those plants by Heinz, Kellogg's, Kraft, Navistar, Xtrata, John Deere, Siemens, and Caterpillar (just to name a few) was an illuminating canary in the mine, demonstrating that not even large, multi-national corporations could continue to face the excessive regulatory red tape and bleak job market created by Dalton McGuinty and Kathleen Wynne.

December's job losses "effectively wip[ed] out all of the jobs created in the first half of 2013" and left "the province with the same stubborn unemployment rate as one year prior – 7.9 percent," said Statistics Canada. The Liberals responded by saying Ontarians should not look "too deeply at month-to-month fluctuations," and instead focus on Ontario's place against Canadian averages.[75] That unemployment rate is 0.7 percent higher than the Canadian unemployment rate. Furthermore, Ontario's youth unemployment rate was 16.7 percent, whereas the Canadian average was 14 percent. Finally, as of January 2014, Ontario's unemployment rate has been higher than the national average for 84 consecutive months – or seven years!

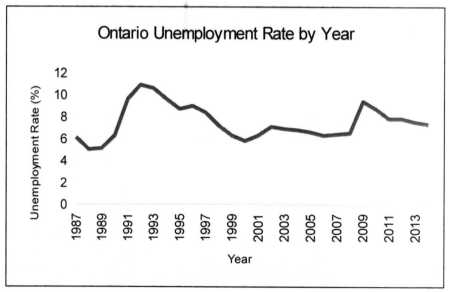

Figure 11: Ontario unemployment rate

Tim Hudak's Conservatives responded to December's job losses with his party's plan to create one million jobs over eight years. In his *Million Jobs Act,* Hudak laid out his plan to begin to undo the destruction and job losses caused by a decade of McGuinty and Wynne governments. That plan includes:

- An across-the-board wage freeze for all government employees (a real one, not a McGuinty "freeze")
- Reducing Ontario's 380,000 regulations by one third over three years
- Ending subsidies for wind and solar power projects
- Ramp up trade agreements with the United States
- Help youth with training in skilled trades
- Lower the business tax rate to 10 percent (a 1.5 percent reduction)
- Better clarify and utilize federal immigration programs to promote Ontario as the destination choice for new Canadians[76]

It did not take long for Liberals and media alike to criticize Hudak's plan, saying the plan was unreliable, not possible, *could* happen but probably would not, would only happen as the result of crippling policies, and so on. Since Hudak was a cabinet minister in the Mike Harris government, they once again dropped the 'H' bomb, as if the Harris name was anything but a positive legacy created during desperate times arising from NDP and Liberal mismanagement. Remember, Harris' government created 1.1 million jobs over his eight years in office.)[77]

Black Females Only

While Tim Hudak's Progressive Conservatives were busy thinking of ways to create jobs and restore hope to the province, the Wynne government was cooking up a scheme to racially divide Ontario's jobseekers. On January 16, 2014, the media released documents that showed the Ontario government was launching a project to help open up promotion possibilities for public servants. In a memo from Deputy Minister of Government Services Kevin Constante to his ministries' employees, the Liberal government explained it was creating "The Administrative Internship Pilot Program." It sounded like an innocent program, until they explained who was eligible: "The purpose of this internship program…is to begin to increase the representation of black, female employees in functional roles (such as) communications, finance, policy and procurement."[78] The problem, Constante said, was that 25 percent of black employees were in administrative positions, eight percent higher than the public service average of 17 percent; and that 46 percent of black employees in administrative roles were "dissatisfied" with their careers compared to the 27 percent of all public servants being dissatisfied with their careers.

Liars

It was a blatant affirmative action program designed to address what the ministry thought was a shortage of black women in more senior leadership roles, and it was a page from Bob Rae's time as Premier, when his government released job ads that explicitly said white men were not eligible to apply. In Rae's case, enormous public outrage caused the Premier to relent and allow white men to apply. Of course, the public's outrage was justified: if Ontarians want and deserve a world-class, high quality public service, then they need to create the conditions for merit-based rather than race- and gender-based hires. It seems absurd, that today in the 21st century, the federal and provincial public services still openly flaunt their intent to cater to people on the basis of their skin colour, race, or gender.

But not only that: the policy itself was ridiculous! It wasn't just for black females – it was for people who "self-identify" as black females![79] It remains to be seen whether the Wynne government will hire a white female who "self-identifies" as black; or even better a white male who identifies as a black female. This is truly the absurd direction this Liberal government is taking – not only is it implementing affirmative action, but it's leaving the interpretation of affirmative action up to anyone who wants to claim they're something they biologically absolutely *are* or *are not*! Will the Ontario public express the same outrage today as they did in 1993?

Hydro One Comes Under Investigation

As a result of the split of Ontario Hydro into Ontario Power Generation and Hydro One in 1998, Ontario was left with a $7.8 billion debt. For over a decade now, hydro customers have been paying 0.7 cents per kilowatt hour on our monthly hydro bills, which shows up as the "debt retirement charge." It works out to about $6-7 per month. As of 2011, the $7.8 billion had been more than repaid: the province had raked in over $8.7 billion from customers who certainly had no say in whether Ontario Hydro should have been sold in 1998. That's over $900 million extra, yet the McGuinty government said the debt retirement charge would remain on hydro bills. Auditor General Jim McCarter criticized the Liberal Finance Minister for failing to state "how much of the debt remains - even though the law requires the Minister to provide such an update from time to time."[80]

As of the winter of 2014, a new Ministry of Finance website says "the Debt Retirement Charge will likely end between 2015 and 2018."[81] On January 29, 2014, Energy Minister Bob Chiarelli said the Liberal government's plan was to phase out both the debt retirement charge and the Clean Energy Benefit at the same time. By removing a charge as well as a bill subsidy they "would balance each other out more or less," Chiarelli said.[82] But the numbers don't add up. As of 2011 the province had paid off over $900 million *more* than what the actual debt was. Why is the Wynne government continuing to charge us for debt retirement four to seven years after it was paid off? Where is taxpayers' money being spent if the debt retirement charge was already paid off? Or was it paid off? Was the money being redirected into another government program?

Documents released in February 2014 revealed that the Ontario Liberals had "borrowed" $4 billion from the debt retirement charge in early 2004, yet did not declare the loan on the books until 2013. For what was the $4 billion intended? Where did it go? Why was it kept off the books for nine years? Why were hydro customers continuing to pay off the debt retirement charge so the Liberals could borrow money to spend on something else? Why are Ontarians paying a debt retirement charge to retire a debt that was already retired? These are basic questions that still need to be answered at the time of writing.[83]

We can't expect any answers from our elected Liberal government; all too often they have demonstrated they are unwilling to answer basic questions, leaving our public defenders – the Auditor General, the Ombudsman, Information and Privacy Commissioners, and others – to give us the answers we deserve. We do know, however, that those answers will not come from a Liberal loyalist: Kathleen Wynne appointed former leadership rival Sandra Pupatello as Chair of Hydro One effective April 1, 2014.[84]

At the time of writing, the Ontario Ombudsman announced it would be investigating Hydro One's "shoddy business practices" such as overbilling customers and failing to answer customers' questions via email or telephone.[85] Trying to get answers from Hydro One was "like wrestling with a slippery pig" the Ombudsman said – a fitting analogy for dealing with most of the Liberal government. If Energy Minister Bob Chiarelli wasn't going to answer for his department's actions, the Ombudsman would. (The investigation is expected to be completed by November 2014, and the Ombudsman will launch a second investigation on separate issues if warranted, he said in February 2014.)

Playing Politics with Health Care and Wine

On January 13, 2014, Kathleen Wynne announced a $26.2 million investment in the Niagara Health System, money that would be used to build a new hospital and two urgent care centres in the area.[86] It was the follow-up to the $75 million "wine strategy" to help Niagara region's grape growers and wine refineries, promising a "cabinet wine secretariat" and a "wine fund" to help support the region's jobs.[87]

Liars

Over the span of just one month, that equated to over $100 million of Ontario taxpayers' money being invested in the Niagara region's health care system and wine producers. It was a transparently partisan investment to make, considering the Niagara seat had been recently vacated by Liberal MPP Kim Craitor, leaving the riding without a representative until a byelection was called.[88] It was a misuse of public money to sway Niagara voters towards the Liberal Party. Obviously, neither the Conservatives nor the New Democrats had over $100 million combined that they could invest in the region even if they wanted to try to buy votes. But with the Liberals controlling Ontario's purse strings, they could easily use Ontario taxpayers' money however they pleased. It was hardly a surprise when Wynne called the byelections in Thornhill and Niagara Falls only two days after her Niagara health care announcement.

The results of the byelections, however, proved that voters could not be so easily bought with their own money. In Thornhill, Tim Hudak's Conservatives won with 49 percent of the vote, easily beating Liberal candidate Sandra Racco, who won 40 percent. Conservative Gila Martow retained the Conservative seat formerly held by Peter Shurman, the Conservative Finance Critic.[89]

In Niagara Falls, Andrea Horwath's New Democrats ousted the Liberals from a seat they had held for over a decade. Liberal MPP Kim Craitor gave up his seat in September 2013, leaving Liberal candidate Joyce Morocco against NDP candidate Wayne Gates and Ontario PC candidate Bart Maves. The Liberal vote plummeted in overwhelming favour of the NDP. The Liberals came a distant third, with Joyce Morocco obtaining less than 20 percent of the vote behind the NDP and Progressive Conservatives. The gap between the NDP and Conservatives was a mere 962 votes despite flagrant campaigning by paid union officials hired by the NDP.[90] But the voters who elected the NDP to represent them will soon realize there is little difference between the NDP and the Liberals: both have the same crippling effect on Ontario's economy, both propose or implement job-killing measures, and both have the same relentless desire to endlessly raise taxes. Just look at the days of Bob Rae's NDP government.[91]

The voters in both Niagara Falls and Thornhill were sending Kathleen Wynne a crucial message: no longer could they be bought with their own money. No longer would they put up with the expensive green energy experiments. They had enough of rising electricity costs and corrupt public servants walking away with multi-million dollar severance packages. Change was in the air in Niagara Falls and Thornhill, a representative sample of what is hopefully to come as residents across Ontario demand change. In her concession speech after losing both elections, the best Wynne could muster was to say the voters in both ridings clearly demonstrated they wanted change, and "I am the change we are bringing to the province of Ontario."[92] What a joke.

A Third Chance for Change?

Wynne's first year in office was marked with scandal after scandal after scandal. The blatant and facetious use of the term "revenue tools" to pay for McGuinty's past and Wynne's future untested and expensive experiments was only one highlight that stood out as Wynne's defining first year as Premier. Somehow, though, despite everything cited above, *The Huffington Post* still felt Kathleen Wynne's first year of Liberal government scored a B- for remaining "competitive despite the baggage of almost 10 years of Dalton McGuinty's time in office."[93]

It didn't have to be this way. Kathleen Wynne had the opportunity to set her Liberals apart from the McGuinty Liberals. In her first year as leader, she had the opportunity to right any number of the numerous wrongs committed under McGuinty's decade of power. She could have undone any one, or two, or dozen of the policies indicative of McGuinty's hijacking. She could have agreed to implement the Drummond Report and made its implementation central to her legacy as Premier.

If she did, here's how her re-election campaign *could* have been mounted: "Dalton McGuinty, the former Liberal Premier of Ontario, commissioned a thorough and non-partisan report on the future of Ontario's government. Well, he's gone now, vacationing in the United States with that other failed Liberal leader, Michael Ignatieff. But I pledge to you, Ontario, that I will heed every word of Mr. Drummond's report and ensure that this government under my leadership fully implements his recommendations. I am not like my predecessor: I will take the advice of economists and experts and make sure our Ontario gets back on track and once again becomes a Canadian leader."

That's how it could have been…inspiring, professional, stateswoman-like, and with a focus on rebuilding for the future. With the Drummond Report as her re-election platform, Wynne would have been able to distance herself from McGuinty and show that she was taking the advice of non-partisan experts. This would have put the Conservatives and New Democrats on their heels to find their own experts to contest Drummond's findings, which would have been hard to do in the span of an election campaign. Instead, Wynne chose to continue down the same destructive path and has made very little progress in fixing Ontario's economy by: making inroads to create new jobs; enforcing a real wage freeze; ending (not just reduc-

Liars

ing) expensive energy experiments; or balancing the books to begin to pay down the debt.

This chapter only stops here because, well, it has to stop somewhere. Without a doubt, there will be more scandals, more expensive experiments, and more issues that will make the news and illustrate how fundamentally incompetent the Ontario Liberals have been – whether under Dalton McGuinty or Kathleen Wynne. The Ontario government under the Liberals has fundamentally transformed our province into something it never was and was never meant to be. They have completely reversed our priorities and failed to take action in the portfolios that *need* action and leadership. They have hijacked Ontario. Thousands of Ontarians are losing their jobs every month, but the Wynne government wants to make sure you know how many calories are in a Big Mac.[94] School costs are soaring,[95] but the Wynne government has no trouble blowing $1.1 billion to cancel some gas plants or increasing wages for lottery executives by 49 percent. More students are failing math at lower grade levels, but instead of addressing that problem, it wants to ban Mother's Day and Father's Day from being celebrated in schools.[96]

These are the priorities of a Liberal government completely out of touch with its constituents. How did we ever allow ourselves to be hijacked and taken so far off course?

There is change ahead. Ontario has turned itself around before, reversing the unthinkable policies of Liberal and NDP governments past, and relatively quickly re-emerging as a leader in the Canadian economy. It both starts and ends with what Ontario voters will tolerate, and for how much longer. Voters in both Thornhill and Niagara Falls completely rejected Wynne's Liberals despite Wynne's message that she was different from Dalton McGuinty. Let's hope Ontario voters feel the same way at the next general election.

1   "Wynne says Ontario Liberals ready to campaign on new tools, transit fees." *CTV News,* last modified September 28, 2013, http://www.ctvnews.ca/politics/wynne-says-ontario-liberals-ready-to-campaign-on-new-tools-transit-fees-1.1474636.

2   Keith Leslie, "Ontario PCs demand Wynne face the music after OPP raid over deleted gas plant emails," *National Post,* last modified February 20, 2014, http://news.nationalpost.com/2014/02/20/ontario-pcs-demand-kathleen-wynne-face-the-music-after-opp-raid-over-deleted-gas-plant-emails/.

3   "Wynne and the Liberals must go, *Toronto Sun,* last modified October 29, 2013, http://www.torontosun.com/2013/10/29/wynne-and-the-liberals-must-go.

4   Robert Benzie, "Dalton McGuinty headed to Harvard for prestigious fellowship." *Toronto Star,* last modified June 28, 2013, http://www.thestar.com/news/queenspark/2013/06/28/

dalton_mcguinty_headed_to_harvard_for_prestigious_fellowship.html.

5   Weatherhead Centre for International Affairs, "Dalton McGuinty," *Harvard University*, http://wcfia.harvard.edu/people/dalton-mcguinty.

6   *Provincial Liberal leadership*, Innovative Research Group.

7   McParland, "Kathleen Wynne Packs her Ontario Team…"

8   McParland, "Kathleen Wynne Packs her Ontario Team…"

9   McParland, "Kathleen Wynne Packs her Ontario Team…"

10   Robert Benzie, "Ontario Finance Minister Dwight Duncan resigning seat next week," *Toronto Star*, last modified February 6, 2013, http://www.thestar.com/news/queenspark/2013/02/06/ontario_finance_minister_dwight_duncan_resigning_seat_next_week.html.

11   "Dwight Duncan," *McMillan LLP*, last modified 2014, http://www.mcmillan.ca/Dwight-Duncan

12   "Rick Bartolucci makes "family decision" to leave politics," *CBC News*, last modified February 7, 2013, http://www.cbc.ca/news/canada/sudbury/rick-bartolucci-makes-family-decision-to-leave-politics-1.1359586.

13   Rob Ferguson, "Energy Minister Chris Bentley to resign his seat," *Toronto Star*, last modified February 8, 2013, http://www.thestar.com/news/queenspark/2013/02/08/energy_minister_chris_bentley_to_resign_his_seat.html.

14   Karen Howlett, Renata D'Aliesio, and Adrian Morrow, "Head of Ontario Lottery Corporation rebuked for pay increases," *Globe and Mail*, last modified April 30, 2013, http://www.theglobeandmail.com/news/politics/ontario-lottery-executives-pay-hikes-are-unacceptable-finance-minister-says/article11639270/.

15   Wayne Lowrie, "OLG resignation signals policy change: MPP," *Gananoque Reporter*, last modified January 29, 2014, http://www.gananoquereporter.com/2014/01/29/olg-resignation-signals-policy-change-mpp.

16   Ontario Liberal Party, "First day," *YouTube*, posted July 16, 2013, http://www.youtube.com/watch?v=ahzerzkqOtA.

17   Employment and Social Development Canada, "Labour Market Bulletin – Ontario: July 2013," *Government of Canada*, http://www.esdc.gc.ca/eng/jobs/lmi/publications/bulletins/on/jul2013.shtml.

18   Brian Lilley, "John Fraser doesn't deserve your vote in Ottawa South," *Ottawa Sun*, last modified July 10, 2013, http://www.ottawasun.com/2013/07/10/john-fraser-doesnt-deserve-your-vote-in-ottawa-south.

19   Kathleen Wynne, "Yes, I'm a woman who can run the economy," *Huffington Post Canada*, last modified September 26, 2013, http://www.huffingtonpost.ca/kathleen-wynne/kathleen-wynne-economy_b_3990668.html.

20   Kathleen Wynne, "Yes, I'm a woman…"

21   "Cancelled Oakville gas plant cost up to $310-million, more than 7 times government figure: Ontario Power Authority," *National Post*, last modified April 30, 2013,

http://news.nationalpost.com/2013/04/30/cost-of-cancelling-oakville-gas-plant-up-to-310-million-not-40-million-government-claimed-ontario-power-authority/.

22   Adrian Morrow, "Ontario could have saved $513 million if cancelled gas plants stayed in GTA: auditor," *Globe and Mail*, last modified October 10, 2013, http://www.theglobeandmail.

com/news/politics/ontario-could-have-saved-513-million-if-cancelled-gas-plants-stayed-in-gta-auditor/article14808495/.

23   "Auditor General report puts total cost of Liberal gas plant cancellations as high as $1.1 billion, *National Post*, last modified October 8, 2013, http://news.nationalpost.com/2013/10/08/auditor-general-report-puts-cost-of-liberal-gas-plant-cancellations-as-high-as-1-1-billion/.

24   Keith Leslie, "Cancelled Oakville Gas plant adds $2 per year to hydro bills: OPA," *CTV News*, last modified December 5, 2013,http://toronto.ctvnews.ca/cancelled-oakville-gas-plant-adds-2-a-year-to-hydro-bills-opa-1.1576255.

25   Morrow, "Ontario could have saved $513 million…," supra note 22.

26   Parker Gallant, "Ontario's power trip: province lost $1.2 billion this year export-ing power," *National Post*, last modified December 2, 2013, http://opinion.financialpost.com/2013/12/02/ontarios-power-trip-province-lost-1-2-billion-this-year-exporting-power/.

27   Keith Leslie, "Ontario police to visit Premier's office in gas plants probe," *Globe and Mail*, last modified November 13, 2013, http://www.theglobeandmail.com/news/politics/ontario-police-to-visit-premiers-office-in-gas-plants-probe/article15414298/.

28   Keith Leslie, S"enior Ontario Liberals broke law by deleting gas plant emails: Pri-vacy Commissioner, *National Post*, last modified June 5, 2013, http://news.nationalpost.com/2013/06/05/senior-ontario-liberals-broke-law-by-deleting-gas-plant-emails-ontario-privacy-commissioner/.

29   Ann Cavoukian, , *Deleting accountability: records management practices of political staff, a special investigation report*, Information and Privacy Commissioner, June 5, 2013, http://www.ipc.on.ca/images/Findings/2013-06-05-Ministry-of-Energy.pdf.

30   "Ontario police pursuing a criminal charge against McGuinty's chief of staff over gas plant scandal," *National Post*, last modified March 27, 2014, http://news.nationalpost.com/2014/03/27/ontario-police-pursuing-a-criminal-charge-against-mcguintys-chief-of-staff-over-gas-plan-scandal/.

31   Antonella Artuso, "Liberal staffer's boyfriend linked to deleted emails had long-term contract," *Toronto Sun*, last modified March 31, 2014, http://www.sunnewsnetwork.ca/sun-news/politics/archives/2014/03/20140331-191502.html.

32   Robyn Urback, "What exactly was Kathleen Wynne hoping to accomplish with a libel notice to Tim Hudak?" *National Post*, last modified April 7, 2014, http://fullcomment.nationalpost.com/2014/04/07/robyn-urback-what-exactly-was-kathleen-wynne-hoping-to-accomplish-with-a-libel-notice-to-tim-hudak/.

33   Ontario Liberal Party, "Never stop," *YouTube*, posted November 13, 2013, http://www.youtube.com/watch?v=x2PXySGHbnk.

34   Ontario PC Party, "Kathleen Wynne – Dalton's legacy running ad," *YouTube*, posted November 20, 2013, http://www.youtube.com/watch?v=TVY4jiAFFs8.

35   "Ontario PCs target Wynne in parody ad, fundraising Campaign," *Sun News Network*, last modified November 20, 2013, http://www.sunnewsnetwork.ca/archives/sunnews/poli-tics/2013/11/20131120-114720.html.

36   Antonella Artuso, "Pan Am games to cost $2.5 billion," *Toronto Sun*, last modified November 20, 2013, http://www.torontosun.com/2013/11/20/pan-am-games-to-cost-25b.

37   Sue-Ann Levy, "Expenses claimed by Toronto Pan Am executives," *Toronto Sun*, last modified September 28, 2013, http://www.torontosun.com/2013/09/28/expenses-claimed-by-toronto-pan-am-games-executives.

38   Sue-Ann Levy, "Mounting expenses for Toronto Pan Am Games executives," *Toronto Sun*, last modified September 28, 2013, http://www.torontosun.com/2013/09/28/mounting-expenses-for-toronto-pan-am-games-executives.

39   Sue-Ann Levy, "Fired Pan Am Games CEO Ian Troop gets $500,000 severance," *Toronto Sun*, last modified January 31, 2014, http://www.torontosun.com/2014/01/31/fire-pan-am-games-ceo-ian-troop-gets-500gs-severance.

40   Ontario Financing Authority, "Borrowing and debt history," *Government of Ontario*, last modified 2014, http://www.ofina.on.ca/borrowing_debt/borrowhistory.htm.

41   Christina Blizzard, "Hudak may hit his stride on jobs issue," *Toronto Sun*, last modified November 28, 2013, http://www.torontosun.com/2013/11/28/hudak-may-hit-his-stride-on-jobs-issue.

42   Antonella Artuso, "Company suspends work on mineral rich ring of fire," *Toronto Sun*, last modified November 21, 2013, http://www.sunnewsnetwork.ca/sunnews/politics/archives/2013/11/20131121-184813.html.

43   Carol Mulligan, "Sudbury mining firm sues province for $110 million," *Sudbury Star*, last modified October 26, 2013, http://www.thesudburystar.com/2013/10/26/sudbury-mining-firm-sues-province-for-110m.

44   Antonella Artuso, "Ontario public service managers get $21 million in bonuses," *Toronto Sun*, last modified October 11, 2013, http://www.torontosun.com/2013/10/11/ontario-public-service-managers-get-21m-in-bonuses.

45   Maria Babbage, "Ontario lowers fee for drive clean emissions test," *Globe and Mail*, last modified December 18, 2013, http://www.theglobeandmail.com/news/politics/ontario-lowers-fee-for-drive-clean-emissions-tests-to-30/article16026439/.

46   "Annual report: Ministry of the Environment – Drive Clean Program," *Office of the Auditor General of Ontario*, 2013, http://www.auditor.on.ca/en/reports_en/en12/304en12.pdf.

47   Richard Brennan and Robert Benzie, "Premier Kathleen Wynne says she is willing to risk fallout from transit levies," *Toronto Star*, last modified December 12, 2013, http://www.thestar.com/news/queenspark/2013/12/12/tim_hudak_blasts_gas_tax_hike.html.

48   Tess Kalinowski, "Ontario transit funding plan could eventually cost drivers $260 per year," *Toronto Star*, last modified December 12, 2013, http://www.thestar.com/news/gta/2013/12/12/ontario_transit_panel_recommends_5centperlitre_gas_tax_hike.html.

49   Gordon Isfeld, "Jim Flaherty favours targeted approach to CPP reform, no need for bazooka," *National Post*, last modified December 16, 2013, http://business.financialpost.com/2013/12/16/jim-flaherty-favours-targeted-approach-to-cpp-reform-no-need-for-bazooka/.

50   Bill Curry, "Tories vote down CPP expansion as seniors warn of waning support, *Globe and Mail*, last modified December 9, 2013, http://www.theglobeandmail.com/news/politics/tories-vote-down-cpp-expansion-as-seniors-warn-of-waning-support/article15834092/.

51   Adrian Morrow, "Wynne stakes Ontario Liberals' fortunes on pledge for new pension plan by spring, *Globe and Mail*, last modified December 18, 2013, http://www.theglobeandmail.com/news/politics/ontarios-new-pension-plan-coming-this-spring-wynne-pledges/article16032806/.

52   Antonella Artuso, "Made-in-Ontario pension plan needs '"mandatory aspect,'" *Toronto Sun*, last modified January 28, 2014, http://www.torontosun.com/2014/01/28/made-in-ontario-pension-plan-needs-mandatory-aspect.

53   "Liberals Think We're Made of Money," *Sun News Network*, last modi-

fied January 24, 2014, http://www.sunnewsnetwork.ca/sunnews/straighttalk/archives/2014/01/20140124-121741.html.

54   Scott Stinson, "Kathleen Wynne backing away from McGuinty's Ontario Green Energy Act," *National Post*, last modified June 24, 2013, http://fullcomment.nationalpost.com/2013/06/24/kathleen-wynne-backing-away-from-mcguintys-ontario-green-energy-act/.

55   John Spears, "Blanding's turtles halt wind farm at Ostrander Point," *Toronto Star*, last modified July 4, 2013, http://www.thestar.com/business/2013/07/04/blandings_turtles_halt_wind_farm_at_ostrander_point.html.

56   *Ostrander Point GP Inc and another v. Prince Edward County Field Naturalists and another*, 2014 ONSC #974.

57   "Woolwich declares emergency as thousands still in dark after ice storm," *CBC News*, last modified December 22, 2013, http://www.cbc.ca/news/canada/kitchener-waterloo/woolwich-declares-emergency-as-thousands-still-in-dark-after-ice-storm-1.2473562.

58   Kevin Swayze, "Power could be out until Christmas for some Waterloo region residents after weekend ice storm," *Kitchener-Waterloo Record*, last modified December 24, 2013, http://www.therecord.com/news-story/4285649-power-could-be-out-until-christmas-for-some-waterloo-region-residents-after-weekend-ice-storm/.

59   "Ice storm means dark Christmas for thousands of Canadians, *CBC News*, last modified December 24, 2013, http://www.cbc.ca/news/canada/ice-storm-will-mean-dark-christmas-for-thousands-of-canadians-1.2475190.

60   Hannah Sung, "Toronto Council split over state of emergency," *Globe and Mail*, last modified December 23, 2013, http://www.theglobeandmail.com/news/toronto/toronto-council-split-over-state-of-emergency/article16096657/.

61   "Ontario Premier ignores Rob Ford, coordinates ice storm recovery efforts with Toronto's Deputy Mayor," *National Post*, last modified December 22, 2013, http://news.nationalpost.com/2013/12/22/ontario-premier-ignores-rob-ford-coordinates-ice-storm-recovery-efforts-with-torontos-deputy-mayor/.

62   Adrian Morrow, "Deputy Mayor Norm Kelly is Ontario's point man for Toronto, Wynne affirms," *Globe and Mail*, last modified December 3, 2013, http://www.theglobeandmail.com/news/politics/ontario-premier-meets-with-toronto-deputy-mayor-over-fords-protests/article15736225/.

63   Antonella Artuso, "Deputy Mayor Norm Kelly apologizes for Florida trip during hydro outage," *Toronto Sun*, last modified December 27, 2013, http://www.torontosun.com/2013/12/27/deputy-mayor-norm-kelly-goes-to-florida-amid-hydro-outage-crisis.

64   Christina Blizzard, "Food gift card campaign thrown together to make Wynne look good," *Toronto Sun*, last modified January 2, 2014, http://www.torontosun.com/2014/01/02/food-gift-card-campaign-thrown-together-to-make-wynne-look-good.

65   "Toronto ice storm: food replacement gift cards run out again," *CBC News*, last modified January 2, 2014, http://www.cbc.ca/news/canada/toronto/toronto-ice-storm-food-replacement-gift-cards-run-out-again-1.2481990.

66   Sue-Ann Levy, "Premier Kathleen Wynne didn't heed her own ice storm advice: neighbour," *Toronto Sun*, last modified January 18, 2014, http://www.torontosun.com/2014/01/18/premier-kathleen-wynne-didnt-heed-her-own-ice-storm-advice-neighbour.

67   "OPG's generous compensation and benefits negatively impact electricity costs," *Office of the Auditor General of Ontario*, December 10, 2013, http://www.auditor.on.ca/en/news_en/13_newsreleases/2013news_3.05OPGhumanresources.pdf.

68   Antonella Artuso, "Three OPG execs fired in wake of Auditor General Report," *Toronto Sun*, last modified December 10, 2013, http://www.torontosun.com/2013/12/10/auditor-generals-report-to-take-aim-at-ontario-power-generation.

69   Christina Blizzard, "OPG to pay $3.4 million to fire three execs," *Toronto Sun*, last modified March 29, 2014, http://cnews.canoe.ca/CNEWS/Canada/2014/03/28/21566406.html.

70   "OPG responds to Auditor General Report on its human resource policies," Ontario Power Generation, December 10, 2013, http://opg.com/about/governance/open/AuditorGeneral.asp.

71   Tom Mitchell, "We commit to do better," *Ontario Power Generation*, December 10, 2013, http://www.opg.com/about/management/open-and-accountable/Documents/131210WeCommitToDoBetter.pdf.

72   Keith Leslie and Tristin Hopper, "Wynne government intends to take control of executive salaries away from resistant OPG," *National Post*, last modified December 10, 2013, http://news.nationalpost.com/2013/12/10/significantly-more-generous-salaries-pensions-and-bonuses-at-opg-increases-cost-of-power-in-ontario-auditor-says/.

73   "Ontario Liberals plan bill to cap public sector executive salaries as NDP push for top compensation of $418,000," *National Post*, last modified December 9, 2013, http://news.nationalpost.com/2013/12/09/ontario-liberals-plan-bill-will-cap-public-sector-executive-salaries-as-ndp-push-for-top-compensation-of-418000/.

74   Ferguson, "eHealth Ontario staff will share $2.3 million…"

75   Matthew Pearson, "Ontario Liberals defend poor December job numbers," *Ottawa Citizen*, last modified January 10, 2014, http://www.ottawacitizen.com/business/Ontario+Liberals+defend+poor+December+numbers/9373138/story.html.

76   Tim Hudak, "PCs have a plan to bring prosperity to Ontario," *Toronto Star*, last modified January 13, 2014, http://www.thestar.com/opinion/commentary/2014/01/13/pcs_have_a_plan_to_bring_prosperity_to_ontario.html.

77   Antonella Artuso, "Conservatives lay out jobs creation plan for Ontario," *Toronto Sun*, last modified January 13, 2014, http://www.torontosun.com/2014/01/13/pc-leader-tim-hudak-lays-out-plan-to-create-1-million-jobs.

78   Antonella Artuso, "Only black women need apply: Ontario Liberals," *Toronto Sun*, last modified January 16, 2014, http://www.sunnewsnetwork.ca/sunnews/politics/archives/2014/01/20140116-210530.html.

79   Artuso, "Only black women need apply…"

80   "Consumers entitled to update on electricity debt retirement charge," *Office of the Auditor General of Ontario*, December 5, 2011, http://www.auditor.on.ca/en/news_en/11_newsreleases/2011news_3.04.pdf.

81   "Debt retirement charge," Ontario Ministry of Finance, last modified 2012, http://www.fin.gov.on.ca/en/tax/drc/.

82   Antonella Artuso, "Hydro debt retirement taking longer than expected: Grits," *Toronto Sun*, last modified January 29, 2014, http://www.torontosun.com/2014/01/29/hydro-debt-retirement-taking-longer-than-expected-grits.

83   Mary Hartill, "Hydro customers hit with another $4 billion," *Metroland Media*, last modified February 5, 2014, http://www.northbaynipissing.com/news-story/4352683-hydro-customers-hit-with-another-4-billion/.

84   "Bernard Lord to take over as Chair of OPG, Sandra Pupatello at Hydro One," *Global News*, last modified March 7, 2014, http://globalnews.ca/news/1194650/bernard-lord-to-take-

Liars

over-as-chair-of-opg-sandra-pupatello-at-hydro-one/.

85 Adrian Morrow, "Hydro One to face major investigation as billing complaints mount." *Globe and Mail*, last modified February 4, 2014, http://www.theglobeandmail.com/news/national/hydro-one-to-face-major-investigation-as-billing-complaints-mount/article16681447/.

86 Donovan Vincent and Robert Benzie, "Wynne calls byelections in Thornhill, Niagara Falls," *Toronto Star*, last modified January 15, 2014, http://www.thestar.com/news/queenspark/2014/01/15/wynne_calls_byelections_in_thornhill_niagara_falls.html.

87 Robert Benzie, "Ontario to allow wine sales at farmers market," *Toronto Star*, last modified December 16, 2013, http://www.thestar.com/news/queenspark/2013/12/16/ontario_to_allow_wine_sales_at_farmers_markets.html.

88 Robert Benzie, "Liberal MPP Kim Craitor resigns, setting up byelection." *Toronto Star*, last modified September 24, 2013, http://www.thestar.com/news/queenspark/2013/09/24/liberal_mpp_kim_craitor_resigns_setting_up_byelection.html.

89 Antonella Artuso, "PCs keep seat in Thornhill byelection," *Toronto Sun*, last modified February 13, 2014, http://www.torontosun.com/2014/02/13/liberal-pc-seats-on-the-line-in-ontario-byelections.

90 Richard Brennan, "Tories launch anti-union attack on NDP in Niagara Falls." *Toronto Star*, last modified February 11, 2014, http://www.thestar.com/news/queenspark/2014/02/11/tories_launch_antiunion_attack_on_ndp_in_niagara_falls.html.

91 Keith Leslie, "NDP would drive Ontario 'into the ditch with the same reckless abandon as Bob Rae,' PC leader Tim Hudak says," *National Post*, last modified January 20, 2014.

http://news.nationalpost.com/2014/01/20/ndp-would-drive-ontario-into-the-ditch-with-the-same-reckless-abandon-as-bob-rae-pc-leader-tim-hudak-says/.

92 "Spring election looms in Ontario as humiliating byelection results further weakens Liberals' grip on power," *National Post*, last modified February 14, 2014, http://news.nationalpost.com/2014/02/14/humiliating-byelection-results-puts-kathleen-wynne-in-tough-spot-ahead-of-expected-spring-election/.

93 "Which Premiers, opposition leaders scored the best in 2013?" *Huffington Post Canada*, last modified December 31, 2013, http://www.huffingtonpost.ca/2013/12/31/canada-premiers-2013-stephen-mcneil_n_4519994.html.

94 Matthew Pearson, "Calorie counts may soon come to a fast food menu near you," *Ottawa Citizen*, last modified February 24, 2014, http://www.ottawacitizen.com/health/Calorie+counts+soon+come+fast+food+menu+near/9545673/story.html.

95 Arthur Cockfield, "Stop soaring school costs in Ontario," *Toronto Star*, last modified January 19, 2014, http://www.thestar.com/opinion/commentary/2014/01/19/stop_soaring_school_costs_in_ontario.html.

96 Joe Warmington, "Getting rid of Mothers' Day, Fathers' Day," *Canoe*, last modified September 25, 2013, http://blogs.canoe.ca/lilleyspad/politics/column-warmington-getting-rid-of-mothers-day-fathers-day/.

Chapter 11

Conclusion – Where Do We Go From Here?

In just 10 years of Liberal government, Ontario has been hijacked. It's been demoted from the economic powerhouse it once was to just another "have-not" province that requires welfare payments from the federal government just to survive. This is the McGuinty-Wynne Ontario.

At the time of writing, the Wynne government had just announced that Ontario's electricity rates would be going up yet again.[1] Combined with the Wynne-approved 40 percent price hike for Ontario's gas suppliers, rising utility bills are just the latest load of new taxes and increased fees to be added onto the backs of Ontarians who can least afford it.

When Dalton McGuinty came to office in 2003, Ontario's debt was $138.8 billion. When he left nine years later, Ontario's debt had almost doubled to a whopping $252.1 billion. In Kathleen Wynne's first year in office, she introduced an $11.7 billion deficit budget and has added an incredible $36 billion to Ontario's debt. These numbers alone are shocking. The first 136 years of Ontario resulted in $139 billion in debt. In barely nine years – in one tenth of the time it took for the first 23 Premiers to accumulate $139 billion – McGuinty *doubled it*. Just *one* Premier spent as much as the first 23, and Ontario has been dug into a deeper debt hole than we've ever seen before.

Liars

We're spending $10.6 billion a year *on interest alone.*[2] Just the interest payments amount to $785 for every man, woman, and child residing in Ontario. Now add another $21,318 to pay for your share of the provincial debt. If the $1.1 billion gas plant scandal outraged you – which it should have – then you should be 10 times more outraged that we waste the equivalent of *10 gas plants* every year just to borrow money from other governments. Debt interest is now our third-largest expense, behind only health care and education.[3] The per-person debt share is more than double that of Mike Harris' Conservatives.

If you were running a company with the same economy and population as Ontario, you would quickly find that such extravagant expenditures on interest alone are not acceptable. Just as Ontario families need to balance their budgets and tighten their belts where appropriate, so should our government. If we were a company, such fiscal mismanagement and scandalous behaviour would have resulted in the leader receiving the swift boot. The leader should embody not only the spirit of the company, but be constantly indebted to his shareholders, ensuring they are constantly receiving the best value for their money. If only Dalton McGuinty or Kathleen Wynne felt the same way.

Kathleen Wynne was elected by the Liberal Party to clean up the McGuinty mess; she was the only hope in restoring not only Ontario's economy, but also the Liberal Party's desperately tarnished brand. Ontario voters had no say in who was chosen, but they have continually expressed their outrage with the Ontario Liberal government through several byelections. Wynne has done nothing to reverse the massively climbing debt or deficit. At the time of writing, Ontario's debt sits at $264,806,834,000 and it's climbing by $372 every *second.*[4]

There is just no excuse for the Liberals' gross incompetence and mismanagement in over a decade of leading Ontario's government. Everything from Dalton McGuinty raising taxes after he said he wouldn't to the numerous scandals with eHealth, ORNGE, OLG, OPA, and the $1.1 billion gas plant scandal (to only name a few)…these cannot be dismissed as rogue, one-off accidents that had no connection to the Liberal government. There is no time for Liberal apologists. Ontario has been fooled two times now because it has failed to kick out this Liberal government.

Time for Change

For the past ten years, Ontario has been on a collision course that desperately needs to be corrected, not because of a sudden and drastic shift to the left as we saw with the 1990 election of Bob Rae's NDP, but via gradual changes. It has not occurred out of necessity for only one emergency stimulus budget, but rather through thousands of incremental legislative and regulatory changes that have killed jobs, reduced wages, increase taxes, and imposed thousands of new regulatory burdens on every business and family. It's death by a thousand cuts or, more accurately: *debt* by a thousand cuts.

Thousands of experts agree with this bleak assessment. As I have shown, everyone from the left-leaning *Toronto Star* and CBC to the right-leaning *Sun News Network* and *National Post* (and everyone in between) agrees that Ontario desperately needs change. Many of the alarming reports on the state of Ontario's government under Liberal rule have even come from the Ontario government itself. This is no longer a debate about left or right, right or wrong. If Ontario continues on its present path it *will* suffer from a catastrophic failure. And when it comes time to pay our bills, and we can't, who will?

But the economic argument is not the only argument for the necessity of change from this corrupt, power-hungry Liberal government. Other arguments presented in this book include the necessity for better education management, better social services, a more responsive government, and updated infrastructure. These are the issues Ontarians are facing that need be addressed by their provincial government. Instead, the Wynne Liberals have further consolidated power in their select few union and Liberal elites. Of all the people she could have named to head the scandal-plagued eHealth Ontario, Wynne named, of all people, her own brother-in-law.[5] The decision reeks of nepotism, yet in the McGuinty-Wynne Ontario, this is business as usual.

The Road to Greece

This is a question Greece attempted to answer in 2008, when its government's massive overspending on social programs and unsustainable public debt finally came due. Greek debt was a whopping 94 percent of GDP in 1999, and when the global economic recession hit in 2008-2009, the country could not sustain its overwhelming debt-to-GDP ratio and high structural deficits. Its debt-to-GDP skyrocketed even higher to 167 percent.

Greece was saved with a €110 billion bail-out with conditions from the International Monetary Fund which required it to:

- Restore fiscal balance through austerity measures
- Privatize government assets worth at least €50 billion by the end of 2015
- Improve government competitiveness and growth through structural reforms

Liars

The response from the Greek people was swift and severe: they did not like an international agency, particularly backed with money from the Germans, telling them they had to return to balance. Quite simply, they did not appreciate being told they had spent too much in the past, and would have to enter a period of deep austerity for the immediate future in order to pay for it.

Ontario should have watched and learned from Greece; instead, the Liberals ignored it. While Ontario is not spending 94 percent of our GDP on debt *yet*, there are other trouble similarities:[6] our populations are within two million people; Ontario's government spending is $121 billion, Greece's is $139 billion. We spend $10 billion on debt interest, Greece spends $12.6 billion. Ontario gives pensions to men and women at 65, Greece gives them to men at 65 and women at 60. Our median age is 39, while Greece's is 42. We're not so different, and we're becoming more similar every year we keep the Liberals in office.

Indeed, that's exactly what a report by the Fraser Institute said in January 2013. In questioning whether Ontario was the next California or Greece, the Fraser Institute concluded: "California has been roundly criticized by news media and the financial markets for its inability to control spending and reduce deficits. Yet Ontario, with a fraction of California's population and a significantly smaller economy, is carrying a debt load almost two-thirds larger than California."[7] In their analysis,[8] they make the same alarming comparisons between Ontario's and Greece's demographics, debt, deficits, and public spending. The same worrisome picture was painted by *Maclean's* following the October 2011 election when it called Ontario "Canada's Greece."[9]

The lessons learned from California and Greece should be alarming. They

Figure 12: The debt hole of Ontario vs. California

200

should be generating changes in government policies, yet neither the Mc-Guinty nor Wynne governments have done anything to get us off the path to disaster. Thus, the changes Ontario needs to see will only come from a conservative government.

A province massively over-burdened by debt and job losses needs more jobs and less government spending in order to pay down its debt. It needs fewer government regulations imposed on those that really create jobs, like small and medium businesses. It needs lower corporate tax rates in order to encourage large businesses to set up shops here in Ontario as opposed to overseas or in the United States. It needs to reduce personal income tax rates in order to take the massive burden of relentless Liberal tax hikes off the shoulders of the people who will work in those jobs. It needs reasonable welfare reforms to take individuals off government-provided subsistence and put them into gainful employment. It needs a health care system that actually provides health care instead of denying brain cancer patients the treatment they need.[10]

These are inherently conservative positions, since California and Greece have proven we cannot spend our way to prosperity. Today, these principles are best embodied in Tim Hudak's Progressive Conservatives. They are certainly not embodied by Andrea Horwath's NDP, which has only called for *more* government regulation, *more* tax increases, and *more* government intervention in programs that should be left to private businesses or charities.

In contrast, for over a year now, Tim Hudak has been releasing White Papers on what a Conservative government would do to fix the mess created by the Liberal government.[11] These papers are thorough, bold, and visionary. They offer a transparent look at how the Conservatives believe the Ontario government should be run, and how Ontario will look as a result of those policies. Neither the Liberals nor NDP have shown such an interest in releasing so many White Papers – essentially policy platforms in advance of an election that voters are entitled to have – even though Hudak's good ideas will undoubtedly be plagiarized again by his competitors.

Everything from fixing the education system to growing Ontario's economy, from getting Ontarians back to work to building great cities is covered by the Hudak government-in-waiting. The media have not given these White Papers the attention they deserve, but they offer a complete agenda for change should the Conservatives be elected in the next election.

The McGuinty-Wynne governments have not been able to emerge from scandal after scandal after scandal to even consider fixing the larger problems with Ontario's economy and government. They have shown no interest in tackling any of the problems outlined in this book, primarily because they have been too busy fighting off scandals surrounding enormous bonuses for public servants here, cancelled gas plants for $1.1 Billion there, multi-billion investments in unproven wind power here, and Liberal cronies' lavish "consulting" contracts there.

Kathleen Wynne's claim that she can manage the economy is simply untrue. Wynne inherited monumental problems from Dalton McGuinty's nine years in office, but she cannot continue to use his name as a scapegoat for her government's problem. Real change needed to start at the top, with a clear direction and focus. Wynne had the opportunity to set a new course for her government, one that was drastically different from the McGuinty legacy. Instead, she *became* the McGuinty legacy by continuing his government, his way, with his projects. It all comes down to the competence of being able to run our province properly, and the Liberals have shown they simply aren't up to it. Without a significant and painful correction, the Ontario government won't have to worry about any scandals *because government won't exist.* If we continue on this course, Ontario won't be able to afford to do anything but pay down debt and dabble in the Liberals' flavour-of-the-day experiment. There will be no money for health care, education, science, infrastructure, or police officers. Unless action is taken, Ontario *will* become the next Greece, and it *will* see massive public riots when an external government or agency finally comes in to bail us out.

Without change, Ontario is doomed to failure with a Liberal government that hijacked Ontario from its path to prosperity.

Why Haven't We Seen the Light?

Ontario knew in 2003 that Dalton McGuinty, the "accidental Premier," wasn't up to the job – his approval rating was just *nine percent* only one month into his term as Premier. Ontario had the chance for change in 2007, but we failed to take it. We had another chance in 2011, but there, too, we failed to fully take it by changing government, instead choosing to leave McGuinty in office with a minority government. This was supposed to force the Liberals to work with the Conservatives and NDP, but both McGuinty and Wynne have shown an overwhelming preference to go only to the NDP for support.

Risky debt levels, incredibly irresponsible spending, massive deficits, unproven green energy experiments, forcing wage cuts on teachers, cancelling gas plants to save Liberal seats, introducing graphic and radical sex education to young children…*these* are the policies of the McGuinty-Wynne government. And they have been the policies of this government for the past decade; this is no longer a shock and can no longer be explained by one or two bad Liberal decisions. *This* Ontario – here, today, right now, in 2014 – is Dalton McGuinty and Kathleen Wynne's Liberal Ontario. Every *minute* we refuse to do something about this government, $22,320 is added to our debt.

Twice now, Ontario has failed to hold the McGuinty-Wynne government to account for their actions. Will we hold them to account when we get a third chance? I hope so. This hijacking will only transpire for as long as we allow it, so take action today to ensure Ontario gets back on course.

In the appendix, I lay out just a few steps that need to be taken to get Ontario back on the right track. I also offer tips for you – the average taxpayer looking for a break – and for political parties, who have largely failed to connect with voters, to really drive home the multitude of the Liberal government's failures. The times ahead are tough, to be sure, but Ontario can once again lead the way as Canada's economic engine.

Look ahead, Ontario! A brighter future can be upon us if we band together, with the first step being the decisive defeat of McGuinty's Liberal government in favour of a conservative government that can ensure Ontario can again lead the way. We cannot bring to power a Conservative Premier, but hold him to minority status. The times call for decisive leadership under a Premier with a majority who can push important legislation through the legislature without being forced to kowtow to other parties' demands.

Change Ahead

Ontario's road back to prosperity will not be an easy one. In order to avoid the anarchy seen in Greece, our province will need strong leadership to cut regulations and taxes, manage its finances properly, modernize services, treat all citizens equally, and uphold the rule of law in order to make it attractive for businesses to bring jobs and wealth to Ontario through start-ups and expansion.

But that shift needs to take place if Ontario is to have any chance of not becoming the next California or Greece. Ontario's present situation did not happen overnight. It came as the result of incremental left-wing governments preaching and implementing left-wing policies, first led by Dalton McGuinty and currently being led by Kathleen Wynne. The road to get there will not be an easy one, but we as Ontarians deserve better than the current government and the current situation with which we are currently faced.

Ontario deserves a bright future with low personal taxes, thriving small businesses, stable large businesses, a minimal social support system in

Liars

place for those who need it, good-paying manufacturing jobs, unions kept in check, and the true Ontario spirit for constant innovation and growth being captured in a thriving economy.

Ontario can get there. Ontario deserves nothing less.

Appendix

An Agenda for Change

What an Elected Government Needs to Do

These are just a few policies the Ontario government needs to implement to get Ontario back on track:

1. Get Big Business and Big Labour out of politics. As with Canada's federal system, Ontario needs to implement its own version of the *Accountability Act.* Set strict definitions for political donations, including restricting them to Ontario residents only. Set a reasonable cap, as in the federal system, around $1,200 per person per year. This would eliminate union and business interference in Ontario's electoral system.

2. Close the gaps in third party advertising and election spending by third parties. Front groups such as the Working Families Coalition do the dirty work of the Liberal Party yet have no accountability for their actions as the Liberals do. Any third party advertising supporting or opposing a political party should be either eliminated or regulated.

3. Implement the Drummond Report. The Drummond Report meticulously analyzed and documented the state of Ontario's public service, economy, and government. It is the most comprehensive document on the subject Ontario has ever seen. It's non-partisan,

it's hard-hitting, and it needs to be implemented. The Drummond Report was limited in making some important recommendations since McGuinty said it could not include conservative approaches to health care (privatization) or liberal approaches to taxes (raise them). Nevertheless, a government coming from the left, right, or centre will eventually have to wake up to the realities presented in the report.

4. Public sector unions need to be outlawed. In addition, any future pay raises for public servants should be done through an independent review committee overseen by the Minister of Labour. Public servants work for the public, yet they are inherently not working for the public while striking for their own self-interest.

5. No taxes should be raised or introduced. If they are, they should be called the McGuinty Tax and be paid directly by Liberal supporters. (I'm mostly kidding.)

6. Re-affirm the government's commitment to the *Taxpayer Protection* legislation introduced under Mike Harris. This legislation was never repealed, yet the McGuinty and Wynne governments have blatantly ignored it for years.

7. Amend the *Taxpayer Protection* legislation to give Ontario residents, collectively and individually, the right to pursue legal action if a Premier breaks their promise under that Act.

8. Introduce mandatory voting that ensures every eligible voter casts a ballot in the next election. This neutralizes any future questions of the legitimacy of the government that is elected, and ensures Ontarians are responsible for educating themselves and casting a ballot for their preferred candidate.

9. Immediately end any "green energy" programs enacted by the Liberals unless they have a clear, positive, and proven benefit to Ontarians and the Ontario economy.

10. Implement strict laws that require a waiting period after leaving a political or ministerial job before being allowed to be rehired as any form of "consultant" or "advisor" for the government. I suggest that period be at least five years, and that it be overseen by the Integrity Commissioner.

11. Progressively reduce the HST from 13, to 12, to 11 percent, just as Prime Minister Stephen Harper did federally with the GST.

12. Reverse the smart meter program: instead of making it more expensive to do laundry before 7:00pm or forcing a family to be up and showered by 7:00am, return to a flat-rate electricity cost. Supplement this with discounts for using electricity during off-peak hours instead of making it more expensive during on-peak hours.

13. Freeze the budget. In 2013-2014, Ontario spent $127.6 billion.[12] In year one, the budget should be frozen and a comprehensive government operations review undertaken. In year two, the results of that review should result in either a five or ten percent budget reduction. Budget reductions should continue at a rate of five percent per year, with payments towards paying down the debt increasing. Government spending should continue to be frozen and reduced wherever possible until the Drummond Report is fully implemented.

14. Split surpluses evenly between reducing taxes and paying down the debt.

15. Amend the Ontario Student Assistance Program (OSAP) to provide loans and grants to students based on demonstrable need, and reward students for exceptional marks or entering a field of strategic importance to Ontario's economy. End the 30 percent-off tuition-for-the-few plan in favour of merit-based grants for all.

16. Update welfare laws to cap the maximum number of months a person can receive welfare. Partner with the federal government to require that anyone receiving welfare is actively searching for employment. *It should be a privilege, not a right, to live off Ontario taxpayers.* The exception to this rule, the proof which lies with the person requesting the funding, should be in cases of temporary hardship where it is to the benefit of the province's taxpayers to assist this person for a short period of time. Ensure welfare funding is paying for the bare necessities of a person's livelihood, not cigarettes, drugs, alcohol, or other privileges outside of basic food and shelter.

17. Eliminate the right of seasonal workers to live on unemployment insurance or welfare while in the off-season.

18. Set welfare funding to decrease over time, meaning by the seventh month, for example, the person is no longer receiving welfare.

19. Cap the total number of people on the Sunshine list to a percentage of the total number of employees in the public sector – say, at 10 percent. The 1996 *Public Sector Salary Disclosure Act*[13] brought in under Mike Harris' Conservative government, is one of the few holdovers from those days of balanced budgets and public sector accountability. In 2003, that list contained 12,000 names, but by 2012 that list had grown to include over 88,000 public servants who made more than $100,000, a growth of over 737 percent![14]

20. Reduce the corporate tax rate from the current 11.5 percent to 10 percent.

21. Strike a Red Tape Reduction Task Force with a view of reducing

or eliminating needless provincial bureaucracy. New regulations should be implemented only after eliminating two unneeded regulations.

What You, a Taxpayer, Can Do

1. Join a political party. I recommend either the Ontario New Democrats or the Ontario Progressive Conservatives as the most likely alternatives to replace the Ontario Liberals. Read up on political parties and join the one that is most reasonable to you. Both have an incredible amount of information available on their websites at http://ontariondp.com and http://www.ontariopc.com. Membership in either party is as little as $10 a year and allows you to participate in at a local grassroots level by helping to elect your riding's candidate. If you're interested in joining another political party, research your options and choose the one that feels best.

2. Write your Member of Provincial Parliament (MPP) on a regular basis. Every time the Ontario Liberal government does something that costs you money or changes a policy for the worse, contact your MPP and demand that they represent your interests as your representative. A listing of their addresses, email addresses, phone numbers, and fax numbers is available here: http://www.ontla.on.ca/web/members/member_addresses.do?locale=en.

3. Write the minister responsible for a portfolio on a regular basis, whether by regular mail, email, or fax. Find their contact information at the link above.

4. Make your voice known. Perhaps you're sick of seeing your taxpayer dollars go into the pockets of Liberal "consultants" and "advisors." Perhaps you want to see more money spent on your local hospital. Maybe you know a small business owner getting ready to close shop because he or she can't withstand the burdens placed by the Liberals any more. Or maybe you are that small business owner. Whatever it is, make your voice known. If you don't believe there's an advocacy group for your topic or issue out there, create one.

1   Antonella Artuso, "Hydro rates going up May 1," *Toronto Sun*, last modified April 16, 2014, http://www.torontosun.com/2014/04/16/hydro-rates-going-up-may-1.

2   Lorne Gunter, "Ontario's debt threatens programs, tax cuts," *National Post*, last modified March 9, 2011, http://fullcomment.nationalpost.com/2011/03/09/lorne-gunter-ontarios-debt-threatens-programs-tax-cuts/.

3   Rob Ferguson, "Drummond report: a reality check on Ontario vs. Greece," *Toronto Star*,

last modified February 17, 2012, http://www.thestar.com/news/canada/2012/02/17/drummond_report_a_reality_check_on_ontario_vs_greece.html.

4   "Ontario debt clock," *Canadian Taxpayers Federation,* http://fpm3.com/debtclock/

5   Rob Ferguson, "Kathleen Wynne's brother-in-law named interim head of eHealth Ontario," *Toronto Star,* last modified April 15, 2014, http://www.thestar.com/news/queenspark/2014/04/15/kathleen_wynnes_brotherinlaw_to_head_ehealth_ontario.html.

6   Ferguson, "Kathleen Wynne's brother-in-law....," supra note 2.

7   Jason Clemens and Niels Veldhuis, "Ontario's debt load larger than California's thanks to big-spending ways; is the province heading for a Greek-Style financial meltdown?" *Fraser Institute,* January 31, 2013, http://www.fraserinstitute.org/publicationdisplay.aspx?id=19281.

8   Jason Clemens and Niels Veldhuis, "The state of Ontario's indebtedness: warning signs to act," *Fraser Institute,* 2013, http://www.fraserinstitute.org/uploadedFiles/fraser-ca/Content/research-news/research/publications/state-of-ontarios-indebtedness.pdf.

9   Frank Gunn, "Why Ontario is poised to become Canada's Greece," Maclean's, October 17, 2011, http://www.macleans.ca/general/why-ontario-is-poised-to-become-canadas-greece/.

10   Andrew Russell, "Milton mother with two months to live devastated after OHIP fails to cover cancer treatment," *Global News,* last modified October 26, 2013, http://globalnews.ca/news/927721/milton-mother-devastated-after-ohip-fails-to-cover-cancer-treatment/.

11   Ontario PC Party, "White papers," *Ontario PC,* http://www.ontariopc.com/white-papers.

12   "2013 Ontario budget," Ontario Ministry of Finance, http://www.fin.gov.on.ca/en/budget/ontariobudgets/2013/ch2a.html.

13   "Public sector salary disclosure 2014 (Disclosure for 2013)," Ontario Ministry of Finance, http://www.fin.gov.on.ca/en/publications/salarydisclosure/pssd/.

14   "Ontario's Sunshine List sees double-digit growth," *CBC News.*

CPSIA information can be obtained at www.ICGtesting.com
Printed in the USA
LVOW08s0224281114

415887LV00001B/298/P